A NEW INTERNATIONAL HISTORY OF THE SPANISH CIVIL WAR

A New International History of the Spanish Civil War

Michael Alpert
Principal Lecturer in Spanish Language and History
University of Westminster, London

St. Martin's Press   New York

First published in the United States of America in 1994

Printed in Hong Kong

ISBN 0–312–12016–8

Library of Congress Cataloging-in-Publication Data
Alpert, Michael, 1936–
A new international history of the Spanish Civil War / Michael
Alpert.
p.   cm.
Includes bibliographical references and index.
ISBN 0–312–12016–8
1. Spain—Foreign relations—1931–1939.   2. Spain—History—Civil
War, 1936–1939.   I. Title.
DP257.A54   1994 1993
946. 081—dc20   93–32764
                                                    .   CIP

Dedicated to the memory of my teacher, a great
historian
Bernard (L. C. B.) Seaman (1911–86)

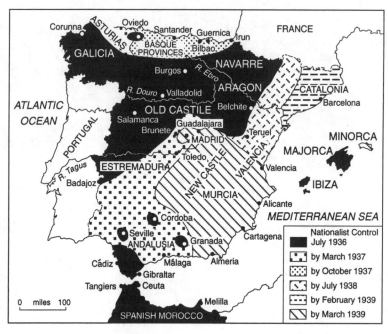

Franco takes control of Spain, 1936–39

Contents

Preface

It is now twenty years since a study was dedicated to the international aspects of the Spanish Civil War. Since then many books, articles and theses have been produced, especially in Spain, now that the Civil War is a subject of scholarly investigation, and archives have been opened. A new synthesis covering the whole of the war and setting it against major events of the later 1930s is overdue.

One view sees the Spanish war as the first struggle against Fascism, an inseparable part of the issues of the interwar years. A contrasting opinion insists that it was an internal working-out of Spanish problems and tangential to the main thrust of European history. This book seeks to discover whether the errors of the age were symbolised by viewing Spain as an unimportant and faraway country upsetting the European concert.

In writing I have contracted many debts. I thank especially Max Platschek and Barbara and Francis MacFarland, who have heard me read the drafts aloud and have read them to me, helping I hope to iron out infelicity and unclarity. I am especially grateful to Paul Preston for his many useful observations, as well as for solving the problem of an unwieldy apparatus of footnotes by suggesting a bibliographical essay. Particular thanks also to my colleagues Lucio Sponza and Ig Avsej for aid with Italian material and for reading Russian for me and to Sheila Ellwood for showing me the Locarno suite at the Foreign Office. I thank the British Academy and the University of Westminster for help to visit Spanish archives.

Prologue

Walking through the West Park – the Parque del Oeste – in Madrid, descending towards the River Manzanares and the French Bridge – the Puente de los Franceses – the scene of bloody battles during Franco's siege of the capital between November 1936 and the end of March 1939 – one suddenly comes across a number of concrete constructions which are recognisable as artillery emplacements. Perhaps they were thought too much trouble to blow up and, since the trees in the Park have now grown again, it is unlikely that the structures will be disturbed. There are few other traces of the Spanish Civil War – at least not physical ones – for the trenches in the open parkland to the west of Madrid, the Casa del Campo, still quite visible twenty years ago, cannot easily be found today, and the churches which were burned by revolutionary mobs in 1936 have long been rebuilt. It is not the physical scars, but the mental ones, which remain after a war, particularly a civil war and above all one which had such a scarring international effect, for the Spanish Civil War expressed for its generation and later ones the great error made by the statesmen of the 1930s in trying to appease the Dictators – Hitler and Mussolini. It is true that Franco did not in the end join them in declaring war against the Allies and that his regime gradually eased its harshness. The frightened anti-Communism of the prewar Right became the determined anti-Sovietism of the Cold War and many of those who had seen the USSR as the only hope for the world in the 1930s were disillusioned precisely by the behaviour of Stalin over the Spanish war. Yet none of this changed the issue of Spain in the collective memory. It was the country where the Democracies failed to defend a constitutional regime attacked by its own army supported by two other countries which were menaces to world peace.

Spain was a third-rate and peripheral country, and yet the dictator and victor of the Civil War, General Franco, during the initial stages of his regime, released a wave of more passionate indignation throughout the world than Hitler. The massacre of Badajoz, the bombing of Madrid and Barcelona and the razing of Guernica, were events to which the public reacted with spontaneous revulsion. There were other elements in the Spanish war which touched the collective European memory: once more the Moors were let loose behind the Pyrenees, but this time as defenders of the Church. As Arthur Koestler put in *The Invisible Writing*, 'The shadows of the middle ages seemed to have come alive, the gargoyles were spouting blood, Goya's Disasters were made to look like topical records: once more a mercenary horde, the foreign Legionaries of the *Tercio*, killed, raped and plundered in the name of a holy crusade, while the air smelt of incense and burning flesh.'

Whatever the exaggerations of Koestler's writing, people did see the Spanish Civil War in this way. The conflict was front-page news, it was in every cinema newsreel and the subject of vast numbers of pamplets, books and public meetings. It has remained until today in the collective memory.

Whether one considered that the Spanish Popular Front Government, against which Franco rebelled, was intentionally preparing the ground for revolution, or merely unable to control its excesses, one could not be unaware of them, for the press emphasised the church-burnings, the murders, the private vengeances, the robberies and the arbitary arrests. Many feared that the class war which the outrages reflected would be carried to countries such as Britain which had hitherto considered themselves immune. Such reports had great effect on the policies of foreign governments.

Perhaps strongest in the collective memory of the Spanish war is the sense of guilt, of fault. Why was the obvious not seen? Was it not evident that the advance of what was generally called 'Fascism' inevitably meant world war? The fact was that, despite the reality of the causes fought over in Spain, it still remained a distant conflict. This is why the words with which George Orwell ends his *Homage to Catalonia* still ring so true: everybody was 'sleeping the deep, deep sleep of England, from which I sometimes fear that we shall never wake until we are jerked out of it by the roar of bombs'.

Part One

Chapter 1

BACKGROUND

At the root of Western European insecurity in the interwar years lay France's fears of a rearmed and *revanchiste* Germany. France had been immensely weakened by the First World War. She had lost her Russian ally. France's only comfort had been the clauses of the Treaty of Versailles which had reduced the German army to a mere 100 000 men, abolished the General Staff and forbidden Germany to have an air force.

On 11 January 1923, French forces occupied the Ruhr in order to force Germany to pay reparations. Lacking British support for their action, the French had to retire. France would never again act without British support. Throughout the interwar years, German fears of France were underlain by resentment of the physical sufferings, caused, the Germans thought, by French demands for reparations. Hitler's acceptance of the invitation to help the Spanish insurgents destroy the Spanish Popular Front in 1936 would be a response to German fear and hatred of France and to what Germany saw as a French-led coalition against the Reich.

For the French, who had suffered so greatly, reparations became a symbol of the great let-down and a cause of the disillusion of French political life in the interwar years. For France, the British were unreliable allies against potential German aggression. Yet France could not afford to alienate British support. France's sense of abandonment conditioned her attitudes in the 1930s. For Britain, the French were making outrageous demands. Britain would not back France, but the French were afraid to make a move without Britain. More than any crisis in the interwar years, the Spanish Civil War would highlight this conflict and demonstrate the absence of an *entente* in the full sense of the word.

Great Britain considered the German threat finished, and refused to get involved in an anti-German alliance. She certainly would not want to risk war with Germany over Spain. People spoke of collective security against an aggressor, but this would mean involvement in foreign wars. Britain could afford to adopt a policy of appeasement or magnanimity to the defeated. Only later did the term 'appeasement' become synonymous with betrayal of democracy to Hitler and Mussolini.

Since there was massive international involvement in Spain, one of the essential questions to be answered is why the League of Nations – the international body set up after 1918 – was impotent to solve the Spanish conflict. Its failure had been evident since the early 1930s, largely because the United States was not a member. During the Spanish Civil War America's indifference to foreign affairs would reinforce American isolationism.

Germany's leaving the League a few months after Hitler took power in 1933, the withdrawal of Japan in the same year, and the absence of the Soviet Union until 1934 were further factors in the League's weakness.

Britain and France laid down the law at the League's headquarters at Geneva. But their aims were different. France wanted to use the League as a system of security directed against Germany, while Britain wanted to develop a general European settlement that would conciliate Germany. British prudence, pragmatism and moderation inclined her statesmen, who could not really comprehend the long-term Nazi–Fascist threat, to be impatient with what they saw as the panicky and unstable French.

When the League of Nations and the quest for disarmament seemed to have failed, only collective security against aggression was left. But this would mean getting rid of deeply-ingrained attitudes hostile to armies and war industries, attitudes which had meant, in concrete terms, that the British and French Left traditionally voted against rearmament. For real pacifists, collective security implied alliances of the sort which had brought Britain into the First World War. People who urged rearmament as a deterrent to aggression were accused of accepting the inevitability of war. Pacifists would accept nothing less than appeasement of grievances within a context of disarmament. Yet the armed intervention of Germany and Italy in the Spanish Civil War would place the pacifist disarmers in a cleft stick, for how could Nazism–Fascism be resisted without rearmament? Governments could easily defend their policies of non-intervention in Spain by asking protesters whether they were willing to risk war.

HITLER AND MUSSOLINI: THE RHINELAND AND ABYSSINIA

The accession to power of Adolf Hitler in January 1933 began a new epoch of constant tension in Europe. This in itself shaped international reaction to the Civil War in Spain.

Germany rejected the Versailles settlement and Hitler announced in March 1935 a new German army. Britain was not prepared to accept a common front against Germany so France now turned to the Soviet Union. But the agreement with Russia had no teeth because a large body of

French opinion felt that it antagonised Hitler unnecessarily and gave offence to Great Britain and Poland.

British Conservatives, strongly anti-Bolshevik and sympathetic to Germany over Versailles, conciliated Hitler with the Anglo-German naval treaty of 18 June 1935 which allowed a new German navy. The French saw the naval agreement as a great betrayal.

The French agreement with the Soviet Union and the British naval treaty with Germany were indications that the *entente* was falling apart. The disharmony and confusion of purpose in tackling the dictators became evident in the two major crises which preceded the outbreak of the Spanish Civil War: the remilitarisation of the Rhineland and the Italian invasion of Abyssinia.

Ignoring the warnings of his generals and counting on the paralysis of the French Government and the deeply defensive spirit of the French generals, on 7 March 1936 Hitler sent troops into the demilitarised Rhineland with orders to withdraw if the French reacted. They did not. The French Right was so anti-Soviet that it would do nothing to hamper Hitler. The French army leaders insisted that they could take no offensive without general mobilisation and, in an election year, this would mean political suicide for a French government which carried it out.

Britain doubted whether the French really would fight. The French in turn supposed, rightly, that they would not be supported by a Britain which saw Germany as doing no more than seeking its rights. Once again, the *entente* was lacking.

Hitler argued that the ratification by the French Assembly of the treaty with the USSR on 27 February 1936 was an encirclement of Germany. But France had signed her pact with the USSR because she could not get firm guarantees from Britain. It was British unwillingness to risk involvement in Europe which lay at the root of European imbalances. Spain would be another vivid example.

The British, French and Belgian leaders met in July 1936, a few days after the military revolt against the Spanish Government. A communiqué of 23 July invited Germany and Italy to a conference to replace the 1925 Locarno Pact by which the Powers had agreed to maintain the European status quo. While both countries accepted the invitation, there was no real progress. The place of meeting would henceforth be the Committee for Non-Intervention in Spain.

Italy's irredentist and colonial aims were not satisfied at Versailles. Britain and France seemed to have a monopoly of empire. In Britain there was much sympathy and respect for Fascism, which took over in Italy at the end of 1922. It was seen in Britain as a bold attempt to crush Bolshevism and to replace impotent Liberal parliamentarianism, with firm yet progressive government. The Italian leader, Benito Mussolini, Il Duce, had many admirers in London. Winston Churchill said to Italian journalists in 1927, 'If I had been an Italian, I should have been whole-heartedly with you from the start to finish in your triumphal struggle against the bestial appetites and passions of Leninism.'[1] But strong government of the Fascist sort implied imperial ambition and the rejection of the usual norms of international behaviour. This was a recipe for conflict which would take shape over Spain.

Under Mussolini the worship of force overcame the acceptance of international standards of behaviour. Fascism defended the conquest of living space for strong and energetic nations. 'War alone', wrote Mussolini, 'keeps all human energies at the maximum tension and sets the seal of nobility on those peoples who have the courage to face it'.[2]

The Italian leader knew that Britain and France were too weak to resist him. Britain spoke in diplomatic terms which Mussolini did not appear to understand, or perhaps understood only too well as meaning that nothing would really be done. He invaded Abyssinia on 3 October 1935. The British Fleet was sent to the Mediterranean. On 10 October the League voted for economic sanctions against Italy and these began on 18 November. But the League was unwilling to impose a blockade on Italy. The Suez Canal would remain open. No country would suspend diplomatic relations with Italy. Many countries would not even agree to restricting Italian imports. The Royal Navy was at risk from Italian air-attacks on Malta, Suez and Aden, and British worldwide imperial responsibilities meant that she could not afford to run the risk of losing ships in the Mediterranean.

At this point, on 14 November 1935, the National–Conservative British Government under Baldwin was returned to power at the general election, thus strengthening its ability to take unpopular decisions. The Hoare–Laval agreement of December 1935 gave Italy two-thirds of Abyssinia in return for very little. The consequent scandal, however, led to the ratification of the Franco-Soviet pact. Hoare was replaced at the Foreign Office by Anthony Eden on 22 December 1935. Eden by now thought that the League was 'physically and morally sick' and virtually unusable.[3] Mussolini ordered the war finished quickly. On 1 May 1936 the Emperor Haile Selassie left his country and on 9 May the King of Italy was proclaimed Emperor of Ethiopia.

Despite talk of sanctions to punish the aggressor, many influential people now, and later in Spain, thought it stupid to antagonise Italy over matters of principle when the real danger was a rearmed Germany. They thought it was essential to keep Italy and Hitler separate. The mistakes of perception were grave. The Foreign Office gave little attention to the role of Fascist ideology. The service chiefs overestimated the ability of the Italian forces. Underestimating nastiness and over-estimating strength imposed policies of appeasement. Public opinion may well have been misunderstood also. The 1935 peace ballot actually showed complete support for the League. Of nine million respondents, 6.7 million had approved nations combining militarily to stop an aggressor. Lastly, it was probably British and French weakness over Abyssinia that suggested to Hitler that he might risk a foreign adventure.

Neville Chamberlain, the Chancellor of the Exchequer, who would be Prime Minister for most of the Spanish Civil War, thought that the League had exacerbated Italian resentment. On 10 June 1936, he called sanctions 'the very midsummer of madness' and, a week later, Eden recommended the ending of sanctions. But Eden resented Chamberlain's interference. In 1938 the consequences of Chamberlain's going behind Eden's back over Spain would be much graver.

On 18 June 1936 the British Government approved the end of sanctions and on the same day the Chiefs of Staff's Subcommittee insisted that Britain must be free of Mediterranean obligations and therefore on friendly relations with Italy if she were to attend to her widespread imperial obligations. The pattern of diplomacy for the Spanish war had been set.

Political reality, not morality, prevailed. The Mediterranean Fleet was withdrawn from Alexandria. But London held back from the final concession of recognising the King of Italy as Emperor. This would be a significant ace in the hand of British diplomacy during the Spanish war.

Abyssinia had been abandoned. Perhaps there was something prophetic in the words of the League of Nations delegate from Haiti, who said, referring to Abyssinia as Ethiopia, 'Great or small, strong or weak, near or far, white or coloured, let us never forget that one day we may be somebody's Ethiopia.'[4]

Wednesday 15 July 1936 was the date on which all measures of sanctions were to come to an end. On that day, in Las Palmas, in the Canary Islands, a privately-chartered British aircraft waited for its mysteri-ous passenger, General Francisco Franco, to arrive from his command on Tenerife. Captain Bebb, a private pilot, would fly Franco to Morocco to take command of the Spanish Army there, spearhead of the insurrection planned for 17 and 18 July.

THE COMMUNIST BOGEY

Europe and America saw the Soviet Union and the Moscow-controlled Communist International as menaces to peace and stability. This fear divided European opinion in the interwar years and paralysed the will to tackle the Nazi–Fascist threat. Many hoped that Nazi Germany would destroy Communism. They saw the Spanish Civil War as the battleground against the invasion of Western Europe by Soviet Revolution.

The USSR was actually very weak. Its lack of military or naval strength to support a firm foreign policy would become evident in Spain. The International, or Comintern, was in reality not a vehicle for world revolution but a tool in Soviet hands for the protection of the revolution at home and, as in the case of Spain, to manipulate matters for the benefit of the USSR.

The USSR was excluded from discussions on the European problem. Yet the fear of world revolution, which was the reason for the ostracising of Russia, was unreal, for the Russian leader, Stalin, despised Western revolutionary movements. The Comintern, in his view, was a 'grocer's shop' and World Revolution an 'idiotic slogan'.[5] The USSR's need of a long period of peace and reconstruction required collaboration, not conflict, with the capitalist world. World revolution was no longer on the Soviet agenda.

Hitler's destruction of the German Left made cooperation with the West essential. The years 1933–35 were a period of readjustment of Soviet foreign policy, led by Commissar for Foreign Affairs Maxim Litvinov. The new Soviet aim was to persuade Britain and France to guarantee European security. Momentous changes were to occur. The Soviet Union, which had always refused alliances with capitalist countries, would now alter its policies and its very language in its effort to persuade the Democracies to stand shoulder to shoulder with the USSR against the Fascist threat. The manifestation of the change in Soviet attitudes was the policy of the Popular Front, formally proclaimed at the Seventh Congress of the Comintern in August 1935.

Some capitalist countries were now to be seen as bourgeois democracies, to be defended by communists against Fascism by means of broadly-based anti-fascist, or Popular, fronts. These were alliances between communist, social-democratic and even conservative parties. In Spain, the Popular Front won the elections of 18 February 1936 and formed a moderate Government. To emphasise its non-revolutionary character, the Socialists and the Communists did not take portfolios. It was, however, in France that the large Communist and Socialist Parties combined with the Radicals to win a triumphant victory in June 1936.

Other countries saw the Popular Fronts as a threat. They did not forget the shock of the Russian Revolution, its repudiation of bourgeois morality and capitalist legitimacy, nor the murder of the Tsar and his family. The Soviet Union was still a pariah, barely tolerated by the international community. At Geneva, Litvinov wanted to make the League a real force for collective security. But Britain and France feared that Russia was trying to involve them in internecine war. They saw Litvinov's defence of the League and collective security as an irritant. So, by the beginning of the Spanish Civil War in July 1936, the Soviet Union was already having doubts about the collective security policy. If Italy had got away with attacking Abyssinia and Germany with remilitarising the Rhineland, in spite of international treaties and the League of Nations, what value could the USSR put on understandings with the West?[6]

During the League of Nations debates on Abyssinia, one Czechoslovak spectator, perhaps already seeing into the dark future for his country, shot himself. When the issue of Spain was to come before the League the small states would be unwilling to get involved. Germany and Italy had got away with flouting international law and solemn treaty agreements, so their arrogance was all the greater and they would be more willing to intervene in Spain than they might otherwise have been. Britain and France, weakened by economic depression, by internal divisions and by the all-pervading fear of a repetition of the tragedy of 1914–18, had shown their incapacity to act determinedly and in concert over Abyssinia and the Rhineland. Nor would they see their way clear to defending the constitutionally-elected Government of Spain against rebels aided by Germany and Italy.

Chapter 2

In Paris, the recent triumph of the Popular Front gave particular poignancy to the annual celebration of the Revolution – the Fourteenth of July. The crowds cheered the soldiers parading down the Champs Elysées. If anyone were to forget the bloody mire and agony of the trenches, the lines of blind veterans led by their guides and the *grands mutilés de guerre* in their wheelchairs would remind them of the reality of war. People thought France was safe behind the fortresses of the Maginot line. Though *Perfide Albion* had let France down over the Rhineland, the talks that were about to be held would, people hoped, give the French firm guarantees.

In contrast to the stability of Britain, where there were only three governments in the 1930s, the French had sixteen in the eight years between 1932 and 1940. The result was to impede any continuity or grand strategy in French policies just at the moment when French governments were faced with the unprecedented challenge of Hitler and Mussolini.

Right-wing movements, heirs to the Nationalist anti-Dreyfusards of the 1890s, inspired by Nazism–Fascism, advocated strong government and friendship with Italy and Germany. Action Française, Les Jeunesses Patriotes and the Camelots du Roi threatened the Republic itself in the notorious battle of the Place de la Concorde on 2 February 1934. Léon Blum's Socialists swung behind the Daladier Government. It was the beginning of the Popular Front. As Blum said: 'Our vote for the government is not a vote of confidence. It is a vote of combat.'[1] On 14 July 1935, Daladier the Radical marched side by side with Thorez the Communist and Blum the Socialist, giving the clenched-fist salute. The great Popular Front election victory was won in two rounds in late April and early May 1936.

The stability of the Popular Front Government was not, however, guaranteed. Half of Léon Blum's Government were Socialists but the other half, including the Vice-Premier, Camille Chautemps, and the Ministers of National Defence, Edouard Daladier, and Foreign Affairs, Yvon Delbos, belonged to the Radical party, which attracted the largest

12

vote because they were seen as repelling revolutionaries on the Left as well as reactionary clericalism on the Right.

The French experience of Popular Front Government had lasted a mere six weeks when it was faced with the challenge of the Spanish Civil War. The Popular Front believed in the League of Nations and in sanctions against aggressors, but they would not act without Britain. This was the French dilemma, and the revolt of the Spanish generals would throw it into relief.

In Spain, the Popular Front faced the threat of a well-organised conservative–clerical party as well as incipient Fascism and an army given to coups. By offering the electorate an alliance of Socialists and middle-of-the road Republicans, the Spanish Popular Front gained a significant victory in the elections of 18 February 1936.

Spain, despite its closeness to France, was an unknown and often despised country. Apart from its value as an exotic symbol for tourists, artists and writers, the land of Mérimée's *Carmen*, the people most familiar with Spain and its ways were those French businessmen who administered the 135 million dollarsworth of French investments in that country. These commercial interests were disturbed by the victory of the Spanish Popular Front in February 1936. Businessmen's fears were communicated to French centre and Right-wing opinion. The history of Spain since the October 1934 miners' rebellion against Right-wing government was seen by the French Right as a warning. France had to be saved from the Popular Front, and this could be done in Spain. In its electoral propaganda, the French Right-wing press launched a campaign against the Spanish Popular Front. The mass strikes and sit-ins in France during May and June, and what the Right saw as Blum's irresponsible and treacherous surrender to working-class demands, fixed attitudes towards the Spanish Civil War even before it began.

BLUM AND SPAIN

Blum learned of the Spanish military rebellion on Saturday 18 July. Perhaps presaging the difficulties Spain would cause for his new Government, Blum said, 'If we succeed, nobody can say that the circumstances helped us.'[2]

Next day, in the stifling Madrid summer, José Giral formed a cabinet and sent a telegram to Blum. It arrived early on the Monday morning, 20 July. The message from Madrid, which was not coded, read:

Have been surprised by dangerous military coup. Request you to help us at once with arms and aircraft. Fraternally yours, Giral.

The events of the next two days are confused. Later on Monday 20 July, Giral advised Cárdenas, the Spanish ambassador in Paris, of the imminent arrival of Spanish Air Force officers to supervise the transfer of aircraft. His message specified the actual requirements of the Republic: eight 75 mm cannon, eight heavy machine-guns and 250 000 cartridges, four million rifle cartridges, 20 000 bombs and twenty bombers. At this stage, this material might have sufficed to put down the revolt in the Peninsula, for Giral had ordered ships to blockade the Spanish Moroccan ports of Ceuta and Melilla to prevent the colonial Army from crossing the Straits of Gibraltar. The next day, Tuesday, 21 July, two Spanish Air Force officers, Captain W. Warleta and Major A., arrived and handed the list of Spanish requests to the Air Minister, Pierre Cot. Blum told Delbos, Cot and Daladier, Minister of Defence, that he wanted to help Spain because a Franco victory would mean German and Italian bases in the Canaries and the Balearics. Cot, though a Radical, was the *bête noire* of the Right, who saw him as treacherously moving further leftwards. He agreed to start preparations to send the bombers at once.

The Spanish Government assumed that its diplomats were loyal, but Cárdenas notified Madrid on 23 July that he was leaving immediately after transmitting his Government's request to the French Government. Major Antonio Barroso, the military attaché, who would become Franco's Head of Operations and end his career as lieutenant-general and War Minister in Franco's Government, contributed to the military uprising by refusing to countersign the cheque for the French armaments and by informing the Right-wing press that Blum was sending arms to the Spanish 'Reds'. The news broke on Wednesday, 22 July. The very Right-wing *L'Action Française* had been informed by French Air Ministry officials of the arrival of the Spanish officers and published the news also on 22 July.

On 23 July, the Spanish Socialist Fernando de los Ríos, who had arrived in Paris to take over the embassy, met Daladier and Cot. The latter gave de los Ríos details of the arrangements that he was making to send aircraft to Spain. Cot telephoned Robert Coulondre, the Assistant Political Director in charge of the Quai d'Orsay in the absence in London of the Foreign Minister Delbos. Cot appears to have spoken in rather high-handed tone, suggesting that he would send the Potez bombers with or without Quai D'Orsay approval. For the first time, the consequences of sending arms to the Spanish Government came under the scrutiny of a professional civil servant concerned with delicate international diplomacy. Coulondre was understandably angered at Cot's actions and cabled the minister, Yvon Delbos, who was in London. By this time the news was common knowledge and concern was mounting in Paris.

Difficulties increased over the next few days. The Potez factory delayed. The Quai D'Orsay refused permission for French pilots to ferry the aircraft to Spain. The idea of selling the planes to a third country – Mexico or Lithuania – or shipping the aircraft without arms, was floated.

The French Right-wing press now launched a hate-campaign against Blum and Cot. Blum was called 'Blum-la-guerre'. The two were reviled as traitors. More lucid writers, such as Henri de Kérillis, wrote that if the French Government sent help to the Spanish Popular Front, this would give Germany and Italy an excuse to intervene. *L'Action Française* wrote on 22 July that, if the rebels won, France would have to deal with a hostile regime to her South.

For the Catholic François Mauriac, writing in *Le Figaro* on 25 July, to send arms to a regime which was murdering priests and burning churches, as was happening in Spain, was to collaborate in the massacre. A French Government which sent arms to Spain was a regime of bandits. Mauriac ended with a threat:

'Faites attention. Nous ne vous pardonnerions jamais ce crime.'[3]

Blum's arrest and trial by the Vichy authorities during the German occupation of France would be the Right's revenge.

In the meantime Blum and Delbos had gone to London on 22 July to discuss the possibility of a treaty to replace the now inoperative Locarno Pact. What happened in London had a grave effect on the two French statesmen.

LONDON

The dominating concerns in Britain were to try to repair the breach with Italy; to keep the USSR out of Western Europe and to guard vital Mediterranean routes. The recent Anglo-German naval treaty and the removal of sanctions against Italy were hopeful signs of a general settlement. Britain was resolved not to be drawn into European wars, either for the sake of French hegemony, as Britain saw it, or even less to support Popular Fronts which might sign alliances with the Soviet Union or frighten the Germans and Italians by appearing to be combining against them. In addition, the British armed forces and the defence industries had been run down. Economies had been made in the defence of the Mediterranean bases of Gibraltar, Malta and Suez.

The consequence of all this was the refusal of Britain to give France guarantees over the Rhineland, and weakness towards Italy. Both Left and Right opinion wanted to reduce British commitments abroad, to spend less on arms and to avoid policies which carried the slightest risk of war. Britain was an insular society for whom 'abroad' was far away. People in Britain knew little about other countries. This attitude suited the general stance of the British way of life: prudence, pragmatism and moderation. But these very qualities were precisely those which made it hard for Britain to empathise with the easily-alarmed French, or to understand the resentment and lack of principles of Nazism and Fascism.

Britain needed Spanish goodwill in order to safeguard the essential Mediterranean route past Gibraltar. It was a cardinal point of British policy that the Balearics and the Canaries should never be allowed to fall under hostile control, and that the Moroccan side of the Straits of Gibraltar should be occupied by a weak yet friendly Spain. Above all, Spain must be kept out of European alliances. A French–Spanish Popular Front alliance in Western Europe, following the French–Soviet pact, would convince Germany and Italy that they were being encircled.

For most Britons Spain was an exotic country, the land of the Inquisition, the subject of adventure stories and historical novels with titles like *Spanish Love*, *Spanish Bayonet* and *Spanish Dancer*. British people thought that Spaniards tended to cruelty and violence. Pre-Civil War cinema newsreels showed Spain as distant and unstable. During the Popular Front period, the newsreels stressed street riots, and this note continued in the earliest newsreels of the war. 'A graphic story of bloodshed and violence in the one-time lazy South', 'The land of smiling tomorrow is grim today', were phrases delivered in the breathless tones of the period. There was no evaluation of the issues which led to the Civil War. Newsreels cut swiftly from church burnings to crowds giving the clenched-fist salute. As always, the sensational made good journalism. The cameramen and editors were not inhibited about the extremely filmworthy events of early Civil War Republican Spain.[4]

There was a general fear, at official British level, of left-wing subversion. People often compared Popular Front Spain and France with the Kerensky period in pre-Bolshevik Russia. Nine days before the War began, the *Daily Express* published a full-page article on Francisco Largo Caballero, the Socialist leader who had adopted the panoply of revolutionary symbols with red flags, the Internationale and clenched fists. 'Will Spain go Red?', asked the headline. Concretely, the Foreign Office had to deal with anguished complaints from British firms in Spain who had been obliged to reinstate previously-dismissed workers. The British Ambassador, Sir Henry Chilton, protested directly to Prime Minister Azaña on 13 March 1936 at the occupation by workers of the property of the Rio Tinto Company. Azaña gave assurances, but the Foreign Office wondered to what extent the Spanish Government could keep its promise.

Naturally British officials were worried about possible revolution in Spain.[5] Foreign Office officials ought to have been able to see beyond their immediate prejudices and view Spanish affairs from the stance of what was in the British interest, a position which, however selfish it might appear, was at least their responsibility. Yet Sir Henry Chilton took Largo Caballero's revolutionary announcements at face-value. He made no analysis of what the Spanish Popular Front actually did nor did he look closely at internal politics in the Spanish Socialist Party, nor tell Whitehall that the Spanish anarchists would never consent to a proletarian State dictatorship. Yet he and the Foreign Office assumed that Largo would grow more revolutionary and that a military coup would neutralise him. On 7 May, Mr W. H. Montagu-Pollock, of the League of Nations and Western Department of the Foreign Office, summarised the reports from Spain. He wrote that the outlook for British firms in Spain, whose rebellious workers would be supported by the Spanish authorities 'at all costs', was poor.

It is difficult, however, to judge to what extent subsequent British actions were affected by these reports. There were occasions when the alarmism was scorned. Did the Foreign Office really fear a revolution in Spain, given that they knew there was nothing that Stalin wanted less? Montagu-Pollock's considered views were expressed in a report on recent developments in Spain. He forecast a military uprising but said nothing of a Communist coup. Neither the Spanish Socialists nor the Communist Party, small in numbers and weak in personalities, took any part in the Popular Front Government of February 1936.

To some extent, the Foreign Office did keep a cool head. Rio Tinto was judged to have been reasonably well-treated despite its complaints of Spanish Government discrimination. Again, when the Royal Automobile Club warned its members against travel in Spain, the British Chargé d'Affaires in Madrid assured Eden that the Commercial Secretary had just completed a lengthy tour with no difficulties whatsoever, and the Assistant Under-Secretary at the Foreign Office, Sir George Mounsey, who was no admirer of Spanish revolutionaries, returning to London after touring Spain, wrote that he could not understand the reason for the RAC's caution.

Foreign Office reactions to Spanish rumours were largely of the 'wait and see' kind. Nevertheless, it was a military coup rather than a Left-wing revolution that was expected. Thus Mr Shuckburgh of the Foreign Office wrote on 6 April, 'There is now very much less chance of a Communist rising.' The burden of the comments was that the military coup would probably come and there was nothing to be done about it. It did not seem to occur to the Foreign Office that the appropriate thing to do was to warn the Government of Spain of the danger and to offer it the support it might need, but the attitude towards Spain – a third-class country which was being difficult – was such that the Foreign Office loftily dismissed the significance of the news that Largo Caballero had lost the leadership of the Socialist Executive Committee to the moderate González Peña. It was really too premature to deduce anything, though hopefully there was a risk of a split in the Popular Front, wrote Donald Maclean, at the beginning of his career as a spy for the Soviet Union.

The Spanish Government had received many warnings about the planned military coup. It should have been aware of what was being plotted in London. For as early as 1932 a small group had been formed there to make propaganda against the Spanish Republic. The group consisted of the Marquis del Moral, a half-Australian and half-Spanish nobleman domiciled in Britain, Luis Bolín, London correspondent of the monarchist newspaper *ABC*, Douglas Jerrold, a director of the publishers Eyre and Spottiswoode, the monarchist Sir Charles Petrie and the Duke of Alba. In 1933, Eyre and Spottiswoode brought out *The Spanish Republic*, an attack by the group on the Republic.

In early July 1936 Bolín was asked by his employer, Juan Ignacio Luca de Tena, owner of *ABC*, to charter an aircraft. Finance was provided by the millionaire Juan March through Kleinwort's Bank. The idea was to simulate a trip by wealthy tourists to Las Palmas, pick up General Franco and fly him to take command of the army in Morocco. Over an expensive lunch, Bolín asked Juan de la Cierva, of the La Cierva Autogiro Company, to search for a suitable aircraft. He soon found a De Havilland Dragon Rapide at Olley Air Service of Croydon. Douglas Jerrold arranged to find three more passengers to offer the appearance of a tourist jaunt. These would be Major Hugh Pollard, a 'huntin' and fishin'' ex-officer, his daughter Diana and a girl called Dorothy Watson, whose devil-may-care attitude and originality struck Jerrold.

Pollard had been in War Office Intelligence and had had experience of the Mexican revolution and British operations in Ireland. One wonders if he informed British Intelligence of Bolín's plans. That neither he, nor his daughter, nor her friend enquired why Bolín wanted their company, as the latter claims, is hard to believe. Captain Olley was also suspicious and asked Bolín for his personal guarantee to meet the loss of the aircraft if the insurers refused to pay because it had been used for illicit purposes. Bolín insisted that under no circumstances should the pilot, Captain Bebb, land in Spain. Furthermore, if Bolín, whose enmity to his country's government was open, was being watched by the authorities, would they not have wondered why he was flying to Casablanca when he had told his wife to put it about that he was going to Oslo? Is it possible that the British authorities suspected what Bolín was up to? During the flight the radio operator turned out to be so incredibly incompetent, nearly compelling Bebb to land in Spain against Bolín's instructions, that Major Pollard had him repatriated by the British consul.[6] This is also intriguing. On what grounds and with what authority could Major Pollard do this? Possibly the radio operator was a plant from the Intelligence Service, who had tried to stymie the operation.

Yet Jerrold, who was a member of the Right-wing Anglo-German Fellowship and would take a leading part in pro-Franco activity, would hardly have tried to harm Bolín's operation by planting Major Pollard. So the story may be even more complicated and the radio operator may have been simply incompetent or paid by agents of the Spanish Government, whose role is unknown, though Bolín was very nervous about the security of the operation. Bebb later said that he fantasised, or perhaps was led to believe, that he was going to fly an exiled Riff chieftain from the Canaries to Morocco to lead an uprising. It probably never occurred to Olley Air Service that, if such was the purpose of the flight, it would cause great embarrassment to the British Government.

The aircraft left Croydon on 11 July, spent 13 and 14 July at Casablanca, and arrived in the Canary Isles the next day. On 19 July, it flew General Franco to Tetuán, where he assumed command of the Spanish Army in Morocco.

GIBRALTAR: BLUM IN LONDON

Britain had taken decisions on the Spanish Civil War even before Blum and Delbos arrived in London on 23 July, for on 21 July, six Spanish warships, hoping to refuel, dropped anchor in Gibraltar. The crews had mutinied against their commanders, suspecting them, with reason, of intending to aid rather than attack the Spanish Army if Franco tried to bring it over the Straits of Gibraltar to Spain. The ships had first dropped anchor in the international port of Tangiers, but the governing body there, afraid that the sailors might stir up the Spanish population of the city and worried by Franco's threats, had requested the ships to leave. All the other harbours in the Straits and on the Moroccan coast were in rebel hands already.

In Gibraltar, the naval authorities suspected that the Spanish navy was run by a soviet of sailors. This was confirmed by a visit to the ships which were dirty and where officers were not to be seen. British naval officers assumed that what they were seeing was a repetition of mutinies like those on the battleship *Potemkin* and at Kronstadt, (the subjects of famous Soviet films), and the refusal of duties by British sailors at Invergordon in 1931. Although investigation would have revealed that the Spanish crews had radioed their loyalty to Madrid and were asking for orders, the Gibraltarian authorities took the view that they should discourage private firms from refuelling the ships. In any case, the longer the ships remained in Gibraltar, the more likely it was that damage would be caused by attacks on them and by ill-aimed anti-aircraft fire by their officerless gunners.

Doubt, rather than duplicity, was the British reaction, for when the Spanish ambassador in London, Julio López Oliván, asked about oil supplies for the ships, his impression was that the British Government would place no embargo on fuel. This was not quite the conclusion of the Cabinet meeting on 22 July, which decided to delay, partly on the grounds that the Spanish Government was at the mercy of armed workers, and partly to avoid seeming to take sides. The private firms declined to supply oil, and the six ships left Gibraltar.[7]

To what extent did the British dissuade Blum and Delbos, now in London to discuss the situation after Germany's Rhineland coup, from supplying arms to Spain?

The question has led to polemics among scholars. Eden reports no discussions on Spain with the French at this stage. Yet, on 27 July, the US ambassador in Paris reported that Great Britain had pushed Blum in the direction of not supplying arms to Spain, which suggests that the rumour must have been flying about. Other sources probably repeat what Blum said to their authors, Pierre Cot and André Blumel, and indicate that British pressure not to send arms to Spain was applied to Delbos and Blum in London. It may well be, also, that Delbos talked to senior British officials and received more clearly-expressed views than did Blum.

After the Second World War, the Assemblée Nationale investigated the events of the prewar years. Blum took the stand on 23 July 1947, and thought back, by coincidence, exactly eleven years. During his brief stay in London, André Géraud 'Pertinax', a French journalist, told him that the British did not like the idea of France supplying arms to Spain. ('ça n'est pas trés bien vu ici'). Blum also recalled that Eden had remarked, during their farewells, having elicited from the French Premier that he was going to help the Spanish Republic: 'It's your affair, but be prudent.'[8] There is also evidence that Stanley Baldwin, the Prime Minister, told Eden to avoid any compromise which might 'bring us in to fight on the side of the Russians'.[9] Although this was after Blum and Delbos had returned to Paris it does make it more likely that Baldwin himself spoke on the subject to Blum and that he may have also telephoned the French President, Albert Lebrun.

It is difficult to know the effect of odd comments. What, for example, did Sir Samuel Hoare, the First Lord of the Admiralty, say to Blum? Baldwin had sat Hoare next to the French Premier at lunch because he spoke French well. While Sir Samuel wanted to talk about politics, Blum talked of art and books. Did Hoare get in a word about his own horror at the French helping what for him were violent revolutionaries? Years later, in old age, Blum said that it would have been exaggerated to speak of opposition on the British part. He added, 'But counsels of prudence were dispensed and sharp fears expressed.'

Individually, these pieces of evidence for British pressure may not be significant; taken together, they must have given Blum and Delbos cause to think very carefully, especially as on their first day in London, Thursday, 23 July 1936, Delbos was given a telegram from Robert Coulondre at the Quai D'Orsay:

> Monsieur Cot has telephoned me to say that he is sending to the department [the Quai d'Orsay] for approval a request presented by the Spanish Government for the purchase of twenty or thirty bombers... The Air Minister [Cot] added that, since this has been agreed with the Prime Minister and the Minister for Foreign Affairs, and in view of the urgency of the matter, he will begin delivery tomorrow, even without having received approval from the department unless he receives a counter-order from the Prime Minister. While I am telegraphing, Monsieur Henri Bérenger has telephoned to tell me of the grave impression produced on the Senate – because of the precedent this would create in present circumstances – by the news of a possible delivery of war material to the Spanish Government. He believes he is reflecting the unanimous view of the *Foreign Affairs Committee* when he asks for an official denial to be made....

What would Blum have made of this? Coulondre seemed to be asking, not that Blum should desist from helping the Spaniards, but that Delbos should deny officially that he was doing so, in other words, lie diplomatically.

Delbos then issued a note to the press:

No delivery of arms can be made to a foreign power without the Quai D'Orsay being consulted. The Ministry of Foreign Affairs has received no such request.[10]

This was the first step backward, the beginning of Non-Intervention.

After lunch with members of the British Cabinet, Blum and Delbos flew back to Paris during the summer evening. A traumatic 24 hours awaited them.

PARIS CHANGES ITS MIND

At 7 p.m. the Vice-Premier, Camille Chautemps, met Blum at Le Bourget and informed him that, while the French leaders were in London, Jeanneney, the Speaker of the Senate, had told him of the anxieties of the upper house, and President Lebrun had called him to the Elysée Palace to tell him that many deputies were alarmed.

Later that night, in Blum's flat on the Quai Bourbon, Vincent Auriol, the Finance Minister, Delbos, Daladier, Cot and Blum met Fernando de los Ríos, the Socialist whom Giral had sent urgently to Paris to represent the Republic in place of the Spanish ambassador. During the discussion Delbos, obviously under pressure from his department, hesitated but, persuaded by de los Ríos that the Spanish war was a not a purely civil one, because of the strategic link with Italy and Morocco, accepted that it was in France's interests to help the Republic.

A commercial agreement signed with Spain in December 1935 included a confidential note or 'secret clause' which obliged Spain to buy up to twenty million francsworth of war material from France. De los Rios found the dossier of the Treaty and the additional note in the Embassy. The discovery of the clause seems to have changed the tone of the following day's Cabinet meeting, perhaps because supplying arms to Spain could be presented as merely fulfilling the terms of an existing agreement.

On the next day, Saturday the 25th, with the Spanish Civil War already one week old, Blum received a warning from the veteran Radical leader Herriot, Speaker of the Assembly. Blum's recollection in *Les Evènements survenus* of Herriot's passionate appeal has reverberated through the years: 'Ah, je t'en prie, mon petit, je t'en prie, ne vas pas te fourrer là-dedans.'

That Saturday afternoon, Fernando de los Ríos sat with Blum from 2.30 until 3.45, just before the 4 p.m. meeting of the Cabinet. 'J'ai l'âme déchirée' ('My soul is torn'), said Blum, 'but I shall maintain my position at all costs and at all risk.'[11]

While de los Ríos talked to Blum, Chautemps tried to persuade the younger ministers of the danger of selling arms to the Spanish Republic. As the French Cabinet began its deliberations, a Spanish civil aircraft touched down at Le Bourget with over £144 000 in gold to begin paying for the aircraft.

The French Cabinet decided to deny that they were sending arms to Spain but to do so by allowing the export of aircraft by private citizens to other private persons or by selling aircraft to a third party, in this case Mexico, a country friendly to the Spanish Republic.[12] They issued a press statement:

> The French Government, after having discussed matters this afternoon in cabinet, has decided unanimously not to intervene in any way in the internal conflict in Spain. This policy ... was unanimously approved. Finally, on the subject of the arms supplies said to have been requested by the Spanish Government, it was stated in official circles, as the Cabinet finished, that it is false that the French Government has declared that it has decided to follow a policy of intervention.

This probably represented the limit of Delbos's persuasive powers. The French Government had decided 'not to intervene in any way'. In addition, it *had not stated* that it was going to 'follow a policy of intervention'. Both statements deny intervention, but the second sentence, relative to arms supplies, is cryptic.

By half-past five in the afternoon the rifles, machine-guns and 75 mm cannon that Giral had requested had not yet arrived in Marseilles. The Spanish ship which had been sent to take them sailed away empty.[13] 'Blum-la-Guerre a dû reculer,' crowed the Right-wing press.

On 27 July, the Quai D'Orsay informed its ambassadors:

> Certain inaccurate press information having given to understand that the French Government was lending support to the Spanish Government to combat the insurrection, I must remind you that the Government has made it a rule not to interfere in the internal matters of other States. In consequence, all delivery of land or air war material to Spain is forbidden, whether it is material belonging to the State or to private industry. However, in accordance with certain precedents, the export of unarmed aircraft by private industry to the Spanish Government is authorised.

Fernando de los Ríos ended his letter to Giral of 25 July 1936 by warning him that telephone conversations were being tapped by the Spanish rebels. Certainly, French decisions to supply Spain one way or another were no secret, and it was armed with this information that General Franco's representatives flew to Germany to ask Hitler for aid on the evening of 24 July just as Blum and Delbos were flying back from London.

Chapter 3

GERMANY

In Nazi Germany there was no Opposition. The Government answered to nobody. The Foreign Ministry – the Wilhelmstrasse – was ignored by Hitler when not closely subordinated to his will. Unlike the leaders of France and Britain, Hitler was not paralysed by the fear of another war. He calculated that the Democracies would do anything rather than face the possibility of conflict. His objectives were to establish Germany as a military power and have the Versailles Treaty revised, to incorporate German minorities into the Reich and ultimately to conquer 'living-space' – *Lebensraum* – in the East.

Once Hitler had established his regime, he was increasingly concerned with Austria, with Czechoslovakia, with Poland and ultimately with France, which he would have to tackle without sacrificing his friendship with Britain. In pursuit of this policy he left the League of Nations in 1933 but signed a naval treaty with Britain in 1935.

Hitler justified his first policy adventure, the remilitarisation of the Rhineland, by the signing of the Russo-French pact on 2 May 1935 and its ratification on 27 February 1936. He claimed that France and Russia were threatening Germany from East and West. Remilitarising the Rhineland became urgent. German forces were ordered to retire at once if the French reacted. The French did nothing. The French generals were convinced that German forces were stronger than they actually were. Hitler justified his action by insisting two hours later to a delirious Reichstag that the French themselves had destroyed the Locarno agreement by allying themselves with Bolshevist barbarity.

Spain had held no interest for Hitler. Even the victory of the Spanish Popular Front in February 1936 does not seem to have changed the German view. There appears to have been no knowledge in German circles about the military plot which developed into the Spanish Civil War. The German Intelligence Service, the Abwehr, did not show any particular interest in Spain before the Civil War, despite the network of espionage and the connections established from 1925 onwards by Admiral Wilhelm

Canaris, later Head of the Abwehr. Several connections were also made in the field of civil aviation and between high-ranking army officers such as General Sanjurjo, whose accidental death at the outset of the Civil War prevented him becoming the leader of the new regime, and with General Franco and Colonel Beigbeder, who had been military attaché in Berlin and would be one of the leaders of the army coup in 1936. Spanish Right-wing personalities visiting Germany received no more than a polite reception. Indeed, Spanish clerical–conservatives were disturbed at Nazi attacks on the Catholic Church. Business was discussed with weapons-dealers, but this had nothing to do with the official decision to send war-material to Franco once the Civil War began.

The military attaché to Spain, actually resident in Paris, General Kühlental, had sent enthusiastic reports to Berlin about the condition of Spanish forces in Morocco, and had stressed the capacities of General Franco and the planner of the coup, General Emilio Mola. These reports may have had some effect on the German decision to send their aid to Franco when the request came, but Kühlental seemed unaware of the imminent coup until Franco and Beigbeder tried to reach him with a request for arms.

What was more important was that General Franco took over immediate command in Morocco where there was a nucleus of Nazi expatriates who were able to direct his emissaries straight to Hitler.

The two Germans who played an important role in the story were Adolf Langenheim and Johannes Bernhardt, businessmen domiciled in Spanish Morocco and on intimate terms with Spanish military circles in the garrison capital of Tetuán. Langenheim was the Ortsgruppenleiter or townleader for the 33 Nazi Party members in Tetuán and as such reported to Ernst Wilhelm Bohle, head of the Ausslandsorganisation – the AO – for expatriate Germans. These three would be the links in the chain that brought General Franco's request for arms to Hitler.

Franco, however, used another channel first. Through Colonel Beigbeder and the German consul in Tetuán, he cabled the Wilhelmstrasse and asked Berlin to request General Kühlental in Paris, whom both Spaniards knew, to send:

> ten troop-transport planes with maximum seating capacity, through private German firms. Transfer by air with German crews to any airfield in Spanish Morocco. The contract will be signed afterwards. Very urgent. On the word of General Franco and Spain![1]

The cable was received in Berlin early on 23 July 1936. It is highly unlikely that Franco had already heard any news of the French decision to aid the Spanish Republic, so his request to Germany cannot be interpreted as a reaction to it.

Later that morning, Von Neurath, the German Foreign Minister, had another cable on his desk from Count Welczeck, the ambassador in Paris, reporting the French decision to supply the Spanish Government with arms. Welczeck stressed that if the French did send bombers Franco's position would be imperilled. The news was telephoned to the German embassy in London. Perhaps German diplomats pressed the British ministers who spoke to Blum and Delbos next day. But did the Germans realise that the British were strongly dissuading the French from sending aircraft? Later that night, a long appreciation of the situation came from the German embassy in Madrid. Counsellor Schwendemann thought that the Spanish Government had all the advantages, but a well-equipped rebel army might change the position. With all this information, the Wilhelmstrasse decided not to give Franco any encouragement. In reply to the cable from Tetuán, the Wilhelmstrasse coldly stated: 'In the view of the Foreign Ministry, compliance with the Spanish request is out of the question at this time.'

However, other channels, far removed from those of diplomacy, were soon to be put to work.

BERNHARDT SEES HITLER

General Franco was military commander of the Canary Islands. He was stationed on Tenerife, whose runway was unsuitable for the British plane due to take the general to Morocco. So Franco went to Las Palmas on Grand Canary, ostensibly for the funeral of his subordinate, General Balmes, who had conveniently shot himself while cleaning his revolver.

On Sunday, 20 July, Lufthansa Captain Alfred Henke flew in from Bathurst and Villa Cisneros with his regular post-flight. He landed his Junkers-52, named 'Max Von Müller', at Las Palmas. Just as Captain Bebb's Dragon Rapide went into history as the machine which flew Franco to take command of the army in Morocco, so 'Max Von Müller' would play a dramatic part in the next few days. On 21 July, the insurgents requisitioned the Junkers to take General Orgaz, who had masterminded the uprising in the Canaries, to Morocco. On the night of Wednesday, 22 July, Henke took off for Tetuán. There, the machine was kept under strict guard.

On 22 July, Franco had spoken to Johannes Bernhardt. The rebels were blockaded in Morocco by the Spanish Government fleet, and the rebellion had failed over many parts of Spain, especially in Madrid, Barcelona, Bilbao, Valencia and the naval base at Cartagena. Bernhardt offered to fly to Berlin and seek help through his contacts in the Ausslandsorganisation. Franco, after all, had been Chief of Staff. His name was not unknown in Germany. Through a Nazi Party member such as Bernhardt he might be able to bypass all the bureaucratic echelons which would block the request for planes which he had sent to Berlin the same day to be passed on to General Kühlental. The opportunity was there. A German airliner stood waiting. A Party member, well-known to the Spanish officers of the Moroccan command, was willing to serve the cause of the Glorious National Movement to save Spain from Bolshevism. Franco seized the opportunity without hesitation.

Henke feared for his job as a Lufthansa pilot which he had only had for a year. Good jobs were hard to come by and he asked Bernhardt why he should risk his position for a 'robber general' (*räubergeneral*). Franco's will, however, was supreme and at 5.30 p.m. on Thursday, 23 July, 'Max Von Müller' rolled down the runway, carrying Bernhardt, Langenheim and Captain Arranz, Chief of Staff of the small Spanish Air Force in Morocco and by chance from the same graduation class as Major Warleta, who had just arrived back in Madrid after his own abortive attempt to buy Potez bombers in Paris for the Spanish Government.

The flight to Berlin would be long and tiring. They spent a night at Seville to make a small repair. Departing at dawn the next day, Friday, 24 July, they flew out to the Spanish coast at Valencia, up the air corridor to Marseilles and then on to Stuttgart and Berlin, where they touched down in the evening dusk at about the same time that French Premier Léon Blum was landing at Paris on his return from London. The German authorities had been advised of the mission and, to attract less attention, they ordered Henke to land at the military field at Gatow, rather than at the civil airport of Tempelhof. The German press had already been ordered to say little about Spain. Even if anybody knew that Franco had sent emissaries to Berlin, the news could not get out. There was no danger of a vicious anti-Government campaign such as the French press was conducting against Blum.

On the morning of Saturday, 25 July, after what must have been a brief night's sleep, Langenheim and Bernhardt contacted Bohle, head of the AO. In the meantime, various messages had been received at the Wilhelmstrasse. From Tetuán a cable had announced the imminent arrival of Langenheim and Bernhardt with a letter to Hitler from Franco. Another telegram repeated the news about French aid to the Republic and conveyed some rumours about Soviet ships with war material.

The Political Director of the Wilhelmstrasse, Hans Heinrich Dieckhoff, wrote a memorandum that same day, 25 July. He noted that Bernhardt and Langenheim had arrived with the letter from Franco. He recalled that the first cable from Tetuán destined for General Kühlental had been stone-walled. More importantly, he noted down that he had strongly advised Bohle not to introduce the two visitors to Party authorities and not to help them. They should do no more than transmit Franco's letter to the Fuehrer. It would, added Diekhoff, be unwise for Wilhelmstrasse officials to have any contact with Franco's emissaries.

Dieckhoff's memorandum was approved by Foreign Minister Von Neurath. However, it displays an interesting stage in the struggle between the Nazi Party, still feeling its way in foreign affairs, and the Wilhelmstrasse. Dieckhoff would not dare to block Franco's letter from reaching the Fuehrer, but he was more sure of himself perhaps when he ordered Bohle not to introduce two private citizens to Nazi Party authorities. Bohle was ambitious for the progress of the Ausslandsorganisation. If he could persuade Hitler to help Franco, this would redound to the credit of the Party against the stuffed shirts of the Wilhelmstrasse.

Few such significant decisions can ever have been taken so quickly as the one to send German aid to Franco. Twenty-four hours after Bernhardt and Langenheim awoke that morning in Berlin, the awesome efficiency of the German machine had gone into operation to free Franco's army from its blockaded Moroccan ports and begin the conquest of Republican Spain.

It was Bohle, head of the AO, who took the momentous decision to ignore the warnings of Dieckhoff and direct Franco's emissaries to Hitler. As he replaced the receiver after speaking to the Wilhelmstrasse, he picked it up again and took the chance of disturbing Rudolf Hess, the Fuehrer's deputy, who was on holiday. Hess grasped the importance of the mission at once and told Bohle to arrange for Langenheim and Bernhardt to fly in Hess's private plane from Berlin to his country estate. Bernhardt and Langenheim were exhausted. Now they were faced with another flight. But they were buoyed up with a sense of purpose and carried along by success. Everyone concerned was immediately located even though it was Saturday, grasped the situation, made telephone calls that connected, obeyed orders and within less than a few hours brought the two Germans from the tiny expatriate community in Tetuán into the presence of the mighty Rudolf Hess, the only man who called the Fuehrer by the familiar 'du'.

Hess heard Bernhardt and Langenheim and decided, at about midday, to telephone Hitler at Bayreuth, where the Fuehrer was attending the Wagner festival. That afternoon they drove the 75 miles to Bayreuth. There, in the

Villa Wahnfried, the Wagner home, they waited for Hitler to return from hearing *Siegfried*.[2] Hitler arrived at a quarter-past-ten and ordered the visitors to be brought in at once, before supper. Did he merely want to hear them quickly and send them away? Or had he been briefed so thoroughly by Hess on the telephone that he had grasped the importance of their mission? It is a matter of debate, then, whether it was up to Bernhardt and Langenheim to awaken Hitler's interest, or whether he only needed information from them. What Bernhardt had to do was to translate Franco's letter and answer Hitler's questions. Franco had written about the struggle against Bolshevism and chaos, stressed his difficult situation and asked for ten aircraft. Hitler checked the information in a dossier which had been assembled for him.

The Fuehrer then proceeded to think his thoughts aloud at length in a monologue. The visitors watched him for two hours as he walked up and down the parquet-floored room formulating and reshaping his ideas on the character of the Spaniards and the Bolshevik peril. Doubtful at first because of the complications which intervention in Spain might create, he steadily produced arguments to convince himself of the need to supply Franco, whom Bernhardt had described as so dangerously isolated in Morocco.

Hitler then told Hermann Goering, President of the Reichstag, Minister for Air, Commander of the Luftwaffe and Commissioner of the Four Year Plan for Economic Development, and General Werner Von Blomberg, War Minister and commander of the Wehrmacht, who were hungrily awaiting supper, that he was going to help the Spanish general, 1500 miles away in Morocco, to cross the Straits of Gilbraltar and save Spain from Bolshevism.

Von Blomberg said that a further complication for the Wehrmacht was unwelcome. Goering, for his part, began to complain about Franco's unreasonable demands, though he later boasted that he had persuaded a doubtful Hitler to help the Spanish general. Hitler said that, with care, an international scandal could be avoided, since Franco did not want troops but merely transport aircraft to airlift his men to the Peninsula. Goering seized the opportunity for his own prestige, as he would be in charge of the whole operation, and changed his tone to one of enthusiasm. As for the financial side of things, Hitler agreed at once to a credit arrangement. There and then it was decided to use the Junkers-52 aircraft ready for delivery to Lufthansa and the Luftwaffe at the factory at Dessau and to form a commercial company to provide the fiction that the German State itself was not intervening in Spain. This was the origin of the famous HISMA (*Hispano-Marroquí de Transportes Sociedad Anónima*). Hitler dismissed his visitors with a dire warning to keep their mouths shut. He would deny any rumour that he was helping Franco as an *infame lüge* or 'dastardly lie'.

OPERATION 'MAGIC FIRE'

The organisation began at once. Senior officials were roused and ordered to be available early next morning. Bernhardt spent his second almost sleepless night discussing at length the details of the Spanish uprising with Goering. When Luftwaffe General Milch and Admiral Lindau arrived they closeted themselves with Goering to plan the shipments. At 4 p.m. that Sunday afternoon, Lindau and Milch returned to their posts. At 7.30, General Helmuth Wilberg was ordered to set up a special staff – Sonderstab W. The operation to aid Franco would be known as Unternehmen Feuerzauber, perhaps recalling the 'magic fire' with which Wotan had surrounded the sleeping Brunnhilde in the opera that Hitler had just heard.

The Wilhelmstrasse was not consulted. Since it was still maintaining diplomatic relations with the Spanish Government, it was against all usage even to discuss helping a rebel general. The Foreign Minister, Von Neurath, may have been at Bayreuth but was simply not told. Indeed Ernst Weizsaecker, the State Secretary, insists that the Wilhelmstrasse was taken by surprise.[3]

The next day, Monday 27 July, a cable announcing the success of the mission was flashed back to Tetuán. All that day, the mechanics serviced the Junkers-52, stripped its seats out and loaded it with extra fuel, for Captain Henke was ordered to fly non-stop back to Morocco. He took off that evening and arrived in Tetuán early the following afternoon. The relief of the Spanish rebels was patent. Franco was overjoyed. Twenty, not ten aircraft as he had requested, were coming, with Heinkel fighters to protect them and 20 anti-aircraft guns to defend the rebels against bombing by Spanish Government machines. Furthermore the material was to be supplied on credit. Franco was now in a better position than his only rivals for the leadership of the rebellion, Generals Mola and Queipo de Llano, both of whose requests for German help had become bogged down in the Wilhelmstrasse. That same afternoon, the exhausted Captain Henke airlifted the first legionaries and Moors of Franco's army to Seville. The second Junkers-52 arrived next day and eight more flew in to Tetuán over the next few days. They had been given civil registrations and stripped of their military equipment. The apertures for cannon above and below the fuselage had been faired over.

The other Junkers and equipment, together with the six Heinkel He51 fighters, sailed in the cargo boat *Usaramo*. On 31 July, the first expedition of Luftwaffe personnel boarded the merchant ship, having travelled to Hamburg disguised as a tourist group. The *Usaramo* sailed at midnight. How well was the secret kept? Some information certainly filtered out. On 27 July, an astute journalist wrote in his diary, 'Party circles are beginning to talk of help for the Rebels', though he admits it was a month before he learnt that aircraft had been sent.[4] Some evidence suggests that surviving anti-Nazi organisations among the Hamburg dockworkers got a message out.[5] There were some attempts by Spanish Republican warships to blockade rebel-held harbours. One or two German ships had to discharge their cargoes in Lisbon, whence they were forwarded to Franco's forces by the good offices of the Portuguese ruler Oliveira Salazar. The *Usaramo* arrived off Cádiz very early on 6 August. There was a powerful German naval presence in the area, ostensibly to protect German property and lives. However, a Spanish Government destroyer spotted the *Usaramo* and fired on it, without scoring any hits. Admiral Carls, the local German commander, was alarmed at the risks that the German Navy, its status now restored by the Anglo-German Naval treaty, was taking in escorting arms-smugglers.

The German officers selected or requested to volunteer for service in Spain had to resign their commissions formally and go on the Reserve so that they were still subject to military law. Refusal to volunteer for Spanish duty meant sacrificing further advancement. On the other hand, there were advantages to be gained. German personnel enjoyed a higher rank in Spain and, as Adolf Galland, the fighter-ace of the Second World War, later recounted.

> One or two of our comrades vanished suddenly into thin air without our having heard anything about their transfer orders...after six months they returned, sunburnt and in high spirits....[6]

Oddly enough, no secret was made of their presence in Spain. The German consul in Seville cabled Berlin on 14 August that the 'Germans who came to Seville to deliver certain materials' were recognised at once and cheered in the streets. The Communist journalist Arthur Koestler, masquerading as a correspondent for a Hungarian Right-wing newspaper and for the London *News Chronicle* while he collected material for a Comintern propaganda organisation, saw the Germans on 28 August at the Hotel Cristina in Seville, where they were luxuriously quartered, wearing white Spanish uniforms with swastikas in the middle of their pilots' wings.[7]

Security was soon tightened up. On their way to Spain, the men were disguised as participants in a 'Strength though Joy' expedition. They were assembled at an air-base such as Gatow and bussed to Hamburg in civilian clothes. They then boarded a ship tied up away from the main harbour at what became known to the stevedores as the 'Franco wharf'. They usually stayed below decks for the trip. After entering the English Channel the ship's name would be altered to one of a vessel known to be in distant waters. Frequently the Panamanian flag was flown and false funnels were erected. Ships would enter Spanish ports at night under escort.

When on leave in Spain the Luftwaffe personnel had orders to remain tightlipped. If hospitalised they were described as suffering from 'malaria'. Their parents were instructed to tell inquisitive neighbours that their sons were 'Away working' or 'in the Foreign Legion'. The men were forbidden to write directly to their families but told to address letters to a postbox known as 'Max Winkler, Berlin SW68', which forwarded their mail. In Germany discussion of Spain was strictly forbidden.

Between 27 July, when 'Max Von Müller' began its task, and 3 August, 1027 men were flown from Tetuán to Seville and to sherry-capital Jerez de la Frontera at a rate of four flights per day. In the next week another 1282 flew. When the *Usaramo* arrived, the ground-crews worked feverishly, some collapsing in the searing August heat, to assemble the Junkers and the Heinkel fighters.

The field commander, Major Scheele, had been forbidden to fly combat missions, but the Republican fleet had to be kept away from the ports where Franco's convoys were landing his men. The order was certainly changed quite soon, perhaps because of the accidents caused by the inexperienced Spanish pilots who flew the Heinkels. Scheele was ordered to organise bombing raids. Two Junkers-52 were altered to carry bombs and attacked the battleship *Jaime Primero* off Málaga on 14 August. Hits were scored. The battleship made port under a heavy list and was long out of action.

A further shipment of Junkers reconnaisance aircraft and several thousand bombs were sent in the *Wigbert* on 14 August. This was one of the ships which had to discharge in Lisbon. Another vital shipment sailed in the *Girgenti*, which reached Corunna on 26 August with ammunition for the Spanish rebels in Northern Spain. On the same day the *Usaramo* sailed again with twenty Heinkel-46 machines.

By 28 August, when both Germany and Italy had agreed formally to take part in the international agreement not to supply arms to either side in Spain, the following German material had been dispatched:

26 bombers
15 fighters
20 anti-aircraft guns
50 machine-guns
8000 rifles

These were the figures given to the head of Italian Military Intelligence, General Roatta, by his German opposite number, Rear-Admiral Canaris, when they met to discuss cooperation between their two countries in supplying Franco with war material.[8]

What were Hitler's reasons for helping Franco? His decision was possibly opportunist, but this is not to say that there was no plan behind it. The Nazi theorist Alfred Rosenberg thought that Germany should stir up tension among France's neighbours; Hitler was aware of the rivalry between France and Spain over Morocco. Consistent in Hitler's actions was a wish not to antagonise Great Britain. There was widespread sympathy in Britain for German complaints about the iniquities of Versailles and irritation at what was seen as the French desire to subjugate Germany. Britain was concerned to appease Germany, as the Anglo-German naval agreement of 1935 had proved. Was there a way to weaken France without creating British enmity? The Spanish war was a good opportunity, for while the new French Government was ideologically hostile to the Franco rebels, the more conservative British administration was neutral with a strong leaning towards the Spanish general.

Naturally, there were strong arguments against participating in the Spanish war. To do so would complicate relations which were then quite good. Hitler's important aims were in the East. This was why the Wilhelmstrasse demurred over Spain. The German generals, for their part, feared that a more resolute French Government than the one which had failed to resist the march into the Rhineland might take some action if German activity in Spain seemed threatening.

The absence of opposition to Hitler, of democratic or pacifist expression of views in Nazi Germany, together with an ideologically unified war machine, meant that no criticism or even contrasting views on German participation in Spain can be traced. If there was a revolutionary-socialist side to the Nazis, that tendency had been crushed before 1936, and a more traditional nationalist stance had triumphed, advocating strength in Europe, a strong Navy and expansion.

ROME

Relations between Spain and Italy had been close. The early years of Fascism coincided with the regime of General Primo de Rivera in Spain. Propaganda had emphasised the Latin and Catholic sisterhood of the two countries. The two dictatorships signed a treaty of friendship in August 1926, according to which each would remain neutral in case of an attack by a third country. Mussolini now had a guarantee that Spain would not allow French forces passage on their way from North Africa to fight a European war. In London and Paris statesmen feared that Spain had promised Italy bases in the Balearics. These were fears which would resurface in the 1930s. None of them came to anything. The weakness of Spain and doubts about the solidity of the Primo de Rivera regime meant that there would be no significant change in the status quo in the Western Mediterranean.

As a counterweight to the pro-French leanings of the Spanish Republic of 1931, Mussolini sought contact with Right-wing groups. For the Duce, the Republic was not a revolution, but a crude copy of out-of-date parliamentary liberalism which, in the new Fascist world, he compared with using paraffin in the age of electric light.[9] Count Dino Grandi, ambassador in London and later to play a major part in the diplomacy of the Spanish war, feared that the proclamation of the Republic meant that Italy had lost the Mediterranean war before it began. Italian fears, though ungrounded, grew about secret agreements to allow France to occupy the Balearics.

Consequently, the Italian ambassador in Spain, Raffaelle Guariglia, was instructed to maintain friendly relations with Spain, to combat erroneous ideas about Fascism and to dissociate Italy from the previous military regime of Primo de Rivera.

Mussolini actually sounded out the Spanish Government about the validity of the Treaty of Friendship of 1926. The Spanish Government ignored this, which may have inclined Mussolini towards Franco when the moment came, at least in the opinion of the Socialist intellectual Luis Araquistáin, later an ambassador of the Republic in Paris.[10]

Keeping on good terms with the Spanish Republic was not easy, given that Italian anti-fascist émigrés had found refuge in Spain. Carlo Rosselli, in particular, hoped to obtain the aid promised him by Republican politicians in the 1920s. Despite some of the hair-brained schemes invented by Air Force Major Ramón Franco, brother of the later *dictatar*, there was no encouragement for anti-fascist exiles. Carlo Rosselli went back to France and raised a battalion (called Giustizia e Libertà) at the beginning of the Spanish Civil War.

By 1934, with the victory of the conservative Spanish Radicals and the clerical CEDA Party, Mussolini had no cause to fear Spain. Nevertheless, Guariglia had orders to maintain secret relations with the Spanish anti-Republican opposition. In April 1932 the Monarchist airman and conspirator, Ansaldo, had visited Italo Balbo, Italian Minister of Aviation, to ask for aid for the coup planned for August under General Sanjurjo. He was promised 200 machine-guns. Sanjurjo's coup was a failure and the arms never arrived. Another pact was signed on 30 March 1934 between Italy and representatives of Spanish Monarchists. The details were discovered at the beginning of the Civil War in the house of one of the signatories, Antonio Goicoechea, and widely publicised as evidence of Italian responsibility in starting the war. Marshal Balbo had offered the Monarchists rifles, machine-guns and grenades, and Mussolini further promised a million-and-a-half pesetas (about £41 000 at the time). In return, the plotters, once successful, were to renounce any secret agreement between France and Spain. Later that summer, 15 Spaniards, referred to as 'Peruvians', began training in the use of the Italian weapons. However, there was no Monarchist uprising and the arms never reached Spain.

The plots came to nothing and Mussolini's interest waned. There had been a *rapprochement* with France when Pierre Laval went to the French Foreign Ministry. There was no 'secret pact' between Italy and Spain. By 1935 Italy was on good terms with France, and Mussolini had his mind on Abyssinia. He had no wish to become embroiled in a Spanish conspiracy. His promises were forgotten.

Even the Spanish Falange, the Fascist party founded by José Antonio, son of the military dictator Primo de Rivera, was supported only half-heartedly by Mussolini. The Duce had met José Antonio in 1933. He realised that Fascism did not amount to much in Spain but nevertheless subsidised it from June 1935 onwards to the tune of 50 000 pesetas (about £1400) per month. This sum was halved the following year and payment ceased when José Antonio was imprisoned in April 1936.[11]

There was, then, no connection between Italy and the Spanish military conspiracy of 1936. Nor did Mussolini encourage Falangists or Monarchists at this time. In June 1936 the Monarchist Antonio Goicoechea asked for a million pesetas, but the answer was no. If, on the one hand, Left-wing governments in Spain were hardly welcome to Italy, on the other, the Italian ambassador, Pedrazzi, wrote from Madrid on 22 April 1936, that the new

Spanish Popular Front Government, composed of middle-class republicans with no Socialists or Communists in it, was friendly.[12]

Nevertheless, whatever the unimportance in Mussolini's eyes of the various Spanish conspirators, and the inopportune moment, from the international point of view, of the July 1936 uprising, those earlier Italian promises of aid must have contributed to the Spaniards' view of their own status and their chances of success. That is why, as soon as the uprising began, they sent to Rome for help.

Mussolini had to hold a delicate balance between Britain and France, on the one hand, and Germany, on the other. He had been successful in Abyssinia, but the democracies still refused to recognise the King of Italy's imperial title. Mussolini was being drawn towards Hitler by his son-in-law and newly-appointed Foreign Minister, Count Galeazzo Ciano. It was hardly the time for another adventure, so the first requests for aid by the Spanish rebels were refused.

On Sunday, 19 July 1936, Luis Bolín, just after accompanying Franco on his flight to Tetuán, took off again for Rome, carrying a letter from Franco, which General Sanjurjo would countersign in Portugal as his last act before he himself flew off for Spain and crashed to his death. The letter authorised Bolín to buy twelve bombers and three fighters. He arrived on Tuesday, 21 July and on the following day, obtained an immediate interview with Count Ciano. Ciano was optimistic but next day sent his Chef de Cabinet, Filippo Anfuso, to say that Mussolini declined to help. Meanwhile, back in Morocco, Franco had spoken to the Italian consul in Tangiers, De Rossi, and the military attaché, Major Luccardi, who cabled Rome that Franco required transport aircraft. The Italian Intelligence service, under General Roatta, who would later command Italian forces in Spain, advised against granting Franco's request and Mussolini scribbled a laconic 'no' on the cable. Luccardi sent another cable to Rome on 22 July, now asking for eight transports with civilian personnel. De Rossi repeated the request on the same day. Luccardi cabled again on the next day and again on 24 July. On 23 July the Italian ambassador in Paris, Cerutti, had wired the news of the French decision to help the Spanish Government.

On 24 July, Ciano cabled Tangiers to ask for more precise information about the situation and again to discover if the airfield at Melilla, at the eastern end of Spanish Morocco, was in rebel hands. This is an indication that Ciano was still ready to try to persuade Mussolini to help Franco. The Italian officials in Tangiers answered on 25 July. Franco now wanted 12 reconnaisance aircraft, 10 fighters, 3000 bombs, 40 anti-aircraft guns and a few transport ships. On 26 July, another telegram from Paris announced that French machines had landed in Barcelona.

On 27 July, Ciano cabled to Tangiers that Italian aircraft were now ready to leave for Morocco, but that the Italian consul should promise Franco nothing. Were the planes still needed? Evidently Mussolini was still hesitating. Only on receipt of De Rossi's next cable did Ciano wire, at 7.15 p.m. on 28 July, that twelve Savoia 81 aircraft could be in Morocco in six hours and further material in four days by ship. The next day he cabled that the planes were ready to leave. The crews were volunteers and could stay with Franco wearing Spanish Foreign Legion uniforms. The Savoias would take off from Sardinia early on 30 July and reach Melilla at 9 a.m.[13]

In the meantime, on 25 July, the Spanish Monarchist and later Education Minister in Franco's Government, Pedro Sainz Rodríguez, accompanied by Antonio Goicoechea, one of the politicians with whom Mussolini had signed the 1934 agreements, was flown to Rome. They had been sent to the Italian capital by General Mola, who was desperately short of ammunition in the north of Spain. According to Sainz Rodríguez, Ciano agreed at once to abide by the 1934 pact.[14]

What led Mussolini to change his mind and authorise the Italian aircraft to fly to Morocco after he had twice refused? The visit of the two Spanish Monarchists may have demonstrated a clear connection between the agreement of March 1934 and the present military rebellion. Alternatively, the insistent telegrams from Tangiers may have had more effect. Certainly by 25 July, when Ciano first began to react positively to the Spanish request, Mussolini knew that the French Government intended to send aircraft to the Spanish Republic and this may have been a consideration. However, this information was in the Italian leader's hands by 23 July, five days before he definitely released his planes. These did not leave till early on 30 July, by which time he probably knew that Hitler too was helping Franco. He also certainly knew of the French decision, taken on the 25th after Blum's return from London, officially not to help the Republic. He knew that the Spanish ship which had waited in Marseilles to take the French equipment, had sailed away empty. The French ambassador told Ciano on 29 July that his Government was not intervening, but that some private firms might send transports. Ciano, about to give the signal to the Savoias to go, replied that 'technically, the bomber and the transport plane are very similar'.[15] On the other hand, the very failure of Paris not to respond fully to the Spanish appeal, as well as the barrage of anti-Blum abuse in the French press, might actually have encouraged Mussolini to go ahead. It is unlikely that Blum's first favourable reaction to Giral's appeal had provoked Mussolini into helping Franco. His motives were more profound.

Mussolini thought that, with a minimum of involvement, he could instal a government in Spain which would relieve Italy of her constant fear of a French–Spanish front in the Western Mediterranean. The risks were small, given that the French had decided not to support the Spanish Republic openly. Britain was looking at Spain with some distaste and was striving to restore good relations with Italy after the end of sanctions over Abyssinia. There were also risks for Italy in letting Franco's movement fail, for fearsome reports were coming in of revolution in Republican Spain. Cables from Spain were describing the Franco rebellion – the Alzamiento – in terms of solidarity against Popular Frontism. It was not just another reactionary military coup. Monarchists, Catholic Republicans and Falangists were uniting around the Army against murderous Bolshevism. While the reports of Red atrocities cannot have failed to concern Rome, the Italian leader also knew well from Moscow cables that the USSR had no intention of intervening with more than verbal and perhaps some financial support. Fear of Communism was less a cause for intervening on Franco's side than concern with the threat to Italy and to Fascism from a Left-wing Spain.

Helping Franco seemed to be a low-cost and low-risk method of making considerable gains. As Ciano wrote towards the end of Spanish Civil War, after Italian blood and treasure had been poured out,

Those silly people who tried so hard to criticise our intervention in Spain will one day perhaps understand that on the Ebro, at Barcelona and at Málaga the foundations of the Roman Mediterranean empire were laid.[16]

So, at three in the morning of Thursday, 30 July 1936, twelve Savoia-Marchetti S81 fighter-bombers of the Regia Aeronautica – the Royal Italian Air Force – climbed into the night sky from Elmas aerodrome near Cagliari in Sardinia. Unlike the silent arrival of Goering's Junkers, the Italian aircraft would become front-page news and lead directly to the formulation of the policy of Non-Intervention in the Spanish Civil War.

Chapter 4

PARIS

Luis Bolín sat in the rear-gunner's turret of one of the Italian Savoias. He might well be satisfied with his achievement. He had organised the flight of the Dragon Rapide to bring Franco to Morocco to take command of Spain's elite troops. Now he was coming back from Italy with the best of one of the most modern air forces in the world to protect Franco's convoys as they took his troops over to Spain.

The flight plan was to locate the Algerian coast and then fly along it westward until just inside the frontier of Spanish Morocco. Unfortunately, fuel-load calculations had not considered the danger of head-winds, and three planes ran out of fuel. One crashed in the sea and another just inside French Morocco. Both crews perished. The third plane made a forced landing and the crew survived.

When the other planes reached Spanish Morocco, the commander, Colonel Bonomi, and Bolín, syphoned all the fuel into one machine and flew to Tetuán. The others had to await the arrival of a tanker with the high-octane fuel that the Savoias required. By 5 August, the nine Italian machines were ready to cover Franco's first convoy across the Straits.

Up till then, no *official* information about foreign aid to Franco had emerged. But the Italian crashes led to a crisis. Late on 30 July, after interrogation of the surviving crew by French authorities in Morocco, Paris was cabled that the Italians carried civilian passports, but other evidence suggested that they were Air Force personnel. The insignia could still be perceived under the new paint on the fuselage. A Spanish aircraft had flown over the crashed Savoia and dropped a parcel of Spanish uniforms and a message in Italian telling the crew to pretend to be Spanish legionaries lost in the desert.

The French press splashed the news. In London, the Foreign Office received the information direct from its consul in Tetuán, who further reported that the rebels hoped to receive many more German and Italian aircraft.[1] Indeed, Franco had said that he now had more planes than the Republic. In regard to modern machines this was true. He had nine Italian and perhaps ten German planes. Despite all the rumours, it is unlikely that any French warplanes had arrived by this date. Franco, added the consul, genuinely believed that Britain was sympathetic to his anti-Bolshevik aims. Eden's memoirs, however, omit any reference at this point to Italian and German armaments. He says only that Hitler and Mussolini were 'openly expressing support for Franco'.[2] Again, that same Thursday, 30 July, the Committee of Imperial Defence showed no particular concern about a possible Franco victory and its effect on the security of Gibraltar.[3]

In Paris, naturally, there was increased pressure to help the Spanish Republic. Blum's speech at a memorial ceremony for Jean Jaurès was interrupted by cries of 'Des avions pour l'Espagne!' It would be easier now to justify helping Madrid. In his 1947 statement to the National Assembly Blum would recall, 'We felt more at ease.' In 1936, speaking to the Senate Foreign Affairs Committee, he denied that France had sent aircraft, but hinted that he reserved the freedom to respond if other countries supplied Franco. On the evening of 31 July, in the Chamber of Deputies, Yvon Delbos declared:

> We could have delivered arms to the Spanish Government, a legitimate government .... We have not done so, in order not to give an excuse to those who would be tempted to send arms to the rebels.

Was this a veiled message? Would the divided French Cabinet use the evidence of Italian intervention to send planes to succour the Republic?

The answer would depend on the French Opposition and on London. Blum got no satisfaction from the former. Instead of accepting that Italy had to be checked, the newspaper *L'Action Française* blamed the Premier for provoking Italy into supporting Franco.

As for London, Blum's close colleague Jules Moch, who was in the British capital on personal business, quoted as typical a comment he had received. 'Here in England we hate both Fascists and Bolsheviks. If they are killing each other, that's all for the good of humanity.'[4]

The French Cabinet met on Saturday, 1 August. The cries of 'Des avions pour l'Espagne!', with which the 20 000-strong crowd at the Vélodrome d'Hiver had greeted Blum the day before, still echoed in the Premier's ears. He insisted that it was in France's self-interest as well as her duty to help Madrid. President Lebrun, chairing the meeting advised prudence, Delbos spoke at length about the warnings coming from London. As the meeting continued, Blum felt that his colleagues were abandoning him. At this point he suggested or agreed with Delbos's suggestion of a 'non-interference' or *non-inmixtion* pact. If this were fully respected by the Powers it could limit the amount of war material that was going to Franco. This formula of non-interference was seized on by the French Government as a way out of their dilemma. It would become 'Non-Intervention'.

'You will add', wrote Delbos the same day to the French ambassadors in the major capitals, 'that while waiting for an agreement to be signed and because of the arms supplies now received by the rebels, the French Government would find it difficult to refuse a request from a normal and officially recognised government and that, in this connection, it reserves the right to freedom of action ....'[5]

Did the French actually send aircraft to Spain during that following week? There is so much contradictory information about dates, quantities and types of machines which flew to Barcelona that it would seem certain that both sides exaggerated: the Right in order to blacken Blum and Pierre Cot; Blum and Cot themselves to show themselves in a better light.

After the 1 August Cabinet meeting, Blum instructed Cot to make aircraft ready for immediate flight to Spain, but to send them without the cannon and bomb-aiming equipment which made them effective. Fourteen Dewoitine D.372 fighters and three Potez 54 bombers were flown to Toulouse where the authorities were ordered to keep them under guard. The Dewoitines had originally been built for Lithuania. They were sold through 'private' transactions to individuals in Spain. The Dewoitine was a difficult aircraft to fly. Experienced ex-Air Force pilots were needed, so the writer André Malraux recruited a squadron of mercenaries at very generous salaries of over 25 000 francs (£328) per month.[6]

The Quai D'Orsay hastened to get the Non-Intervention agreement accepted by the major Powers before Blum and Cot gave the green light for the French aircraft to take off for Barcelona. On 2 August, the French chargé in London handed the proposals to Sir George Mounsey, an Assistant Under-Secretary at the Foreign Office. Sir George's view was that the agreement, to be effective, should be 'practically universal'. This was wise, because to tie only Italy down, as the French seemed to want, would make it difficult to smooth Mussolini's feathers, still ruffled as they were by the imposition of sanctions over Abyssinia. Whitehall was also irritated by the French insistence on reserving the right to supply Madrid. At this stage, however, Eden accepted the French proposal, while stressing the need to secure the agreement of Germany and Portugal, for he knew quite well that those two countries were aiding Franco as well. There was really no alternative to accepting the French suggestion. If it came to nothing Blum would probably resign or France would descend into chaos and perhaps incipient civil war.

Nevertheless, Blum had not abandoned hope of persuading the British that it was in their interest to help the Republic. On Wednesday 5 August, he sent Admiral Darlan, Chief of the Naval Staff, and Rear-Admiral Decoux to see the First Sea Lord and Chairman of the joint Chiefs of Staff Committee, Admiral Chatfield. The French admirals presented a strategic argument. While the British Government might balk at supporting what it considered murderous Reds, it could hardly ignore the warnings of its own admirals that its strategic interests were imperilled by German and Italian help for Franco. Such was the burden of Darlan's message.

Chatfield was not impressed by the French arguments. He saw no reason to think that Hitler and Mussolini had designs on the Balearics and the Canaries, as Darlan claimed. The British admiral said that Franco was a patriot who would resist the Dictators' demands. Chatfield was strongly hostile to the Spanish Republic particularly because of the mutinies and murders of officers in the Spanish fleet. He was followed by the First Lord of the Admiralty, Sir Samuel Hoare, who insisted that the strategic risk of a Franco victory was hypothetical. Britain and France would be mistaken if they antagonised Germany and Italy, especially if the result was to keep a revolutionary regime in power. In a note attached to Chatfield's memorandum of the meeting, Hoare insisted that 'On no account must we do anything to bolster up Communism in Spain, particularly when it is remembered that Communism in Portugal, to which it would probably spread and particularly in Lisbon, would be a grave danger to the British Empire,' These words illustrate all Sir Samuel's ideological prejudices, which blinded him to the dangers of Italy and Germany, at a moment when those countries' intervention with the most modern weapons, directed from the highest sphere of government, was known.

In Paris, the Blum–Cot group hesitated. Should they go ahead and send aircraft to Spain, hoping the Republic could crush Franco there and then, or was this really too much of a risk? Would they be better advised to try the diplomatic method of persuading Germany and Italy to stop supplying Franco? This might work. In any case, it was what the British wanted and their support was vital, for Berlin had made threatening noises, André François-Poncet, the ambassador in Berlin, had cabled a dispatch. He had been told that France would bear grave responsibility if she supported the manoeuvres of Moscow, as the Germans put it.[7] Would Britain abandon France if Germany threatened her? This was her nightmare.

NON-INTERVENTION AGREED

By this time French diplomats were calling at every foreign ministry in Europe with their Non-Intervention plan. On 3 August, Count Ciano insisted that the Italian aircraft that had crashed in Morocco were private exports. In Berlin, Von Neurath told the French ambassador that Germany was not sending arms to Spain and that any Non-Intervention agreement must include the Soviet Union. He also threw a smokescreen over German activity by attacking France for sending arms. Real Non-Intervention would be impossible unless a universally-accepted sea blockade was introduced, to which every country trading with Spain would have to agree.

The Italians and Germans procrastinated because they were shipping war-material to Franco. Had they really been concerned that France and the Soviet Union were aiding the Republic they would have been the first to agree to the French Non-Intervention proposal. To delay even more, on 12 August the Wilhelmstrasse blamed the impasse on the Spanish Government for refusing to release a Junkers which had landed in Republican territory by error. Berlin insisted that the aircraft was intended for evacuating German civilians, but the absence of seats and the very temporary metal sheeting over the gun positions led the Spanish Government to conclude rightly that it was one of the machines on its way to help airlift Franco's troops, Madrid had asked earlier for an explanation of the presence of German aircraft in Spanish Morocco but Berlin had decided to ignore the enquiry. Consequently the Junkers was kept under guard, though the crew were freed.

By 24 August, when the Soviet Union had agreed to Non-Intervention, Germany changed its mind. To refuse to accept the agreement would mean that France would no longer be able to resist internal pressure to support the Spanish Republic, which it could do more easily than Germany, with no common frontier, could help Franco. Now that other countries had accepted the French plan, to go on supporting Franco was very risky. Hitler decided to accept the French proposal.

In Rome, Ciano also temporised. On 6 August he complained about the pro-Republican solidarity meetings that were taking place in many countries, about the press campaigns and the public subscriptions and the enrolment of volunteers to fight against Franco. He claimed that these were just other kinds of intervention. What was the use of a Non-Intervention agreement between States, asked Ciano, if the activities of private citizens could not be stopped, forgetting perhaps that he had recently insisted that the Italian aircraft had been private exports. The truth was that Italy had to delay long enough to supply Franco with his needs, but not too long. If Italy refused to agree to Non-Intervention, the Blum–Cot group in the French Cabinet would prevail and France would equip the Spanish Republic.

So, during the early days of August 1936, while Italy and Germany prevaricated, they strove to supply Franco with what he needed for a quick victory. As early as 4 August, the chiefs of the respective military intelligence services, General Roatta and Admiral Canaris, met to discuss cooperation.[8]

Finally, on 21 August, after a persistent diplomatic assault by the British and French representatives in Rome, Ciano agreed to the Non-Intervention proposals.

In the meantime, the French planes waited at Toulouse. On 6 August, Blum and Cot played their last card and ordered the planes to leave for Barcelona. That night, Jean Moulin, Chef de Cabinet in the Air Ministry and later a hero of the French Resistance, telephoned Toulouse, only to have his orders countermanded by the Ministry of the Interior.[9]

Evidently, some parts of the French administration were acting independently. Even Delbos, the Foreign Minister, thought that five Dewoitines had in fact gone to Spain, and confessed as much to Sir George Clerk, the British ambassador, in an interview on 7 August.

This meeting was crucial. Although in his report Clerk insisted that the opinions he expressed were personal, the evidence suggests that he was encouraged by London. In reality he was supporting one half of the French Cabinet against the other, not a very proper practice. This explains why he laid such stress on his personal initiative when he asked Delbos to do what he could to prevent aircraft going to Spain. How did Delbos know, asked Clerk, that the Spanish Government was not just a screen for extremist Anarchist elements? The Foreign Office had been well-informed about the atrocities taking place in the Government Zone. Clerk actually quoted one of the large number of outrages which had taken place in Madrid, but he had nothing to say about the executions that the rebels were carrying out in the territory they held and where the consuls, had they wanted to, could have reported what was happening. Clerk's double standards were evident. French help for Republican Spain, continued Clerk, would make close cooperation between their two countries difficult. This was a diplomatic way of threatening not to help France if she got into difficulties. Clearly worried that the document might be leaked, Clerk once more stressed that he had spoken without instructions. The Foreign Office, however, lauded Clerk's words: 'Your language is approved and appears to have had good results.'[10]

Those results had been a unilateral declaration of Non-Intervention by the French Government at its meeting on 7 August, immediately after the Clerk–Delbos interview. After the main Cabinet meeting on Saturday, 8

August, a communiqué announced that in view of the 'almost unanimously favourable replies so far received' to the French Non-Intervention proposal, the Government had decided to suspend exports to Spain. This was a somewhat misleading statement. The German, Italian and Portuguese replies had been hostile, if anything.

The argument in the French Cabinet had been long and bitter. Delbos had led the case for Non-Intervention, and Blum, possibly affected by a letter he had received earlier from Winston Churchill, justified the policy against Pierre Cot's protests.[11] Socialists, including Auriol and Salengro, were against Non-Intervention, but others supported the policy. The Radicals were also divided: Cot, Jean Zay and Gasnier-Duparc, the Navy Minister, were against it, while Delbos, Daladier and Vice-Premier Chautemps supported Non-Intervention. The deciding card was the risk of isolation and the danger of forfeiting British support.

That evening Blum told the two Spaniards who were running the Paris embassy, Luis Jiménez de Asúa and Fernando de los Ríos, that he was heartbroken. He suffered stomach pains and insomnia for several nights. One of the Spaniards recalled that Blum, with tears in his eyes, said: 'Nous sommes des salauds si nous ne tenons pas nos promesses.' (We are bastards if we don't keep our promises). He wanted to resign. But it was better for Spain if Blum stayed in office and the Spaniards persuaded him not to go.

During that tense Cabinet meeting on 7 August, Pierre Cot tried to dispatch the Dewoitines and the Potez bombers, but the pilots, except for one who did reach Barcelona that night, refused to go because of approaching darkness. The next day, while the French Cabinet was finally deciding its policy, all six Potez 54s, including three that had arrived the previous day, left for Barcelona, as did the Dewoitines. Nevertheless they went unarmed and Spanish mechanics had to rig up various generally unsuitable arrangements for mounting cannon and bombing equipment. So hard were the Dewoitines to handle that three were damaged on landing. No further dispatches of war-material were allowed. Pierre Cot, however, did his best to sidestep the Cabinet decision. The Right wing in France would later accuse him of depriving the Air Force of essential machines and thus of contributing to the 1940 defeat. The issue was never fully discussed although it was brought up at the trial of Blum by the Vichy regime. However, with some exceptions, the French aircraft that went to the Republic were training, sporting and transport machines. Another Potez went on 27 August and seven more in October 1936. In the first week of December five Loire 46 fighters, without proper armament, ostensibly destined for the Middle East, landed at Barcelona.

Until 8 September aircraft could pass through France to Spain if they had been bought in other countries. Spanish Republican machines sometimes landed in Spain to refuel or escape pursuit. This was known as 'navigational error'. In a civil war, the normal rules concerning the internment of belligerents did not apply and the planes were refuelled and sent back. Spanish militia were allowed to pass through France from the Catalan frontier to the Basque side until General Mola's forces took Irún and closed the western exit.

This was known as 'La Non-Intervention Relâchée'. But one French Ministry checked the other. While Vincent Auriol's customs men organised the smuggling of arms, the Sûreté circulated orders that 'every suspicious flight going to Spain must be stopped'. Arms smuggling must be 'rigorously watched'.[12]

During August the Italians and the Germans were also sending material. On 7 August Rome sent 27 fighters, five tanks, 40 machine-guns and various other items. The German ship *Wigbert* left Hamburg on 14 August with eight aircraft and ample supplies of bombs. The *Kamerun* sailed on 13 August with aviation fuel which it had to discharge in Lisbon because it was intercepted by the Spanish Government cruiser *Libertad*. This was the occasion of a German threat to attack any ship which interfered with German cargo-boats. The Spanish Government had announced a blockade of rebel-held ports, but other countries had refused to recognise it.

Blum was faced with the task of defending a policy he disliked, without being able to admit that France could not stand up to British pressure. On 3 September, his name was booed at a meeting at the Vélodrome d'Hiver addressed by the Spanish Communist leader Dolores Ibarruri, known as 'La Pasionaria'. Two days later he was threatened with a metal-workers' strike. He decided to use a giant meeting of the Socialist Federation of the Seine on Sunday 6 September, the day after Irún fell before the eyes of French citizens watching from Hendaye, to defend his Government's actions. He said,[13]

My eyes are not closed to reality... I don't want there to be a cruel misunderstanding between the masses and the Government....

The cries of 'Des avions pour l'Espagne !' continued, but died away as Blum went on,

Does anyone think I have changed in the last three months?... Do you think I don't share each and every one of your feelings?...Do you think I did not share the agony of the last militiamen of Irún?

Cries of 'Vive Blum !' came from parts of the audience. He continued,

> I know you want arms for the Spanish Government. But if we send them
> other countries will help the rebels.... What would be the result of an
> arms race in Spain?...Even for Spain it is better to have an international
> agreement which would benefit the Spanish Government.... Non-
> Intervention has probably already avoided a European war.
>
> I have to fulfil a duty to the Party and to the nation...When I cannot
> do both I shall resign. Remember also that this is a coalition, not a
> Socialist or working-class cabinet.

Blum reminded his audience of the ingrained pacifism of the popular
mood and insisted that he would do all he could to avoid war, while
remaining faithful to his engagements to the Socialist party; to his
colleagues in the Popular Front and to the convictions that he shared with
the audience.

His speech was a triumph. There was an ovation which lasted several
minutes. The audience stood shouting 'Vive Blum!' and then sang the
Internationale.

Blum had used every ounce of his skill, but was he sincere? He knew
that a war over Spain would isolate France, but he did not say this, because
it would have suggested capitulation to British pressure. On the other hand,
did he really believe that sending arms to Spain would precipitate a
European war? It was a danger he could not risk, especially since, as he
reminded the audience, the Soviet Union had also agreed to the French
proposals for an international embargo on arm supplies to Spain.

MOSCOW

In Spain the Spanish Communist party, the PCE, failed to obtain a mass
following until it began to cooperate with other working-class forces during the October 1934 rebellion in the Asturias coal basin, which propelled
Spain into the forefront of the Left struggle. At the February 1936
elections the PCE obtained 16 seats. Its biggest success was possibly the
merger in April 1936 of the Communist and the Socialist youth movements into the United Socialist Youth, which would provide so many of
the political commissars and new officers of the Popular Army of the
Spanish Republic. The PCE programme for the elections had reflected the
Popular Front stance, which also met the interests of the USSR, desperate

to keep the Spanish bourgeoisie from turning towards reactionary political forces.

Soviet interests were hampered in Spain by the revolutionary stance of the Socialist leader, Francisco Largo Caballero, by the Anarchists, who refused any compromise with the bourgeoisie, and, lastly, by the particular *bête noire* of the Comintern: the dissident revolutionary Marxist party, the Partido Obrero de Unificación Marxista or POUM.

The USSR expressed public sympathy for the Republic, combined with official reticence. Yet the Soviet Union could not afford to stay distant if it was to retain its leadership of the anti-fascist world. This created conflicts, and the process of Soviet decision-making over Spain is unclear. There may have been a meeting of the Comintern on 21 July which resolved to help with money and the recruitment of a volunteer force. This, however, is denied by Palmiro Togliatti, the Italian Communist leader.[14] A meeting was held on the 26th in Prague to discuss channelling funds to Spain. The plans for the volunteers were probably left in abeyance. While there was still so much uncertainty about what was going on in Spain it can hardly have been in the USSR's interest to have a military force there.

There was no holding back in the propaganda onslaught, however. The Communist *International Press Correspondence* devoted the issue of 1 August to Spain and on 3 August there was a demonstration in Moscow's Red Square. On 6 August, the Secretary of the Central Soviet of Trade Unions announced that over twelve million roubles had been collected by voluntary deductions from Russian workers' wage packets. With later collections, the total is stated to be 47 million roubles.[15]

Communist front organisations, such as the World Committee against War and Fascism and the International Workers' Aid, called for solidarity with Republican Spain. Willi Muenzenberg, the Comintern director of Agitprop for Western Europe, employed the journalist Arthur Koestler to write a book on Francoist atrocities: *Menschenopfer Unerhört*, widely translated and appearing in English as *Spanish Testament*. At the same time, based on research that Koestler had done in Spain, Otto Katz, Muenzenberg's right-hand man, wrote *The Nazi Conspiracy in Spain*, also published in English, as one of Gollancz's Left Book Club series in 1937. There was no question, however, of military aid to Spain. When Francoist propaganda claimed that a Soviet tanker was refuelling Spanish Government ships off the Moroccan coast, Moscow declared,

The Spanish Government has never asked for assistance and we are convinced that they will find in their own country sufficient forces to liquidate this mutiny of Fascist generals acting on orders from foreign countries.[16]

The Soviet dilemma was complicated. Within the USSR, the internal struggle was reaching a climax. Leon Trotsky, the exiled advocate of world revolution, was furiously attacking Stalin. To be a Trotskyist, in Stalin's language, was to be a provocateur, a saboteur and in league with Nazis and Fascists against the true interests of the USSR. Just as the Spanish Civil War was beginning, the old Bolsheviks Kamenev and Zinoviev were about to face trial on charges of Trotskyist counter-revolutionary conspiracy.

In foreign affairs, fundamentalist Bolsheviks tended to dislike Maxim Litvinov's conciliatory approach to the West. However, Stalin shared Litvinov's concern not to alienate the Western Democracies by seeming to encourage revolution. The war in Spain was worrying, because it was accompanied by revolutionary excesses of murder, robbery, expropriation and the more typically Spanish killing of priests and burning of churches. It was a poor advertisement for the new Soviet policy of reassuring the Western bourgeoisies.

The Soviet Union could no longer delay if it wanted to put the brakes on the Spanish revolution. However, no Soviet representation had yet been arranged in Spain. So the USSR now appointed an ambassador and a consul-general, who arrived on 27 August. They were Marcel Rosenberg, a senior counsellor in the Paris embassy and ex-Deputy Secretary-General at the League of Nations, and an old Bolshevik and hero of the storming of the Winter Palace, Vladimir Antonov-Ovseenko. They were accompanied by a suite of counsellors and a military mission. General Berzin would run Russian military intelligence in Spain, General Goriev would be the senior adviser, Generals Voronov and Pavlov would advise and in some cases command artillery and tanks. Captain Kuznetsov and Colonel Svieshnikov were en route to act as naval and air attachés respectively.

The earliest Russian arrival was, however, the *Pravda* journalist Mikhail Koltsov, who reached Madrid on 8 August. He was Stalin's personal representative in Spain. Koltsov was later recalled and executed as were many of the Russians whom Stalin sent to Spain and even more of the non-Russian Communists who died in the Great Purges of 1937–38 because they criticised the methods used by Stalin's agents in Spain.

Early in September 1936, Alexander Orlov was sent to Spain to set up a branch of the NKVD, in order to control the Russians and the Comintern operatives functioning there, and to channel the Spanish revolution in the interests of the Soviet Union, while Walter Krivitsky, head of Soviet Military Intelligence in Western Europe, was ordered to set up a ring of purchasing agents in European countries to buy military supplies for the Republic.

The USSR had welcomed the French proposal for Non-Intervention. A spoke would be put in German and Italian wheels. Furthermore, Non-Intervention would free the Soviet Union from blame for having, so it appeared, abandoned the Spanish Popular Front. In fact, some Soviet officials were opposed even to sending money and medical supplies because they feared, rightly, that Germany and Italy would use Soviet aid to justify their own supplies of arms to Franco.[17] The USSR was opposed to the formation of volunteer units to fight the Spanish rebels. So the Italian exile Rosselli would recruit his Giustizia e Libertà battalion from non-Communist Italian exiles.[18] Other volunteers would make their own way to Spain. Some, like Felicia Browne, the London sculptress, killed on 25 August, had come to attend the Popular Olympics, due to open on 18 July 1936 in rivalry with the Olympic Games held that year in Berlin.

Seeing that Italy had agreed to Non-Intervention on 21 August, and that Germany was about to follow suit, the Soviet Union finally accepted the French proposal on 23 August 1936, on condition that the USSR was not responsible for Comintern actions; that Germany and Italy must cease to aid Franco; and that Portugal must accept Non-Intervention. The Soviet adherence to Non-Intervention was the best of a set of alternatives. The Russians calculated that if Non-Intervention failed because Italy and Germany continued to send weapons to Franco, the French would be more eager to put some teeth into their military agreement with the USSR. Non-Intervention might even work and, if it saved the Republic, it would do so without fuelling suspicion that Russia was meddling. These views seem more convincing than the strongly anti-Soviet one which ascribes Machiavellian cunning to Stalin and suggests that he wanted Non-Intervention because he calculated that it would provoke a war between Britain and France and Germany and Italy, from which he could pick up the pieces. In reality, Stalin had little alternative. He could hardly pose as the champion of the Popular Front against Fascism and ignore the plight of the Spanish Republic. Nor, on the other hand, could he flood Spain with Soviet weapons.

In August and September 1936, the desire to aid the Spanish Popular Front crystallised the internal Russian opposition to Stalin's international policies. The Soviet press was hostile to the whole idea of Non-Intervention. Indeed Bukharin, one of the ablest of Stalin's rivals and editor of *Izvestia*, took the view, as did other old Bolsheviks, that Fascism was not just a sign of capitalist breakdown, as Stalin thought, but a menacing mass phenomenon which threatened the Soviet Union.[19]

The decision to send military aid to Spain may have been taken at a session of the Central Committee of the Soviet Communist Party in early

September, while Stalin was away on vacation. At this time an attempt was being made to save Bukharin from trial and condemnation, which was temporarily successful and might have coincided with the decision to aid Spain.[19a]

This was followed possibly by a meeting on 14 September to discuss the organisation of arms shipments. According to Krivitsky, the decision to send war material to Spain was divulged neither to the Soviet Foreign Ministry nor to the Comintern. Krivitsky had been recalled to Moscow on 19 August to give the Russian leaders full information about German and Italian aid to Franco, so it is possible that the Soviet decision to help Spain took a further month to mature and reflected a power-struggle.

The first Soviet supply-ship to reach Spain was the *Neva*, which dropped anchor in Alicante on 25 September. This ship carried food, though the German chargé in Spain was informed by a harbour official that packing cases marked 'pressed meats' actually carried rifles. However, reports from informers often tell their paymasters what they think the latter want to know and are hardly reliable. On 28 September, the German chargé in Moscow informed Berlin that he had no concrete evidence that the Soviet Union was sending weapons, but there might have been more than food in the *Neva*'s holds. Access to Black Sea docks was more restricted than usual. On 16 September, the German consul-general at Barcelona reported that 'a reliable source' had told him that 37 aircraft, some already assembled, had been landed a week earlier by the Russians at a small Spanish harbour. Did the readers of this dispatch in Berlin wonder how a Russian ship large enough to carry assembled aircraft had managed to dock and unload its cargo at a small harbour? Reports of Soviet arms shipments at this time are not convincing. This does not mean that the Russians were not planning to send arms. The Soviet authorities had already sent Captain Kornievski, of the Long Distance Shipping Service, to survey Spanish ports and plan the details.[20] Nevertheless, Soviet shipments of weapons did not begin until October, which means they were set in motion in September after the USSR realised that its moderation made no difference to the conduct of the Non-Intervention Committee and that Germany and Italy and, in particular, Portugal, were brazenly helping Franco.

LISBON

For Portugal, the emergence of the Spanish Republic in 1931 had been alarming. Would revolution spread to a Portugal that was only just establishing the New State, based on corporative principles and led by

Antonio Oliveira Salazar? Newly-progressive Spain sheltered Portuguese political refugees and, while no real help was given to them, the Spanish Republic did not trouble to reassure Lisbon that it had no hostile intentions. When the Spanish Communist newspaper *Mundo Obrero* actually forecast a joint Iberian Popular Front, Salazar's fears were confirmed. The weakness of Communism in Spain and the physical distance from the Soviet Union made no difference.

After the Popular Front victory in Spain in February 1936, some 15 000 Spaniards, including significant monarchists and conservatives, took refuge in Portugal. They included General José Sanjurjo, who had escaped from prison to which he had been condemned for his attempted coup in 1932 and who was amnestied by a later Right-wing government, and Juan March, the Majorcan millionaire, who would finance the beginning of the Spanish uprising. Despite pleas from Spain, the Portuguese police ignored the plotting of the exiles.

Although the Popular Front Government, alarmed by reports of conspiracies, tried hard to win Portuguese friendship by sending the distinguished historian Claudio Sánchez Albornoz as its ambassador, he found his hosts suspicious and hostile. Spain seemed to be tolerating conspiracies by Portuguese exiles. For the Salazar regime, the anarchy prevalent in Spain was the precursor of a full-blown revolution.

One can only speculate on whether detailed arrangements had been made in Portugal for the approaching coup in Spain. It would seem likely at least that officials had been ordered to provide all facilities for the rebels. Lisbon ignored Madrid's request to stop Sanjurjo leaving for Spain on 20 July 1936 to preside over the new regime. However, Salazar obliged Sanjurjo's pilot, Major Ansaldo, to take off in full public view without the General on board, to land secretly and to pick up his passenger from a temporary airstrip on a race course. The Portuguese could then plead ignorance of Sanjurjo's movements. Ansaldo crashed soon after and his passenger perished. Ansaldo's own account of the episode blames Sanjurjo's immense cabin trunk which obliged the pilot to keep the nose of the plane down till the last moment, which led to a stone or a hard clod of earth damaging the propeller. Sanjurjo's death meant that the leadership of the insurgent movement was open for Franco to seize.

Portugal continued to maintain uneasy relations with the Spanish Republic until 23 October 1936 when the Spanish Government publicly accused Portugal of contravening the Non-Intervention agreement. This was true, but Portugal had signed the pact unwillingly and only after intense British pressure.

Portugal's activities at the beginning of the war embarrassed the British. Salazar facilitated the arrangements of the Spanish rebels. He provided medical equipment and refuelled Spanish seaplanes flying from northwest Spain down to the Straits of Gibraltar to join Franco. Portugal supplied the insurgents with radio equipment, explosives and ammunition.[21]

Portugal's answer to British pressure to stay neutral was that she feared an invasion by a Sovietised Spain. Naturally, she sought reassurance from her traditional ally, Great Britain. On 30 July, the Foreign Minister, Armindo Monteiro, expressed his fears to Anthony Eden, but the latter found them 'hardly credible'. Eden suggested to the French Government that they invite Portugal to accept their Non-Intervention proposals.

Britain then pressed Portugal to accept the French plan, but Lisbon retorted that the Soviet Union was helping Spain, a statement which at this stage was quite false. If Portugal remained quite neutral, asked the Portuguese, would the British guarantee her against a Spanish attack?

Obviously the Portuguese were delaying while they helped Franco as much as they could. But their fears seemed genuine and Britain was their only guarantee. Portugal's strategy was a high-risk one, for she was liable to find herself completely isolated if Franco was crushed.

The British reply was that Non-Intervention was a better safeguard for Portugal than helping Franco. Of course, Britain would respect her treaty guarantees to Portugal but not in any circumstance. On 13 August, faced with no alternative, the Portuguese Foreign Ministry grudgingly agreed 'in principle' to the French Non-Intervention plan.

On 14 August, the frontier city of Badajoz was taken by the Nationalists, as the Spanish insurgents called themselves. Franco's legionaries and Moors and General Mola's conscripts and volunteers in northern Spain now had a tenuous but continuous left flank. Portugal's frontier was secure and she wanted to recognise the Nationalists as the *de facto* rulers of the territory they controlled and as belligerents in the international legal sense. This irritated Britain, and Eden penned a particularly testy draft message to Lisbon:

> His Majesty's Government would find it extremely difficult to reconcile the Portuguese Government's request for assurances of their support in the event of an attack by the Spanish Government with the tendency now becoming apparent on the part of the Portuguese Government to throw in their lot with the rebel factions.

Behind the diplomatic phrases, the intention was clear. If, by helping Franco, the Portuguese provoked a Spanish invasion, they could expect no support from Britain.

Portugal was, of course, protecting her own interests. She had no intention of respecting Non-Intervention because she did not believe France was doing so either. On the very day, 21 August, that Portugal, with many reservations, finally accepted the French plan, she allowed two German ships, the *Kamerun* and the *Wigbert*, prevented by the Spanish Government blockade from entering Cádiz, to dock at Lisbon, and dispatched the war material they were carrying into Francoist territory. As the German chargé in Lisbon reported, 'Prime Minister Salazar removed all difficulties by his personal handling of details.' A few days later, Franco thanked Salazar for 'valuable assistance received'.[22]

Salazar might have been acting behind the back of his Foreign Minister in order to free him from the accusation of deliberate lying over his country's intervention, yet the sheer dishonesty of the process, which must have been known to Great Britain through its intelligence services, is breathtaking.

Portugal remained very nervous. Subversion threatened the regime, for on 8 September, three warships mutinied in Lisbon harbour with the intention of joining the Spanish Government fleet. In full view of two thousand British passengers on four cruise-liners, coastal artillery battered them into submission. The mutiny offered Salazar a perfect propaganda point. In an official statement the next day, he stressed the dangers of the spread of revolution from Spain. He said that the Spanish war was an international struggle and that revolutionaries were plotting against Portugal. He called for a disciplined force to be recruited for the eventuality of an invasion from Spain. This would become the Portuguese Legion, officially founded on 30 September, which itself would have a role to play in the Spanish Civil War.[23]

CONCLUSIONS

On the afternoon of Saturday, 24 August 1936, André Charles Corbin, French ambassador in London, joyfully came to tell Anthony Eden that Berlin had accepted the Non-Intervention proposals. The French Government felt that a committee would have to be set up to deal with the conflicts which would inevitably arise when infringements of the Non-Intervention agreement came to light. Could London, the most neutral of the European capitals, give the committee hospitality? The following day Britain agreed to act as host of the Non-Intervention Committee and the first meeting of the new body was convened on Wednesday, 9 September.

So ended, apparently, the immediate crisis of the Spanish Civil War. Blum and Delbos had been at the end of their tether until Germany and

Italy had accepted the French proposal. Both these powers calculated that the Non-Intervention agreement would not really prevent them supplying Franco. The German chargé in Rome cabled to Berlin on 28 August:

> That the Italian Government has attempted...to reserve far-reaching freedom of action for all contingencies is just as obvious as that it does not intend to abide by the declaration anyway.

And on 29 August, Dieckhoff wrote to Von Neurath,

> I hardly believe that the plan could really entail any serious danger for us. The word 'control' does not appear in the French note....

Franco himself was advancing towards Madrid up the Tagus valley. His left flank against the Portuguese frontier was secure. He could bring his forces across the Straits of Gibraltar without any problems. Most of Western Andalusia was secure. Within a week the fall of Irún would close the frontier with France. Within a couple of weeks Franco would be elected Head of the new Spanish State and Generalissimo. In Republican Spain on 5 September the Giral Government had resigned and been replaced by a broad-based administration, in which Communist ministers participated for the first time in Western Europe, under the veteran Socialist Francisco Largo Caballero. The Republican militias were to be formed into a proper army and the revolutionary excesses curbed. Now began the great struggle for Madrid, whose successful defence would constitute another important moment in the international conflict over Spain.

Part Two

Chapter 5

LIMITED VALUE OF THE NON-INTERVENTION AGREEMENT

Non-Intervention sought to limit the Spanish conflict, but it suffered from several fundamental disadvantages, quite apart from its refusal to accept that the Spanish Government was trying to suppress an internal rebellion and was therefore fully entitled to international support.

Firstly, the agreement did not have the legal force of a treaty. It was no more than a statement accepting, often with caveats, the essence of the French note of early August.

Secondly, the perceived need for Non-Intervention was based on mutual errors. Germany and Italy on the one side and France on the other, feared that their rival was able to help the favoured side more efficiently than they. According to Blum's Chef de Cabinet, André Blumel, 'Non-Intervention was essentially an attempt to prevent others from doing what we were incapable of achieving.'[1]

For Great Britain, Non-Intervention was a method of improving relations with Italy and reassuring Germany that Britain and France were not trying to combine in a bloc against her. This stance was based on overestimates of German preparedness for war and of Italian strength.

Non-Intervention warded off probably unreal dangers at the expense of the legal government of Spain, but legality was overshadowed, for many, by the perceived incapacity of Spanish governments to control revolutionaries and by the pervasive fear that the Soviet Union was encouraging revolution through the Popular Front. The disorder in Spain of the summer of 1936 and the widely reported outrages which took place from 18 July 1936 onward in the Republican zone only confirmed these fears.

Thirdly, Non-Intervention removed the need for a declaration of neutrality by the Powers, which would mean granting the belligerents control over the movements of neutrals in the war zone. Britain, with hundreds of merchant vessels trading with Spanish ports, balked at the prospect of allowing the Republic's mutinous navy or Franco's completely unrecognised navy to stop and search ships flying the Red Ensign. It would have been correct in international law to concede such a right to the Republic, an internationally-recognised regime, but this would mean taking sides against Franco and would bring Britain and France into conflict with the navies of Germany and Italy, who would defend their own shipping. Thus the vicious circle was complete.

Fourthly, Non-Intervention was full of loopholes. Germany and Italy were persuaded to agree only when reassured that the Committee would not have any real power to act and that it would hear accusations only from its own members, cutting out both Spanish parties and any independent persons.

Thus, while Léon Blum was defending Non-Intervention before 60 000 Socialists at Luna Park on Sunday, 6 September, in London, 15 000 people in Trafalgar Square stood bareheaded for two minutes in the rain as they honoured the Spanish dead. Huge placards bearing images of heroic Spanish militia covered the plinths of Nelson's Column. After the speeches, a two-mile procession wound past the Italian embassy protesting against Italian intervention.

In these circumstances, the first meeting took place of what was to be known ponderously as The International Committee for the Application of the Agreement for Non-Intervention in Spain. After the first two meetings the Chairman for the rest of the war would be the Earl of Plymouth, Parliamentary Under-Secretary to the Foreign Office, fifteenth Baron Windsor, and one of the largest landowners in the country. Solemn and refined, never rude, the image of self-confident aristocrat, he was the perfect chairman of a committee whose task it was to do very little, but pretend to do much.

The Committee Secretary was Francis Hemming, a civil servant and eminent entomologist. Hemming's patience was enormous, as was his ability to suggest endless variations in forms of words of the communiqués which had to satisfy all the delegates.

At noon on Wednesday, 9 September 1936, the Chairman welcomed the ambassadors of 26 European countries. Eden, in bed with chicken-pox, could not be present to receive them. Around the oval table in the high-windowed and vaulted room in the Foreign Office, in order of their countries' names, sat representatives of Albania, Austria, Belgium, Bulgaria, Czechoslovakia, Denmark, Estonia, Finland, France, Germany, Great Britain, Greece, Hungary, the Irish Free State, Italy, Latvia, Lithuania, Luxemburg, Norway, the Netherlands, Poland, Rumania, the USSR, Sweden, Turkey and Yugoslavia; that is, every European country save Spain, Portugal and Switzerland, which had agreed to Non-Intervention but declined to compromise its neutrality by taking part in the discussions.

The Chairman proposed that the replies to the French proposal for Non-Intervention and the various national regulations about exports of war materials should be collated and published. At this point, the German chargé d'affaires in London, Prince Otto Christian Archibald Von Bismarck, a descendant of the Iron Chancellor, and Dino Grandi of Italy, asked to speak. Bismarck had been told not to antagonise Corbin by making accusations against the French Government, but rather to let the Italian delegate make the running, and to delay agreeing to anything in order to postpone as long as possible the earliest date from which contraventions of the agreement would be investigated. He was to resist any suggestions for positive control measures. Grandi, a distinguished officer in the World War, had led the Fascist movement in North Italy and had been Minister of Foreign Affairs before coming to London as ambassasdor in 1932. He was a popular man with a small beard in the fashionable Fascist style. He had done a lot to ease tensions between Britain and Italy. As he sat in the Foreign Office, he had before him Mussolini's instruction to draw the Committee's attention away from Italian aid to Franco by harping on French aid to the Spanish Republic and about the propaganda and fund-raising campaigns organised by the Left in Paris, London and Moscow. (In 1943, Grandi proposed deposing the Duce. Grandi had to flee and enjoyed a lucrative business career in Brazil. Returning to Italy, he lived until 1988, fifty years after his able defence of his country's actions at the Non-Intervention Committee.)

That evening Bismarck cabled Berlin with a summary of the proceedings. There was no need for alarm, he said, for Britain and France were not interested in taking any urgent steps but merely in pacifying their respective Leftists.

EARLY MEETINGS OF THE NON-INTERVENTION COMMITTEE

The next day, Hemming and Plymouth decided that the Chairman should not himself raise the question of breaches of the agreement unless a member country did so and that when complaints came they should be ventilated in a sub-committee consisting of those countries immediately concerned.

At the meeting on 14 September, Grandi assured the Committee that 'the existing embargo is being most strictly and scrupulously enforced in my country'. At this point Samuel Cahan, the Russian chargé in ambassador Ivan Maiskii's absence, said that the British Government knew, because Madrid had told it so, that 24 Italian aircraft had arrived at the northern Spanish seaport of Vigo. The Chairman cut him short. He should wait till the agenda reached the item of 'complaints'. But Cahan insisted that this was the point of the Committee. Grandi agreed because this allowed him to accuse the Soviet Union of intervening. The Chairman said that he would not allow complaints about the past, to which Corbin said helpfully that a good date limit was the date when individual countries had forbidden their nationals to sell arms to Spain. At this point the Chairman proposed the creation of a sub-committee consisting of Britain, France, Germany, Italy, the USSR and three countries with substantial arms industries: Belgium, Czechoslovakia and Sweden.

On 21 September, Lord Plymouth announced the ground rules. Complaints about contravention of the agreements would be taken only from a country which was a party to Non-Intervention. The accused country would be asked for an explanation. What would happen after that was doubtful. If fact, nothing at all could be done, even if the stage of proving an accusation were reached.

Cahan, not really aware of the purpose of the committee, naively seemed to think that it would do what it was officially appointed to do and impatiently asked when they were going to listen to his accusations. He did not enjoy the diplomatic skills of Guido Crolla, the Italian chargé, who skilfully diverted Cahan's attack by bringing up the question of what he called the 'indirect intervention' of propaganda campaigns and monetary contributions. Cahan angrily replied that this was not within the jurisdiction of the committee and asked why were they not discussing Portugal's behaviour, which he had put on the agenda before but which the chairman had avoided discussing?

The Portuguese representative, Francisco Calheiros e Meneses, whose English was not quite up to the standard of the others and who always spoke in French, said he had not understood what Cahan had said. (The skills of Samuel Borisevich Cahan lay elsewhere than in diplomacy. He was Resident Director of the Soviet Secret Intelligence service in Britain and on the look out for socially well-placed young dissidents. His abilities enabled him to recruit the notorious spies Philby, Maclean, Burgess and Blunt.)[2] Corbin whispered in Calheiro e Meneses' ear. Perhaps he not only summarised the Russian's statement but also advised the answer, because the Portuguese representative asked for notice of the Russian accusation in writing, which would helpfully permit a little more prevarication.

So far, then, it had been possible to deflect any investigation into German, Italian and Portuguese help to Franco. However, the Spanish Republican Minister of Foreign Affairs, Julio Alvarez del Vayo, had sent notes detailing violations to these countries, asking for an explanation of their hostile acts towards a country with which they still had official relations. No answer came from Berlin, Rome and Lisbon, which were only waiting for Franco to take Madrid in order to break off relations with the Republic. The Non-Intervention Sub-Committee agreed to ignore del Vayo's note, as Spain was not a member.

On 25 September, del Vayo publicised his complaints in a speech at the General Assembly of the League of Nations in Geneva. He cited concrete examples of Italo-German Intervention, but the Secretary-General refused to publish it as an official document. Del Vayo appealed privately to Eden, who 'gave him no encouragement to think that we would modify our policy'.[3]

Indeed the League was not at all sympathetic to the Spanish Republic. Only about twenty of its members had democratic systems and these were dominated by Britain and France. Most of the Latin American countries, with the exception of Mexico, were conservative. Furthermore, the Secretary-General, Joseph Avenol, was making great efforts to bring Germany back into the League and to reconcile Italy, still smarting from the sanctions of 1935. After the humiliation that the League had suffered over Abyssinia, no action under its covenant was likely to be successful. The answer of the British and French Foreign Ministers, who did not want Spain discussed at Geneva, was that the Non-Intervention Committee had been set up precisely to try to limit the war and cut off its supplies. This was the obvious get-out for the many League countries which considered Republican Spain a nation of uncontrolled revolutionaries.

Del Vayo's memorandum had, nevertheless, not been ignored by British officials, who had felt some moral discomfort in refusing to sell arms to the Spanish Republic. On 7 September, as the untrained Spanish militia fled back along the Estremadura highway towards Madrid, del Vayo had made a moving appeal to the British chargé d'affaires in Madrid, George Ogilvie-Forbes, stressing Spain's friendship with Britain, her loyalty to the principles of the League and her vulnerability to the Franco rebels, supported as they were in all manner of weapons by Italy, Germany and Portugal. What price British fair play, asked del Vayo, who had spent several months in his youth at the London School of Economics? The Foreign Office commented extensively on the cable, concluding that it would be dangerous to give the legal government of Spain the facilities 'to which it was undoubtedly entitled', and no answer was sent. In contrast, the ghastly reports of nightly assassinations of persons often well-known to embassy staff reassured the Foreign Office that its actions were correct.

However, by October, the Foreign Office began to think that it ought to do something to restore the balance, and this consisted in putting del

Vayo's accusations before the Non-Intervention Committee on 9 October. The situation had evolved over August and September to such an extent that it had become politic to take this step.

THE BRITISH LABOUR PARTY AND THE TUC

By now, the Spanish conflict was front-page news. The British Independent MP Eleanor Rathbone set up a Commission of Enquiry into Alleged Breaches of the Non-Intervention Agreement in Spain, which was to act as a kind of unofficial correction to the Non-Intervention Committee. Members included Professor J. B. Trend, holder of the first Chair of Spanish at Cambridge University, Philip Noel-Baker, the noted international civil servant and Labour MP, Lord Faringdon, Geoffrey Bing, a later Labour MP and Attorney-General of Ghana, a journalist, John Langdon-Davies, author of a perceptive book on the beginnings of the Spanish Civil War, the well-known Communist barrister, D. N. Pritt and the politician and father of a later leader of the Labour Party, Dingle Foot. These names would often reappear on the many committees set up in Britain to aid and propagandise for the Republic. This body began its deliberations on the afternoon of Thursday, 24 September, when the Communist activist Isabel Brown produced the parachute in which an Italian pilot had baled out when his fighter had been shot down.[4] The Commission of Enquiry published its report at the same time as the British press published the evidence produced at the League by the Spanish Foreign Minister. At this point the Labour Party also began to show discomfort at the course of British policy towards Spain.

After the failure of the League of Nations to prevent Italian aggression in Abyssinia, opinion in the Labour Party was coming round to the idea of collective security – that is, international pacts against aggression. This, however, required a sea-change in Labour Party attitudes. To urge the Government to take a strong line on Spain meant accepting the risk of European war and therefore voting for and not against the defence estimates. But on the other hand, the Party could not risk policies which went against the mass of public opinion. Tellingly, Sir Walter Citrine, General Secretary of the Trades Union Congress, said to the Labour intellectual, Hugh Dalton:

Our own people are passionately concerned about Spain, but the great mass of the public are not. This might be deplorable but it is true.

Dalton himself did not see Franco as a menace as serious as the German and Italian dictators. Moreover, he thought that the Spanish Left, with its revolutionary agitation and propaganda, had been partly responsible for the breakdown of democracy. Nor was he enthusiastic about the slogan 'arms for Spain' if that meant selling arms which Britain might need for its rearmament programme. Supporting Spain, reasoned Dalton, would not help Labour win an election.[5]

On 7 August, the Deputy Leader of the Party, Arthur Greenwood, told Foreign Office officials that the Labour rank and file were pressing for a campaign in favour of Madrid but that the leaders were 'damping things down'.

Greenwood, Citrine and other Labour officials saw Eden on 19 August. They questioned him about the rumour that the French Non-Intervention initiative had really come from London. Eden, of course, denied this. The Labour leaders knew nothing of his warning to Blum to be prudent, nor of the pressure exerted by Sir George Clerk on Delbos, just before the French Cabinet meeting on 7 August which finally accepted the Non-Intervention policy.

After the Labour leaders had met Eden for the second time and the Foreign Secretary had given assurances that Non-Intervention would be applied fully to both sides in the civil war, they decided that they would not oppose the Government over its Spanish policy.

The conference of the Trades Union Congress, held at Plymouth from 7 to 11 September, defeated an amendment attacking Non-Intervention. Though delegates stood in silence in support of the Republic, the General Secretary, Sir Walter Citrine, questioned whether the TUC should bind Labour to war, which, he said, repeating what Eden had told him, would inevitably break out if other countries poured arms into Spain. In contrast, another speaker, Mr Zak of the Furnishing Trades Union, told Conference that

Far from preserving peace it [Non-Intervention]...draws us closer to war because it increases the audacity of the Fascist powers.[6]

These two stances exemplified the argument over Non-Intervention. As it happened, Mr Zak was right, but the appeasers, as they would come to be known, hoped that if Germany and Italy were allowed a little leeway, they could be inclined towards more acceptable behaviour. Whether trades union and Labour Party members believed this or not, pacifism was so deeply ingrained that Citrine took the conference with him when he said:

I know that in our movement there are those who...every time there has been under consideration the question of force to be exercised against aggressors, have evaded facing it. I thought to myself that in the British Labour movement we shall require some heartsearching before we can give a definite, clear reply as to what we shall do on that question.

The block vote system ensured that the motion against Non-Intervention was defeated by 3 029 000 to 51 000 votes.

The 1936 Labour Party Conference at Edinburgh, which opened on 5 October, had before it the Spanish Government's *Libro Blanco* (White Book) denouncing German, Portuguese and Italian intervention.

That afternoon, Arthur Greenwood defended the Labour Party Executive over Non-Intervention. He challenged any delegate to propose action which would mean that 'a lighted match was dropped into the powder barrel'. While Ernest Bevin, of the Transport and General Workers, together with other big union leaders and Major Attlee, the Party leader, also defended the Executive, several delegates accused the leadership of being ready to help Spain but only with 'sympathy, accompanied by bandages and cigarettes'.[7] Aneurin Bevan, the Labour firebrand, roundly attacked the Party leadership for their lack of a long-term view. If Spain was overrun by Fascism, said Bevan, Blum's Government would collapse and Europe would lie prostrate before the Dictators.

In spite of Bevan's rhetoric, the Executive's motion in support of Non-Intervention survived by 1 836 000 votes to 519 000.

However, on the Wednesday morning, 7 October, two new figures appeared on the rostrum. They came from Spain as fraternal delegates from the Spanish Socialist Party. First to speak was Luis Jiménez de Asúa, Vice-President of the Spanish Cortes. He spoke briefly in French and asked the Labour Party to help Spain to buy arms. He was followed by Isabel de Palencia, the Republic's ambassador to Sweden. She spoke in English about Scotland, which she had known as a child, of Walter Scott and Robbie Burns. She was a Catholic and was probably one of the first people to remind audiences that not all Catholics supported Franco. She described the suffering of Spanish women, and their fate at the hands of Franco's Moorish troops. She finished in the tones of a Scottish minister:

Now you know the truth. Now you know what the situation is in Spain. Come and help us. Scotsmen, ye ken noo!

She hurled her clenched fist into the air as the audience rose and sang the Red Flag. Then delegates shouted 'What about Non-Intervention now?' The Executive was plainly embarrassed and met during lunchtime. When the afternoon session began, the Chairman of the Executive, Hugh Dalton who, incidentally, seemed to think conference had been addressed by the Spanish Communist leader Dolores Ibárruri, announced that the speeches would be published. Attlee and Greenwood, would go to London at once and discuss the situation with the acting Prime Minister, Neville Chamberlain.

One wonders whether some of this was expected, given that the previous week the Executive Committee of the Labour and Socialist International had voted a resolution to allow the Spanish Government access to the arms market. The following day the British National Council of Labour had cabled Eden at Geneva to insist that del Vayo's White Book required examination. William Gillies, the Party's international secretary, had acquired two thousand copies of a pamphlet defending the Republic from a Catholic point of view, to try to counteract the bad effect on the Labour Catholic vote of press publicity about anti-clerical outrages. All this somehow suggests that an attempt was being made to overturn the Executive's stance. In the end, of course, it made no difference. The block vote ensured a majority from the major unions, and Dalton took the view that the opponents of the party leadership were 'wallowing in vicarious valour' and 'unrepresentative of the vast mass of their countrymen'. Curiously enough, Eden later repeated the expression, writing 'The Labour Party had always had its share of vicarious warriors.'[8]

Attlee and Greenwood rushed to London, returning on the Friday, 9 October to tell Conference that they had demanded an investigation of the Spanish accusations, and proposed that, if they were found to be true, the Party should change its view on Non-Intervention. The resolution in those terms was unanimously accepted. In reality, this resolution would mean nothing unless the Non-Intervention Committee really investigated the Spanish charges and found them to be true. It was unlikely that it would do so. All the same, the Labour Party Conference had had some effect on the British Government, which now presented the Spanish complaints to the Non-Intervention Committee.

ITALIAN INTERVENTION WORRIES BRITAIN

Events were overtaking the delaying tactics of the Foreign Office. On 6 October, Cahan wrote to Hemming, drawing attention to del Vayo's White Book, which the Committee's rules did not allow Spain to submit directly. He wanted an immediate discussion of the complaints. The next day, he wrote to Lord Plymouth that the Spanish Government had proved breaches of the Non-Intervention agreement. The USSR had raised the question many times. It was not prepared to turn the Committee into 'a screen shielding the military aid given to the Rebels'. Unless the violations stopped, wrote Cahan, the Soviet Government would 'consider itself free from the obligations arising out of the Agreement'.

This was strong meat. Cahan demanded the end of violations, not merely their investigation. A week later, the first Russian arms ship would dock at Cartagena. The Soviet decision had been taken. Italy was increasing her supplies of war material to Franco in the hope that Madrid would be taken before the mounting scandal forced the Non-Intervention Committee to act. Twelve Fiat fighters were unloaded in Morocco on the night of 12–13 August.[9] One of them was shot down on 31 August and its pilot's parachute was displayed at Miss Rathbone's Commission of Enquiry. A further nine fighters were sent to Vigo at the end of August, followed by another nine on 3 September. In addition, twelve RO-37 reconnaissance aircraft arrived in Vigo on 23 September, so that by mid-September, 42 planes had arrived in addition to the nine which had landed at the end of July. In September, the *Città di Bengasi* docked at Vigo with tanks, flamethrowers, cannon and anti-aircraft guns, together with 200 men.

Italy was being sucked into the quagmire of the Spanish war, but Ciano and Mussolini did not know how long they could keep the Non-Intervention Committee at bay. At the end of September, according to Italian records, there were fewer than 400 Italians in Spain.[10] However, disturbing reports were coming from the island of Majorca.

Franco had held Majorca since the outbreak of war. However, on 16 August a Government invasion force had established a bridgehead on the island and over the next two weeks tried to press inland. Six Italian planes arrived on the night of 27–28 August. The local Falange chief had little confidence in the military command and asked Italy for an adviser to help him. Since Majorca in Republican hands would constitute a potential strategic danger for Italy, Mussolini, who could not send a military force openly, dispatched one of the legendary figures of the Spanish Civil War, a black-uniformed and -booted, red-haired, bearded Fascist called Arconovaldo Bonaccorsi, alias 'General Count Aldo Rossi', Festooned with grenades and small arms, wearing a white cross around his neck, he swaggered about the island on a white horse or in a fast sports car, announcing to the staid Catholic bourgeoisie of Palma that he needed at least one woman a day. The Spanish military command denied Bonaccorsi any official role, but he created a Fascist militia. With a combination of theatricality and brutality he galvanised the somewhat passive insurgent forces and, aided by Italian aircraft and supplies and the presence throughout this time of an Italian cruiser in Palma harbour, he succeeded in expelling the invading Spanish Government forces.

Bonaccorsi posed as Liberator of the island. His escort, the so-called Dragoons of Death, left a trail of corpses behind them. Of course, there were complaints from the Spaniards and indeed from the Italian consul. Ciano himself advised Bonaccorsi to moderate his activities and, in particular, refused to allow him to attack the Government-held island of Minorca. Nevertheless, neither the Duce nor Ciano appears to have expressed disapproval of plans drawn up by Bonaccorsi and the Falangist leaders on Majorca to overthrow the Spanish military command and set up a fully-fledged Fascist regime.

The Foreign Office worried that Italy was using the Spanish war to weaken British seapower in the Western Mediterranean. It was important to make Mussolini understand that Britain would not accept any alteration in the balance of power in that area.

The Chiefs of Staff had already been asked to consider the effect on British interests if Italy upset the existing balance. Their report appeared on 24 August. Somewhat self-contradictorily, they said that while an Italian occupation of Majorca would not affect essential British strategic interests, it would nevertheless bring Italian forces 250 miles nearer to Gibraltar and be a direct threat to French communications. The Chiefs of Staff concluded that Italy could be dissuaded only if she were convinced that Britain would respond with force. Britain would be better advised not to do this, they wrote, because Italian forces were fully mobilised and prepared for battle. Britain should avoid measures which would alienate Italy, and hope for the success of the Non-Intervention Committee.

Thus years of neglect of the armed forces and poor perception of the nature of Fascism led the Government to accept a military view which subordinated British interests to the success of a low-level international committee which had no teeth.

Ten days later further information alarmed London. It seemed as if the Italians were intending to stay on Majorca. On 2 September the Cabinet decided that Eden should send a warning to Italy at the appropriate moment. In the meantime a British warship would be stationed in every Spanish port where there was an Italian naval vessel. Eden ordered Mr Ingram, the chargé in Rome, to tell Ciano, in the carefully-chosen language of diplomacy, that 'any alteration in the status quo in the Western Mediterranean must be a matter of the closest concern to His Majesty's Government'. Thus, quietly and as part of a friendly note, the Foreign Office made its point. It was not until 12 September that Mr Ingram saw

Ciano and conveyed Eden's exact words. Ciano assured Eden that he would not engage in negotiation with Franco to change the status quo.

While Italy was determined to break British Mediterranean hegemony, she interpreted the term 'status quo' narrowly, as referring to territorial expansion. She was willing to behave as an international gangster to destroy the Popular Front in Spain.

These were the circumstances in which the British Government decided to bring the Spanish Government's complaints to the Non-Intervention Committee. Military intelligence confirmed the truth of the accusations against Germany, Italy and Portugal. This, of course, embarrassed the Foreign Office, which would have been happier if the accusations had been Leftist propaganda. Walter Roberts, Head of the Western and League Department, wrote a report which included this paragraph, a masterpiece of incomprehensible double-talk.

> The facts alleged by Señor Del Vayo are confirmed by our own information as may easily be seen from the attached secret report. But these facts alone...do not prove a breach of the Non-Intervention Agreement by any one of the three Powers. This is not to say that the Agreement has not been broken. The same report proves conclusively that it has been broken at least by Italy and, although the evidence does not prove a case against Germany, it is at least doubtful whether Germany has kept her undertaking. The evidence against Portugal is also not sufficient to convict her of a breach of the agreement.[11]

If Mr Roberts had looked at 'Notes on air aspects of the Spanish Civil War' of 20 August 1936, from Air Ministry Intelligence, he would have read that 'there is indisputable evidence that the German Government and the Italian Government have been materially assisting General Franco, particularly in large aircraft and also, in the case of Germany, with artillery, ammunition and bombs.'[12] Military Intelligence had reported on 6 August that there were thirty large aircraft at Tetuán with foreign pilots. On 14 September the same source reported that reports of Russian and French help to Government forces were unsubstantiated while it was indisputable that Germany and Italy were aiding the insurgents.

Britain put the Spanish Republican case forward because of the widespread publicity given to Nazi–Fascist activities in Spain. A warning to Berlin and Rome was probably in order. Even so, Eden thought the moment 'peculiarly inopportune' for raising the question at the Non-Intervention Committee and was forced to do so in the end by Cabinet pressure.[13] Italian intervention had been widely reported, and embarrassing parliamentary questions were inevitable when the session began on 29 October.

For this reason, the Russian delegate's threat to abandon Non-Intervention just at that moment was an error. It is just possible that the combination of the protests of the Spanish Government, the press, and the Labour Opposition, together with the fears expressed by the Chiefs of Staff, could have led Britain and France into taking action which would have at least slowed down Italian and German aid to Franco.

Chapter 6

THE RUSSIANS ARRIVE

On 15 October 1936, the *Komsomol* dropped anchor in the naval base of Cartagena. On the bridge stood a Soviet officer, Colonel Semyon Krivoshein. Odessa, his port of departure, had been under strict security, so he was astonished to see the Spanish pilot guide the *Komsomol* past a British destroyer, HMS *Grafton*, and a German torpedo-boat, the *Luchs*.[1] British and German officers carefully examined the Soviet ship through their binoculars.

The moment was highly delicate. Francisco Largo Caballero's new coalition Government had been in office for one month. It contained Communist ministers who pressed for Soviet policy to be followed. The Communist view and that of most Spaniards who were not Anarchists, was that only if the revolutionary forces in Government Spain were disciplined could the war against Franco's Nationalists be successfully fought. The Soviet advisers and the Comintern representatives insisted on a highly-disciplined army with a regular structure. It would be the price paid for Soviet aid. Yet the Russians would have to go carefully, given the deep Spanish Arnarchist and revolutionary tradition.

There were fierce clashes between the Spanish Premier and the Soviet Ambassador, Marcel Rosenberg, who regularly visited the Prime Minister. On one occasion he was pressing an irritated Caballero for a series of dismissals and appointments. The conversation became heated. Alvarez del Vayo, the Foreign Minister, was interpreting. Voices were raised and staff in the outside office looked at each other aghast as Largo Caballero was heard to shout:

> 'Out you go! Go out! You must learn, Señor Ambassador, that the Spaniards may be poor and need aid from abroad, but we are sufficiently proud not to accept that a foreign ambassador should try and impose his will on the Head of the Spanish Government. And as for you, Vayo, you ought to remember that you are a Spaniard and Minister of Foreign Affairs of the Republic, instead of arranging to agree with a foreign diplomat to exert pressure on your own Prime Minister!'[2]

These clashes reflected the extent and success of Communist influence in Republican Spain. Reassuring signs of law and order came back gradually from September 1936 onward: there was a regular army rather than militia, a police force rather than self-appointed patrols, respect for private property, the re-establishment of some sort of legal system, and freedom to walk along the street in collar and tie without being arrested as a potential enemy of the Republic. It was the Communist Party, immensely larger in size and prestige than before the war, which strove to keep the revolution within strict bounds.

On 16 October 1936, *Pravda* published Stalin's telegram to the Secretary-General of the Spanish Communist Party, José Diaz. It was the Russian leader's first open statement of support.

The workers of the Soviet Union are only doing their duty in rendering all possible aid to the revolutionary masses in Spain. They are well aware that the liberation of Spain from the yoke of Fascist reactionaries is not the private concern of the Spanish but the general concern of all advanced and progressive humanity.

A week earlier, Anthony Eden had stopped off at Paris on his way back from Geneva, and lunched with Léon Blum. Both statesmen had been briefed about the Soviet threat at the Non-Intervention Committee, but the Soviet Foreign Minister, Maxim Litvinov, had told Blum that Cahan's actions had come as a complete surprise to him. If this is true, it seems hardly possible that Cahan, a mere chargé d'affaires, could have acted off his own bat. Therefore he must have had direct orders from Moscow. Moscow may well have kept Litvinov in the dark, though he must have been aware that the entry of Communist ministers into the Largo Caballero Government in early September marked the beginning of a closer approach of Republican Spain to the Soviet Union, an approach which was followed by the shipping to Moscow of 500 tons of the Spanish gold reserve, by the arrival of the first volunteers for the International Brigades, and by the appointment of a Spanish ambassador to Moscow.

On the same day that Colonal Krivoshein and his Soviet tanks landed, the Spanish Premier told the Soviet Ambassador that the Government wanted to transfer most of the Spanish gold reserve – 510 tons, mostly in gold coins – to safety in the Soviet Union. The gold would have to be melted down and sold to produce funds for the Republic to pay for weapons anywhere it could acquire them. If the gold were sent anywhere else, it would not be safe from some form of sequestration under the Non-Intervention agreement.

Meanwhile the Comintern, with Soviet approval, had decided to show solidarity with the Republic by organising the recruitment of foreign volunteers for the Republic. The centre of organisation was Paris, under the French Communist Party and refugee Communists from other countries. The first contingent arrived at their Albacete base on 13 October. These volunteers, whose recruitment had been complained of by Italy at the Non-Intervention Committee, cannot be reasonably compared with the forces, however badly-trained, that Italy later sent to Spain. Most Internationals were too young to have served in the First World War and had little or no military experience or training. Nor did they have the military, industrial and political organisation of nations like Germany and Italy behind them. They did, however, enable the USSR, through the Comintern, to demonstrate international Communist backing for the Spanish Republic. In the autumn of 1936 they were arriving at the rate of several hundred men a week. Commanded by an ex-officer of the Austro-Hungarian army, who used the *nom-de-guerre* of Napoleon's general, Kléber, and by a Hungarian Communist, Matias Zalka, alias Pavel Lukaçz, the Internationals suffered heavy casualties in the battles around Madrid in the late autumn and winter of 1936.

Most of the prewar Spanish diplomatic corps had resigned and formed the nucleus of Franco's unofficial representation in foreign capitals. On 19 September, Largo Caballero appointed Luis Araquistain, brother-in-law of Foreign Minister del Vayo, to be ambassador in Paris, Pablo de Azcárate, an Assistant Secretary-General of the League of Nations, went to London, and the Socialist professor Fernando de los Ríos to New York. While these men were individuals of considerable ability, most of them lacked diplomatic experience. Some of the impression of desperate incompetence displayed by the Spanish Republican diplomatic correspondence during the Civil War may be explained by the sheer shortage of staff. As the Foreign Minister wrote to his brother-in-law in Paris on 11 February 1937, he had now dismissed the last six officials from the old regime who remained in the Ministry. He conducted all the diplomatic correspondence himself, dictating to a secretary. Even so, security was unreliable. On 18 March 1937, he wrote that there were leaks in Paris, Prague and London and that the enemy knew what he was writing.[3] In contrast, Franco's unofficial ambassador in Rome, Admiral Magaz, wrote on 8 September 1936 to the head of Franco's diplomatic office that all the embassy personnel in Italy were in the service of the Nationalists.[4]

The first Spanish ambassador to the Soviet Union was warmly welcomed and assured of Soviet support on 7 October. This was Dr Marcelino Pascua, a medical statistician who had been Director-General of Social

Welfare in Spain and was a personal friend of Dr Negrín, the Spanish Socialist Minister of finance and later Prime Minister.

The Soviets had crossed the Rubicon. Fifty-seven years later it is still difficult to know why and how the decision to send massive aid to Spain was taken. Probably a set of compromises had been made between conflicting demands and views. Perhaps the Soviet leaders were concerned to win back the sympathy lost in progressive circles because of the show-trials of Old Bolsheviks and Trotskyites. Possibly the USSR had thought that the Non-Intervention Committee would actually stop Hitler and Mussolini helping Franco and now realised its error. This at least was the view of diplomats. Mr MacKillop, the British chargé in Moscow, wrote on 20 October: 'though of course no conclusive evidence is available...one is inclined to ascribe that fact [the change in policy] to a growing sentiment on the part of the Soviet leaders that that policy is failing to produce the hoped-for results and that there is consequently less reason to allow it to inhibit doctrinal or class sympathies'. On 24 October, Alexis Léger, Secretary-General at the Quai D'Orsay, sounded out the Russian chargé in Paris. The latter said quite openly that the USSR intended to stop the march of Fascism. In the Russian view, such an intervention on their part in Spain would not lead to the war that Léger so feared. The French concluded that the followers of Trotsky and Lenin had been too strong for the Russian leader, who had taken on the risks of intervening in Spain to protect himself against internal opposition. All this remains supposition and speculation. Such was the mystery of internal Soviet affairs that the Permanent Secretary to the British Foreign Office, Sir Robert Vansittart, lamely ended a letter to Eden on the subject of Soviet intervention in Spain, with the words: 'the urge to world revolution must be much stronger in Russia than anyone had believed in the last two or three years'.[5]

This erroneous view of Soviet strength and intentions coloured Eden's attitude when he spoke to Maiskii, the Soviet ambassador in London, on 3 November. Though the Russian insisted that Moscow had no desire to encourage revolution or set up a Communist regime in Spain, this cut no ice with the Foreign Secretary. Maiskii's attempts to alarm Eden about the influence that Germany and Italy would have over a victorious Franco, and the risk that the two dictatorships would be encouraged in their aggression if they were allowed to get away with it in Spain, were airily dismissed by the Foreign Secretary.[6] The Foreign Office doubted whether Franco, whose imminent victory was expected, would allow Hitler and Mussolini any advantages in Spain. Britain had remained incontrovertibly neutral and was well-placed to gain economic and political influence over the new Spain, which would be recognised, so the Foreign Office had recommended, when Madrid fell. Russian intervention, at this stage, was a massively embarrassing factor.

Colonel Krivoshein's tanks were unloaded from the *Komsomol* in full view of everybody. He drove to his base at Archena. Passing through the provincial capital, Murcia, he reported to the local Party offices, whence he spoke on the telephone to José Díaz, Secretary-General of the PCE in Madrid. This cannot have been accidental and it must be assumed that the Soviet Colonel's orders were to keep in close touch with Spanish Communists. Almost certainly the reason was to keep the weapons under the control of units which were fully militarised and untainted by Anarchist indiscipline or Spanish professional military torpor.

The *Komsomol* was followed by the *Stari Bolshevik* and the *Kruschev*, with trucks, tanks and aircraft. German agents observed ship after ship passing through the Dardanelles *en route* for Spain: the *Karl Lepin* and the *Transbalt*; on 23 October the *Shachter*, with war material for Alicante; in the following days the *Kuban*, the *Varlaam Avanasov*, the *Kursk*, the *Blagoev* and the *Komsomol* again, all bound for Spanish Mediterranean ports. There were estimated to be 23 journeys in Russian ships and 10 in ships in other nationalities carrying arms, tank drivers and Soviet pilots from Russian to Spain before the end of 1936. They also brought Soviet military and naval advisers. Admiral Kuznetsov, the Russian naval attaché during the Spanish Civil War, speaks of 'more than twenty great transports until September 1937'.[7] Spanish ships also brought material, and some British ships were chartered to bring cargoes to Spain from the Soviet Union. Jack Billmeir, in the course of expanding his Stanhope Shipping Company, was carrying material to both sides, as he admitted to Board of Trade officials when interviewed on 30 October. Claude Angel, Sons and Co. of Cardiff had a ship, the *Hillfern*, loading a cargo of war material for Spain in Danzig. Angel boldly told the Board of Trade that he was doing nothing illegal in chartering his ship to the Spanish Government and that he hoped the Royal Navy would extend the protection to him which was his right. Angel was correct in this. Officials judged that something would have to be done to avoid an incident between British ships and Franco.[8]

AT THE NON-INTERVENTION COMMITTEE

The Non-Intervention Committee met again on 9 October. Complaints were to be received for the first time through the official procedure. The

Portuguese representative, however, refused to discuss his country's conduct in the presence of the Soviet delegate, and left the meeting. This led to much rhetoric about procedure, interrupted at last by Samuel Cahan, who complained that the whole issue was being drowned in points of order. Why not have it all out now? At this stage, Lord Plymouth decided it was time for lunch. The Committee would reassemble at 4 p.m.

On his return, Cahan bitterly asked why the Portuguese behaviour was tolerated. The violations of the Agreement, he complained, had turned the Committee into an empty procedure and a screen for some countries to aid the Spanish rebels.

This was what the skilful Italian, Dino Grandi, wanted. He now attacked the Soviet Union for proposing the investigatory commission before the Portuguese could answer the accusations (ignoring the fact that the Portuguese had refused to do so). The USSR, sneered Grandi, had refused to discuss the question of the recruitment of volunteers for the International Brigades and the collection of funds in the Soviet Union and by the whole apparatus of Communist and Popular Front organisations in Western Europe. The USSR, Grandi went on, was trying to destroy the edifice of Non-Intervention by threatening to abandon it before Soviet accusations had been answered. Why such indecent haste? The previous day, Grandi had made a last-ditch attempt to stop the discussion of Madrid's complaints. The Foreign Office had taken fright and wondered whether the Italians would withdraw from the Committee and topple the entire delicate house of cards of British policy in Europe and the Mediterranean. Far from doing this, the next afternoon Grandi was posing as a champion of the Non-Intervention Committee and managing to isolate the Soviet Union as a threat to peace. Only now did Grandi begin to list his own accusations against Russian intervention. It was just the right moment. Grandi read out 18 accusations that Soviet ships had unloaded war material in Spanish ports. 'These are the facts. This is the truth of the situation', said Grandi. He continued: 'the Italian Government, however, do not threaten to withdraw from the Agreement because of these facts. The Italian Government have too great a sense of responsibility towards European cooperation and peace, and have adhered to the Agreement on Non-Intervention with too much loyalty to endanger its existence by showing false zeal or invoking doubtful pretexts.'

This was Grandi's task, to alarm Great Britain about the Soviet threat in the Mediterranean. Rather than deny Italy's participation in Spain, he had to divert attention from it and even justify it by attacking the Soviet Union. In his reports, Grandi showed exactly how aware he was of his success. Italy's delay in accepting Non-Intervention, he had written, 'has given us another precious month in Spain'. His attack on Russia at the meeting of 9

October had, thought Grandi, removed the threat of a French–British–Soviet bloc against Italy, which was what Mussolini really feared. As for the Germans, who had let Grandi make the running, he wrote, 'we have dragged them in with us'.[9]

Cahan now hit back. He ridiculed Grandi's 18 accusations. What if some Russian ships had sailed to Spain and back again? This proved nothing. Why had there been no news of a single Soviet aircraft being shot down in Spain? Had any Soviet airmen been captured? Yet, he asserted, the world's press was full of reports of Italian and German intervention.

That was the end of the discussion. A long time – 16 pages of minutes – was now given up to the wording of a communiqué. Hemmings suggested the words: 'The Committee took note of the communication received from the USSR and of the declaration made at the ensuing discussion.' Cahan cavilled for a long time, trying to get the other delegates to make some concrete proposals. But they, aware of British wishes, kept silent.

During the two weeks between Cahan's warning of 7 October 1936 and the Soviet statement of 23 October, which openly announced that the USSR was helping the Republic, there was a massive build-up of arms shipments to Spain. Up to 29 September, the arrivals of German and Italian aircraft had been as follows:

German: 20 Junkers-52 transports/bombers arrived between 28 July and 10 August
24 Heinkel-51 fighters arrived on 6 and 17 August, and in early September
29 Heinkel-46 reconnaissance machines arrived in mid and late September

TOTAL 73

Italian: 9 Savoia S.81 bombers arrived on 30 July; 36 Fiat CR32 fighters arrived on 14 and 28 August and 3 and 29 September. 1 Cant Z.501 naval reconnaissance seaplane arrived 20 September.
10 IMAM Ro37 reconnaissance biplanes arrived 29 September 1936.

TOTAL 56

In addition, Italy supplied 12 more aircraft to Mallorca in August 1936, giving a total of 68.[10]

Thus by 7 October, when the Russians made their threat, Germany and Italy had provided the Spanish insurgents with 141 aircraft and a large amount of other war material. The pilots and ground crews were members of the respective German and Italian air forces. Now Russian material would pour in and Germany and Italy would match it.

Soviet arms came at a vital moment. The 14 Dewoitine fighters and 6 Potez bombers that Pierre Cot had managed to send to Spain, often unarmed and flown by heterogeneous crews, together with almost all the thirty or forty other machines bought here and there from small airlines or dealers and smuggled, had been lost by October.

The first Russian aircraft to arrive were 18 Polikarpov I-15s, which were landed at Cartagena from the *Stari Bolshevik* on 15 October. They were observed and reported to the British authorities. Six more I-15s arrived the next day. These 24 I-15s, known as *chatos* or 'snub-noses', were fighter biplanes, the most modern in Soviet production. They went into action on 4 November. Fifteen landed at Bilbao in the Government's Northern Zone, on 1 November. A wing of 31 I-16s, only just delivered to the Soviet Air Force and the most advanced low-wing monoplane of the time, went into action on 15 November. It was equal to the Messerschmitt 109 and the British Hurricane and Spitfire designs. The I-16, known in Russian as the 'fly', was given the same nickname in Spain, 'Mosca'. Its performance in speed and manoeuvrability was unequalled, though it needed very experienced piloting. Another wing of 31 R5 reconnaissance and day bombing biplanes arrived in November and carried out its first mission on 2 December. Probably the most advanced Soviet aircraft supplied at this time was the SB fast bomber, known in Spain as the 'Katiuska'. A wing of 31 Katiuskas went to Spain in October 1936. Their speed was unequalled, but the aircraft was vulnerable if hit and often needed to be escorted by slower fighters, which removed its own speed advantage.[11]

Between 15 October and early November, 132 Soviet aircraft arrived in Spain. In addition, Russia dispatched other material, including tanks and armoured cars, cannon, small arms and ammunition.

Italian forces were also significantly increased at this time. Italian Whippet tanks went into action on 24 October. The number of Italian ship arrivals increased rapidly from 10 October onwards. Italian experts mounted artillery on the new Nationalist cruiser *Canarias*, which was as fast as, better-armed, and with greater range than the modern Republican destroyers and older cruisers. At about the same time, an Italian naval and military mission arrived. On 21 October, during the crucial fortnight, as Russian supplies arrived, a squadron of Italian cruisers took up station off Sicily to keep watch on ships heading for Spain, while a powerful Italian fleet maintained its presence in Spanish waters.

Franco had no submarines, because all twelve Spanish boats had mutinied against their officers in loyalty to the Republic. Consequently, in October, Franco's naval officers, disguised as a Latin American mission, went secretly to Italy to arrange for four Italian submarines to operate secretly for the Spanish Nationalists.[12]

In Germany, Admiral Raeder had told Hitler that, if he seriously wanted to help the Spanish insurgents, more substantial aid would have to be sent. German and Italian collaboration in Spain had been an established fact from the time that Admiral Canaris, head of Abwehr, the German secret service, had met General Roatta, head of Italian Military Intelligence, in August. For one thing, the joint decision to channel supplies only to Franco had been a major factor in establishing the Spanish general as generalísimo and head of the Spanish Nationalist Government. On 24 August Hitler decided to send a military mission, which led to the dispatch of more forces in September 1936.[13] Earlier the *Usaramo* took 20 Heinkel-46 aircraft to Spain, while the German War Minister, General Von Blomberg, sent Lieutenant-Colonel Walter Warlimont to be in general charge of German forces in Spain. Highly conscious of security and still under the alias of 'Guido', Warlimont, accompanied by Roatta, saw Franco on 5 September. When Warlimont learned that the Nationalist forces had no tanks, anti-tank guns or heavy artillery, he suggested supplying these items. In October, 28 anti-aircraft guns, four of the famous 88 mm cannon which could also be used effectively as anti-aircraft, anti-tank or ground artillery, 24 anti-tank guns, 41 Mark 1 tanks and armoured cars, with 10 officers and 225 men arrived under Lieutenant-Colonel Von Thoma[14] (who was to command a Panzer division in North Africa in the Second World War).

At this time two or three German ships were entering Spanish harbours every week. Their journeys to Spain were organised by a special section, the Schiffahrtsabteilung, within Sondertstab W. The German Government had taken a very aggressive stance against threats of blockade of its ships by the Spanish Government navy. A German squadron – the battleship *Graf Spee*, the cruisers *Nürnberg* and *Leipzig* and the destroyers *Jaguar, Wolf, Greif* and *Falcon* – patrolled menacingly in Spanish waters. German arms-carrying cargo-ships were carefully camouflaged, provided with false names and silhouettes, and ordered to keep radio silence.

Thus Italian and German intervention had increased considerably in October. Count Ciano arrived in Berlin for his first visit as Foreign Minister on 20 October 1936. He discussed Spain with Von Neurath. Both parties agreed to await the imminent fall of Madrid before recognising Franco's government. The Duce, said Ciano, intended to make a decisive military effort to bring about victory, and would send not only more aircraft but also submarines. Would Germany associate herself with this effort?

On 24 October, Ciano was received at Berchtesgaden. Germany, said the Fuehrer, had committed herself to crushing Bolshevism in Spain. She had no territorial or political aims, though Hitler omitted to mention his economic aims in the Peninsula. The Fuehrer approved of the Italian decision to make a final push to take Madrid and agreed, in rather vague terms, to match it. These were days when the precise volume of Russian arms-imports was still unknown and no Soviet aircraft had engaged in combat. Hitler may not yet have decided substantially to increase German arms supplies to Franco. Mussolini, for his part, may not yet have given up hope of an agreement with Britain and decided to throw in his lot with Hitler. Nevertheless, the formal coming-together of Italy and Germany was announced in Mussolini's speech at Milan on 1 November where he referred to the term 'Axis', which would be much-used in future years.

Ciano's own record of events, however, does not suggest that Soviet intervention was the trigger for augmented German and Italian shipments of arms to Franco. The German and Italian *entente* has to be seen within the context of a general hostility toward the League and the revival of the Locarno agreements of 1925.

There were also other pressures at work. The Italian Fascist regime was at the height of its prestige. Yet there were grave economic problems which should have counselled against the expense of intervening in Spain. This was not, however, the Fascist style. To a considerable extent, the Fascist *milizia* used the Spanish conflict to counterpoise the status achieved by the victorious Army in Ethiopia. The Army and particularly the Navy, which was the least Fascistised of the armed forces, were not all that enthusiastic about getting into the Spanish morass; the regime itself had held back. In particular, Franco was not heralded as the great anti-Bolshevik crusader. It was the Vatican newspaper *L'Osservatore Romano* which took this line first with its reports of 23 and 26 July 1936 of the anti-clerical outrages in the Republican zone. Serious Italian thought, as for example in Giuseppe Bottai's *Critica Fascista*, saw intervention in Spain as bearing the duty of expanding Fascism as well as the imperialism of the new Italy. This, of course, was incompatible with the politics of reality, since it would never be tolerated by other Powers, who sympathised only with the anti-Communist side of Italian intervention. Indeed, there was some dismay in the Fascist movement itself about aiding the grossly reactionary aspects of Franco Spain. As a young Fascist wrote:

'We speak of a proletarian revolution, while we defend the most reactionary generals, landlords and exploiters in Europe.'[15]

A more down-to-earth consideration was the fear, confirmed by reports from the Italian Secret Police, the OVRA, that the Spanish conflict might reawaken dormant Left-wing ideas in Italy itself. On 26 August, an agent in Milan reported: 'in some workers there is an implicit sense of solidarity with the Spanish Communists. The echo of the revolution has awakened the dormant sense of class in them, in spite of all the regime's precautions.' The authorities were worried by the activity of Italian anti-Fascist exiles, in particular Carlo Rosselli's Giustizia e Libertà column, now in Spain, and the significant participation of Italian exiles in the International Brigades. Mussolini, an avid reader of exile newspapers, feared Rosselli's capacity and prestige. The leaders of the exiles had understood this and at a meeting at their Paris headquarters on 23 July 1936 had decided to fight Fascism in Spain even if this provoked Mussolini. Spain offered Italian anti-Fascists a chance to fight. This accounts for their propaganda effort, the loudspeakers at the battlefront and the significance given to Italian anti-Fascists capturing Italian troops sent by Mussolini and presenting them in public, before the world's press, as dupes of the Italian regime. It also explains the powerful broadcasting stations established in Barcelona and Valencia by Italian anti-Fascists, which were eagerly listened to by Italian workers. Rosselli launched the slogan 'Today in Spain, tomorrow in Italy!' ('Oggi in Ispagna, domani in Italia!'). This was broadcast on 13 and 14 November 1936. What influence did it have on Mussolini's determination to give Franco victory with Italian arms even at the cost of abandoning any possibility of good relations with Great Britain?

THE CONDOR LEGION

On 30 October, Admiral Canaris told Franco that Hitler had decided on a huge increase in aid. He was going to send an air force, to be known as the Condor Legion. The decision seems to have been a result of the conversations with Ciano. Perhaps Hitler thought that he could not afford to be less enthusiastic than Italy in helping Franco take Madrid. Perhaps the Fuehrer was being pressed to commit himself more to Franco's aid. And just how much material were the Russians sending in the ships whose passage through the Dardanelles was so faithfully reported to Berlin?

The question whether the increase in German participation came as a result of or coincidentally with the Russian escalation is one for which not enough evidence is available. Possibly it was less the threat of Soviet intervention than anticipation of complications with Britain if the war continued that determined Hitler to try to get it over with as soon as possible.

While Franco urgently wanted more Italian war material, which he could keep under his control, the escalation of German aid should be seen differently, for the generalísimo himself had not asked for it and indeed, told Lt-Col Warlimont that he did not want it.[16] Foreign aid which was not under Spanish control might be worse than no aid at all. While for Franco, the struggle against Bolshevism constituted the ideological background to his aim of restoring the values of traditional Spain, for Germany a Popular Front Spain was a contribution to her paranoia about encirclement. Whether Franco wanted it or not, the Condor Legion would fly against the Spanish Reds. What is more, it would fly under German command.

In the meantime, the Non-Intervention Committee had met again on Friday 23 October. Ivan Maiskii sat for the first time at the long, polished table. Opposite him sat Dino Grandi and, to his left, the Swedish representative, Baron Erik Palmstierna, who was currently writing a book recounting his conversations with messengers from the other world. Understandably, the following year his Government retired him as soon as he reached the minimum age.

Maiskii was struck by the sepulchral silence in the room, though with deputies, secretaries and experts there were possibly one hundred people present. Whoever spoke did so in a whisper. Reserve and tact were clearly more important than home truths. They were, after all, guests of the British Government.

After Stalin had openly proclaimed that the Soviet Union was helping Republican Spain, Maiskii again wrote to Lord Plymouth. The only way out of the present impasse was to give the Spanish Government the right to buy arms. The Soviet Government, wrote Maiskii, 'cannot consider itself bounded by the Agreement for Non-Intervention to any greater extent than any of the remaining participants of the Agreement'. Maiskii refused to discuss the exact meaning of the statement, and discussion on it was put off to the sub-committee where the Russian was at last successful, for the body agreed to investigate the possibility of sending teams of inspectors to Spanish ports and frontiers.

The Committee then went on to discuss the German reply to the accusations made by the Spanish Government. Count Bismarck insisted that most of the charges referred to dates before Germany had agreed to Non-Intervention. Anything else was completely without foundation. Maiskii bitterly criticised the German reply, but nobody would support him, and Lord Plymouth proposed that the German reply should be taken as satisfactory.

Maiskii's tactic was to show up the Committee as a useless farce, so he deliberately tried to provoke the urbane Lord Plymouth. In what way, he asked, did the Chairman find the German reply satisfactory? Plymouth rose to the bait: 'Really, I am not here to be cross-examined by members of the Committee!' he retorted. After some further discussion the next two hours were spent in arguing about the form of the communiqué. The meeting had started at 4 p.m. At 9 that drizzly October evening, Maiskii and Cahan emerged from the portals of the Foreign Office. 'We've been sitting there for five hours without a break,' grumbled Cahan, 'and nobody even offered us a cup of tea at tea-time. It's not like the English at all.' 'Yes,' said Maiskii, 'even the age-old English traditions can't take the strain.'

The following Wednesday, 28 October, at 3 p.m., the Committee assembled again. Maiskii was on top form. Grandi replied to the accusations made on 9 October against Italy. When he insisted that most of the facts referred to events before Italy had agreed to Non-Intervention, Maiskii cuttingly asked why the country of Marconi could not recall its ships by radio if they were *en route* to Spain at the crucial moment. What about Majorca, which had become, in Maiskii's words 'some sort of principality with an Italian, Rossi, as head of the administration'? Lord Plymouth, however, insisted that the Italian reply was satisfactory and asked if anyone else wanted to speak. Nobody did and Plymouth passed on to the next item.

The Portuguese delegate had agreed to answer the accusations against his country. His reply was 67 sheets long. Maiskii sarcastically observed that Portugal had to make the best of one of the very rare occasions where it had a chance to cut a dash on the international stage, and it deserved top marks for diligence. But the substance of the reply was to cast the Soviet Union as a villain in an old melodrama. It was, remarked Maiskii, the 'nightmare of a frightened parochial...or an actor trying to scare the audience to death with his rendering of the Communist devil, complete with horns and tail'.

It was now five o'clock. If the meeting went on as long as the previous one they would be there until late that evening. Maiskii assumed an innocent expression and raised his hand on a point of order. What was he going to say? Would he upset the smooth rejection of the charges against Italy and Portugal by bringing up some tiresome point of protocol? 'May I suggest', said the Russian gently, 'that we have a break now for a cup of tea?' A sigh of relief went round the table. No arrangements for tea had been made. Plymouth called for fifteen minutes' rest during which he arranged for tea and sandwiches to be available at six-thirty. From then on, tea was regularly served at the proper time.[17]

After the break, Lord Plymouth went through the accusations against Portugal one by one, declaring himself satisfied with the explanations given. Moscow had anticipated this, and Maiskii made a third statement, this time saying that nobody need consider themselves morally bound by the Non-Intervention Agreement.

Nevertheless, the Soviet Union was not abandoning the Committee, which was the important thing. The entire basis of British policy was that, whatever the disagreements, none of the signatories to the Agreement was ready to break it. For Eden this was proof of its practicality, as he said in his speech in the House of Commons on 29 October, the first occasion for debate after the recess.

'The chief complainant among the nations against the working of the Non-Intervention Committee is Soviet Russia,' said Eden. This was rather like the traditional answer: 'Nobody has ever complained before.' 'Nor have we any information whatever to support the Soviet charges,' he continued, which was untrue. 'There is no alternative policy except to allow the free export of arms to either side.'[18]

In the meantime, Germany was organising the Condor Legion. On 30 October 1936, Von Blomberg handed Admiral Canaris and Major-General Hugo Sperrle, commander of the Condor Legion, their orders. They were to tell Franco 'most emphatically' that his 'hesitant and routine' tactics so far were not likely to be successful. He would receive greater support from the Luftwaffe but all German units would be under German command. Sperrle would be the sole adviser to Franco on the use of German forces and responsible only to Franco. If Franco accepted these conditions 'without reservations' more aid would be sent.[19] The Germans were, of course, already committing aircraft and pilots to Franco, which seemed to justify their brusqueness. Yet one may well imagine the irritation with which the Spanish Nationalist command received this tactless, even arrogant, note. In view, all the same, of the news of major Soviet support for the Republic, Franco had no choice but to swallow his pride and accept the German conditions.

On 31 October, Major-General Sperrle left for Spain, accompanied by the Chief-of-Staff and later commander of the Condor Legion, Baron Wolfram Von Richthofen, a cousin of the 'Red Baron' of the First World War.

The Condor Legion had 36 Ju-52 bombers, added to the 18 still operational in Spain, 27 He-51 fighters and 9 already in Spain, 12 He-45, He-46 and He-70 reconnaissance machines and a Dornier-17, together with 14 sea reconnaissance aircraft. This was a total of 117 aircraft, to which were added 48 tanks, 60 anti-aircraft guns, a training battery, a searchlight section and an ammunition train and five companies of air-communications specialists. For the first time there would be a considerable presence of German personnel in Spain, probably about 5000 men, accompanied by 1500 vehicles. In addition, there was a naval section, the Nordseegruppe, with ten officers and 70 mine and signal specialists sailing on the warships *Deutschland* and *Admiral Scheel*, which acted as spies to enable Franco's own navy to intercept transport bound for Republican ports.

Operations code-named Unternehmen Winteruebung and Unternehmen Hansa dispatched the Condor Legion in 25 ships between 9 and 19 November 1936.[20]

Thus by the end of November the Soviet Union and Germany were heavily committed to the Spanish war. This throws an even more ironic light on the contemporaneous meetings of the Non-Intervention Committee. The sessions of 4 and 12 November were particularly lively. The German and Soviet delegates replied to their mutual accusations. Maiskii denied that the Russian ships *Neva* and *Kuban* had carried war material, but the Committee got itself into a technical argument about the capacity of the ships. The ships had been weighed down to the Plimsoll line. There was strong suspicion that there were weapons and ammunition in with the foodstuffs. Judgement on this was suspended and Plymouth sagely commented that even with facts and figures the Committee could not come to any decision. A system of supervision and control over imports to Spain was the only solution. As for the *Komsomol*, which had been seen to unload tanks, Maiskii, taking a lesson from his opponents, lied and said they were lorries, allowed under the Non-Intervention Agreement. But people had seen the tanks, insisted Grandi. Who were these eye-witnesses? asked Maiskii. Probably paid spies. Of course they would tell the German and Italian consuls what they wanted to know. There were heated accusations and counter-accusations. At this point somebody in Grandi's suite passed him a sheet of paper, allegedly from Franco's headquarters, which announced that two Soviet planes had been brought down. Quickly Maiskii said 'I think that all of us are grateful that the Italian representative has such fresh news from the front.' Grandi retorted, 'Yes, news from the front where your friends are being beaten', to which Maiskii reposted, 'Rira bien qui rira le dernier' and then made the point that Grandi's statement only went to show how close relations were between Italy and the Spanish Nationalist rebels.

On 12 November, the accusations petered out. Lord Plymouth took the discussion on to the next stage. What about the supervision scheme? This was agreed in principle and would be studied in the sub-Committee.

While the committees bickered, Madrid resisted. Soviet aircraft ruled the skies of Central Spain; the defence of the capital was conducted by a delegated committee (Junta delegada de la defensa de Madrid) while the Government went to Valencia from where it intended to continue the struggle should Madrid fall to Franco. The resistance of Madrid led to a further step in favour of Franco's Nationalists by the Axis Powers, who now recognised his Government.

Chapter 7

ITALY AND GERMANY RECOGNISE FRANCO

Late on Friday, 6 November 1936, Alvarez del Vayo told the British chargé in Madrid that, as Madrid was in imminent danger, the Government was going to leave early next morning for Valencia. Overcome with emotion, he could not go on.[1]

The next day, one Franco column planned to cross over the Puente de los Franceses. Pockmarked even today with cemented-over bullet holes, it carries the railway line to the North. The column was to advance through the Parque del Oeste, then round the north of Madrid to plunge down the long Castellana Avenue. Another column was to debouch from the Park and race round the northern boulevards – today the traffic-choked Alberto Aguilera, Sagasta and Génova Streets. A third column would emerge from the park and drive straight down the Calle de la Princesa and the Gran Via into the very heart of the city.

The defenders had to hold out at all costs. When the battle began, resistance, inspired by propaganda and fortified by trenches and barbed wire, was fierce. The Nationalist columns did not advance very far. The first three International battalions were moved into line to protect the Puente de los Franceses. After several days of hand-to-hand battle, Nationalist troops at last forced their way across the bridge and into the open area of the University City, where the battle raged among what had been libraries, lecture halls and laboratories. The German Condor Legion began to bomb the city and Russian fighters criss-crossed the skies. Madrid held and on 23 November, Franco called off his direct assault.

Given the stalemate, the question of recognition of Franco was left in abeyance by the British Government. This was not so, however, with Franco's three main supporters: Portugal, Italy and Germany. On 23 October, Lisbon broke off relations with Madrid, but was persuaded by Britain not to recognise Franco, and did not do so until May 1938. Salazar told a demonstration in Lisbon that the Non-Intervention Committee had justly exonerated Portugal from the accusations of helping Franco, but he did not deny them. The Portuguese were still facilitating supplies to the

Spanish rebels. Spanish agents reported that a convoy of one hundred lorries organised by Radio-Club Portuguez had taken food and clothing into the Franco zone.[2] This broadcasting station, run by a Portuguese army officer, had been serving Nationalist interests by tendentious propaganda and false military information.

In the meantime, seeing that there was no point in waiting for Franco to take Madrid, Germany and Italy recognised him. The political advantages for Germany and Italy of this act were considerable. While at one level, the two dictatorships had accepted the Non-Intervention agreement, at another, recognition of Franco absolved them from the accusation of aiding a rebel against a recognised government. An international demonstration of anti-Comintern solidarity, such as the recognition represented, might have the effect of intimidating the USSR, especially as the Anti-Comintern pact between Germany, Italy and Japan had recently been signed. International recognition of Franco might offset the prestige which the successful defence of Madrid had brought to the Republic.

On the other hand, the dictatorships had burnt their boats, for now their prestige was irrevocably attached to Franco's. They could not allow him to lose. Germany had already committed the Condor Legion. Within a few weeks, Italy would throw several infantry divisions into the fray.

Germany and Italy assured Britain that they would remain on the Non-Intervention Committee. In view of this, a meeting of British Ministers on 22 November decided to continue to refuse belligerent rights – and thus the right to blockade – to both sides in Spain. Eden had argued that giving belligerent rights was tantamount to conceding recognition to Franco, while Sir Samuel Hoare, the pro-Franco First Lord of the Admiralty, had argued that to deny the Spanish general those rights was to prevent him from winning, which, in Sir Samuel's view, was not impartial. The fierce differences between Eden and Hoare over Spain were becoming evident. Eden wrote in his diary that he would not grant Franco belligerent rights because he wanted, as he put it, to 'show a tooth in the Mediterranean'. 'Still less', he continued, 'do I want to facilitate an attempt at a blockade that is maybe intended to starve Madrid.'[3]

The Foreign Secretary's attitude had changed. While the Foreign Office's earlier cool neutrality had harmed the Spanish Republic, now Eden worried about the consequences of a Franco victory achieved with massive German and Italian support. While earlier, Eden's policy had been to recognise Franco when Madrid fell, now he did not even want to give him belligerent rights. Was this because he was gradually realising that he and the British Government had made an error about Spain?

The British Left was outraged at Italy's and Germany's recognition of Franco. How long would the British Government maintain the farce of Non-

Intervention? At Question Time in the Commons on 19 November, Mr Gallagher, the Communist member for West Fife, rose to ask Eden whether he did not agree that the recognition was 'an open and deliberate breach of Non-Intervention' and whether the Government proposed 'to meet this new aggression by their policy of "do nothing"'. Eden replied that while Germany and Italy recognised Franco, most other natios recognised the Republic. There was no reason why Non-Intervention should not continue, he declared.

Eden added a rider: 'so far as breaches are concerned, I wish to state categorically that I think there are other Governments more to blame than those of Germany or Italy'.

By 'other Governments', Eden meant the USSR. Information about unloading of Russian war material had flowed into the Foreign Office. On 11 November, Donald Maclean, newly-appointed to the Foreign Office and already recruited as a Soviet agent, noted what he called the most striking example of Soviet arms shipments since the last summary provided by London for the Non-Intervention Committee on 25 October.[4] The Russians had been less security-minded than the Germans or the Italians, which meant that information about the latter was not so easily available as well as less specific. Nevertheless, the War Office did not agree with the Foreign Secretary. Four days later, the Foreign Office knew this and a note read: 'The War Office has no evidence to show that there are other governments more to blame than those of Germany and Italy.'[5] But the massive and barely-concealed Russian intervention had got Eden off the parliamentary hook.

The British Government had accepted Eden's recommendation not to grant Franco the right to stop neutral ships, but what if he did so, just the same? This would involve Royal Navy protection for British ships and lead to dangerous incidents. So it was decided that the best thing to do was to forbid British merchantmen to carry war material to Spain from any-where. The result was the Merchant Shipping (Carriage of Munitions to Spain) Bill, which came into law on 3 December and empowered ships of the Royal Navy to take any British merchant ship suspected of carrying arms for Spain – from any destination – into a British port (probably Gibraltar or Malta) to be searched. Royal Navy captains had complete power, according to the new Act, to require the master of a suspected ship to make his vessel available for inspection. However, force could not be used to make a ship heave-to. The fine was not stopping was £100. Given the huge increase in freight rates to Spain and the potential profits, some people thought the fine derisory. In the debate in the House of Commons on 23 November, Eden was evasive when questioned about the safety of ships inside the three-mile limit of territorial waters. Franco had warned that he would bomb Republican ports. Territorial waters were normally under the jurisdiction of the Government which controlled the shoreline. In this case, it was the Spanish Republic, so did merchant ships have the right to protection by the Royal Navy if attacked by Franco's ships within the three-mile limit or should the Royal Navy keep out? Since Franco's Government insisted on a six-mile limit the issue became even more complicated and would, over the next two years, cause many headaches in the Foreign Office. For London, the failure of Franco to take Madrid, which led to his recognition by the two dictatorships, had placed the international aspects of the Spanish Civil War on an entirely new plane.

ITALY SENDS TROOPS TO FRANCO

Italy and Germany sought certain advantages for themselves in the new Spain for which they were laying out so much treasure and compromising their relations so severely with Britain and France. In November 1936, a decision was taken in Rome to organise a division of Fascist militia to go to Spain. Italy asked relatively little in exchange. Filippo Anfuso, Ciano's Chef de Cabinet, travelled to Spain with the text of an agreement stating that Italy had no territorial ambitions in Spain and that no future enemy of either Spain or Italy would be given facilities by the other, which was only a repetition of the Treaty of Friendship of the 1920s, aimed at preventing the granting of facilities to France which Mussolini was convinced the Republic had secretly conceded. Another clause could be interpreted as meaning that, in case of war, Italy could apply for the use of bases in, for instance, the Balearic Islands, though the Treaty did not guarantee her such rights.[6]

The British view was that a victorious Franco was unlikely to offer Mussolini any important military facilities, but it was always possible. It was important to establish better British relations with Italy, but without conceding anything important in exchange. Three days after Mussolini's mention of the Italo-German Axis in his Milan speech of 1 November, he suggested to Ward Price, a journalist on the pro-Italian London *Daily Mail*, that a 'Gentlemen's Agreement' on the Mediterranean would be valuable.[7] Eden was not ready to make any concessions, particularly over Abyssinia, but he hoped that the Italian Government would respect the territorial *status quo* in the area. Discussions were lengthy, for it was important to find a form of words that compromised and threatened nobody. Italian activities on Majorca were still bothering Eden, even more than the substantial supplies flowing to Franco on the Spanish mainland. 'Count Rossi' was still on Majorca and making violently anti-British speeches. On 17 October he was reported to have proclaimed that the

Italians would stay for ever on the island. Could he be making these statements without the consent of his Roman masters? The British Government recognised his youth, but it would be a good thing if he refrained from red wine before speaking in public, said Sir Robert Vansittart, the Under-Secretary for Foreign Affairs, to Grandi. Grandi promised to try to influence his superiors.

On 6 December, Sir Eric Drummond, British ambassador in Rome, told Ciano that he was concerned about the increase in the enrolment of Italian 'volunteers' for Spain. Ciano replied that Italy had always warned about this but now that there were masses of Russians in Spain (he meant the International Brigades, who were not Russian), he thought that banning volunteers was no longer feasible. It seems obvious that Mussolini and Ciano saw the Italian presence in Spain as compatible with a promise not to change the status quo. In the end, Ciano consented to a 'gentlemen's agreement' whose most important sentence was that the two governments 'disclaim any desire to modify or, as far as they are concerned, to see modified, the status quo as regards national sovereignty in the Mediterranean area'.

Mussolini genuinely thought he was meeting the British concern. He had no intention of altering the status quo in the Balearics. For Italy, the Popular Front regime in Spain was a serious threat which legitimised Italian intervention. As for 'Count Rossi', Ciano insisted that he had no status.

Mussolini was consistent and truthful in his assurances that he had no territorial interests in Spain. In fact Franco's correspondence with the Italian authorities at this time reflects selfless Italian generosity. Whatever Franco needed to fight the war would be given to the limit of Italian resources and on generous credit terms. On 18 March 1937, Mussolini again told Ward Price that he would respect Spain's territorial integrity. For him assuring Franco of victory was not hostile to Britain but part of the battle against the Bolshevik threat.

Some time during November 1936, as a result of Italian recognition of Franco, of the rival German build-up of aircraft and of growing disillusion with Franco's methods and strategy, Mussolini decided to send a sizeable military force to Spain. The Non-Intervention Committee seemed at last to be going to try to keep a closer eye on material going to Spain, so the quicker the war finished the better. Ciano's Chef de Cabinet, Filippo Anfuso, had written to him from Spain that Franco was in the mould of colonial soldiers, satisfied with small, limited successes. Italy would now take a more dynamic 'Fascist' attitude to Spain. On 27 November, Ciano informed Von Hassell, the German ambassador, that he was going to send a division of Fascist Blackshirts. The first four battalions were already organised. They would show Franco how to fight the Reds.

The decisive meeting was held at the Palazzo Venezia under Mussolini's chairmanship on 6 December 1936.[8] The Italian Chiefs of Staff and Admiral Canaris were present. The Duce wanted to send more aircraft and to use up to eight submarines to intensify the blockade of Spanish ports. At the moment he would prefer to keep large units in reserve unless the Soviets sent divisions. However, by 16 December, Mussolini had decided to send three thousand Blackshirts, to be followed by further units. They left on 18 December. A special department, the Ufficio Spagna, was set up under Ciano's direct authority. Its role was to centralise the requests of the Italian Military Mission in Spain and to coordinate the responses to them. The Ufficio Spagna was out of the control of the military ministries. Italian forces in Spain, known as the Corpo di Truppe Volontarie or CTV, were placed under the overall command of General Mario Roatta, known in Spain as 'Mancini', and his Chief of Staff, Colonel Emilio Faldella.

Franco had not asked for these troops. He had said that he needed officers only.[9] However, according to General Faupel, the newly-appointed German representative in Franco Spain, Franco had asked for a division each of German and Italian infantry.[10] Though this is perhaps an elaboration on Faupel's part, the frequent references to Franco's cold-shouldering of the Italian reinforcements may be part of a carefully-fostered legend to support the picture of a war fought entirely by Spanish forces, in contrast to the Republican side which, according to the Franco regime's propaganda, were mostly Russians, French and the sweepings of the world's gutters. On 13 February 1937, Colonel Faldella was received by Franco. The Italian noted that Franco did not congratulate him on the recent capture of Málaga, largely by the Italians. Nor did he thank him when two Italian officers handed him the mummified hand of Saint Theresa of Avila, which had been found in the office of the last Republican commander of Málaga after being stolen in Ronda by Government militia. Franco would cherish this relic for the rest of his life. He was angry. He had accepted independent Italian units, but not entire brigades and divisions with high-ranking officers to command them. He could not use such a large number of men together. This argument was the beginning of Spanish–Italian tension.[11]

Franco's pride seems to have precluded graciousness. On the other hand, a proclamation, tactlessly distributed to Spanish officers, made by General Arnaldi of the Blackshirt division somewhat blasphemously known as the 'Dio lo vuole', spoke of Italian victories over the whole of Spain. Whatever the reasons, the decision to send a major Italian force to Spain was taken without proper consultation with Franco and throws a curious light on the workings of Mussolini's mind.

The purpose of the Blackshirt troops, in Mussolini's view, was to give some energy ('*innervare*') to the war effort. Luigi Barzini, the journalist, wrote in *Popolo d'Italia,* 'A division or two, of an army like ours, would cut like a knife through butter.'[12] It is difficult to understand how Mussolini could have thought that his army troops, and much less the Fascist militia, were tougher than the Legionaries and the Moorish troops who were making no headway as they battered against the defences of Madrid. While undoubtedly some of the Italian troops who went to Spain were well-trained, many of them had not in fact fought in Abyssinia and had no experience of war. Serving soldiers and Fascist militia were asked if they wanted to take part in an enterprise which was vital for the destiny of Italy. Some were enthusiastic regular soldiers, especially the NCOs and officers, who saw Spain as a chance to win promotion and earn generous bonuses. Others were recruited with little care. Ages were varied. Some were alcoholics or suffering physical defects. Many were fathers of large families, others enrolled for the bonus which would free them from backbreaking peasant debt. This was especially the case with the disproportionately large numbers recruited from the poor regions of the South and Sardinia. There were even some fugitives from justice and others later claimed that they thought they had been recruited as extras to film the epic *Scipio Africanus* in Libya. This was the case with the Littorio division, which consisted of older men.[13] Its commander, General Bergonzoli, known as 'Barba Elettrica', claimed to a journalist that he had two thousand men with grey hair. A large number were evidently ill-adapted to the harsh conditions of fighting in Spain. This was widely confirmed. The American military attaché, Colonel Stephen O. Fuqua, visited Italians in a Republican prison camp near Valencia. They were, he reported, mostly married peasants and he found them a sad lot.[14]

The Italian volunteers set sail on 18 December 1936. They passed Gibraltar without lights and observing radio silence. Yet they took no precautions on landing at Cádiz on the night of 22 December.

By the end of 1936, just over ten thousand Italian troops had arrived in Spain to fight for Franco against Bolshevism. Ciano had told Pedro García Conde, Franco's minister in Rome, that he hoped to organise a division of 20 000 men.[15] He was underestimating. By 18 February 1937, the nine Savoia aircraft of six months earlier had become 48 823 Fascist militia and Army personnel. Six Italian generals commanded them. Italy had sent 277 pilots and 702 non-flying Air Force officers. As for the spectacular amount of weaponry, by 18 February 1937, Italy had dispatched 248 aircraft, 542 cannon, 105 000 rifles, two million hand-grenades, over a million shells, 140 million cartridges and nearly four thousand vehicles.[16] Sixty-two ships had transported this great force, and none of them had been impeded in the slightest by the Republican Navy, whose Soviet advisers insisted that the Spanish Republic's modern destroyers limit themselves to protecting convoys from Russia, while the Republican Government itself was so concerned not to anger Britain that it did not insist on its rights to seize cargoes going to its enemies.

The Franco naval officers who had been training on Italian submarines completed their course and, on 8 November, the *Naiade* sailed for Spanish waters, followed at close intervals by three other Italian submarines. They had orders to sink only Spanish or Russian ships, if possible without witnesses or survivors. Their great triumph was the torpedoing on 22 November, of the Spanish Government cruiser *Miguel de Cervantes*, which was anchored just outside Cartagena harbour. This was a major achievement, which put the cruiser out of commission for over a year. The Spanish Nationalists put the rumour around that the mystery submarine was one of the enemy's which it had captured and refloated. Technical inspection of an unexploded torpedo by the Spanish authorities confirmed that it was Italian. Nevertheless, in spite of protests in Parliament, the First Lord of the Admiralty, Sir Samuel Hoare, at the time a great admirer of Franco, refused to go further into the matter, thus barring discussion at the Non-Intervention Committee. Italy saw the green light and, by the end of 1936, had sent up to 24 submarines to Spanish waters, though with the strictest orders to attack only inside territorial waters and only Spanish and Soviet ships.[17]

On 19 November, senior German and Italian naval officers met and divided the Spanish coast between them. Another conference was called on 29 December, on board the Franco cruiser *Canarias*, anchored in Cádiz. Italians and Germans were critical of the apparent inactivity of the Spaniards, but agreed to watch the Republican fleet, and particularly the routes of arms-carrying ships. Franco's admirals wanted German and Italian ships to be placed under their command, which was, of course, unacceptable. The Germans, in particular, wanted the Nationalists, in spite of their small and weak forces, to be much more active in stopping cargo ships. The Republican Navy, despite its size, was thought, not too inaccurately, to be a paper tiger because of its lack of officers and its indiscipline. A notable result of this conference was more efficient information about the routes of merchant ships with arms for Spain, and this, over the next two years, would lead to the virtual strangling of the Republic's marine lifelines.[18]

GERMAN ECONOMIC AGREEMENTS WITH FRANCO

After Germany recognised Franco on 18 November 1936, retired General Wilhelm Faupel was appointed chargé d'affaires and then ambassador at

Franco's capital, the ancient Castillian city of Salamanca. Faupel had been a military adviser in Argentina. Returning to Germany he was made head of the Ibero-Amerikanische Institut in Berlin. He was a close associate of Bohle, head of the Ausslandsorganisation, who prevailed on his superior, Hitler's deputy Rudolf Hess, to send Faupel to Spain. He was to take an adviser with him for dealing with the Spanish Fascists, the Falange. This suggests that at high levels there was some idea of using the Falange as a spearhead of a Nazi-like regime. Faupel was ordered not to concern himself with military matters, an instruction which seemed to have proved difficult for this old soldier to obey.[19]

The German and Italian embassies to Franco arrived at the same time by ship in Seville, where they were brilliantly received. A torchlit demonstration was held that night in the square outside the great Town Hall of the Andalusian capital, followed by a banquet. In a way, the German delegation's telegram to Berlin of 24 November constituted a clear agenda for the future, for their first impression of Franco Spain was of a lack of seriousness and a surfeit of frivolity. There was no programme to solve the social injustices which had caused the war. Franco should be made aware that he had to start to pay for the supplies he was getting and the best way to do this was by regular shipments to Germany of Spanish minerals. Faupel wrote that British economic influence was a real danger for Germany. By 5 December, Faupel had studied the situation closely and concluded that Madrid could neither be taken by Franco nor abandoned. The siege would continue. Either Germany should leave Spain or it should send a division, whose 'superior training and leadership' would, in conjunction with Franco's armies, 'trained under our guidance with the greatest energy', gain a quick victory. The Wilhelmstrasse's reaction was one of alarm for, even with Italian cooperation, Germany could not take on the responsibility of winning the Spanish war for Franco.

This was not a very encouraging response to Faupel's suggestions, but he had been warned by Lt-Col Warlimont, the first German liaison officer at Franco's HQ, not to try to tell Franco how to win his war. After meeting Franco on 30 November, Faupel wrote that the Spanish general's estimate of the situation and its possibilities was frivolous. Faupel reported that Franco had asked for a German division to be sent as well as an Italian one.[20] If Faupel's report was accurate, it suggests that Franco was not as unwilling to accept foreign troops as his previous attitude had suggested. Perhaps he recalled his admiration for the German army while on a visit in 1928.[21] Von Neurath sent Faupel's report to Von Blomberg, the War Minister, with the comment that he did not consider sending a German division feasible. Warlimont, who seemed to understand the Franco mentality, resigned his post in protest at General Faupel's tactlessness.[22]

A conference was held in Berlin on 21 December. Hitler, Goering, Von Blomberg, Generals Von Reichenau and Von Fritsch, Admiral Canaris, Faupel and Warlimont attended. Faupel now suggested the dispatch of no less than three divisions to Spain. The others opposed him and Hitler agreed with them. He wanted to endanger neither his delicate foreign relations nor the German programme of rearmament, even if the consequence was a slow war in Spain. Hitler's probably correct instinct was that diplomatic pressure, particularly from Britain, would stop the Russians sending the Republic enough arms to win the war. In any case, at this stage in German rearmament, to send three properly armed and supplied divisions would drain the Wehrmacht and the French might even take advantage of Germany's temporary weakness.

The more Machiavellian side of Germany policy was suggested in a long and perceptive report from Von Hassell in Rome on 18 December. For him, the important aim was to prevent Italy from being drawn into the Anglo-French orbit. Italy had more political interests in a Franco victory than Germany, whose only concern was to prevent Bolshevism getting a toehold in Spain. However, the outcome of the war was doubtful and the Spaniards might yet sign an armistice and turn against all foreigners. So the best thing was, suggested Von Hassell, to let Italy involve herself deeply in Spain. This would lay bare the natural conflicts between Italy and Britain, thus drawing Mussolini ever more closely into the German orbit. Von Hassell's view became the official Wilhelmstrasse position.[23] Baron Ernst Von Weizsaecker, Director of the Political Department at this time, confided a private note to his memoirs. Italy, he wrote, was more concerned than Germany with the peril of a bolshevised Spain. Therefore she should take the lead and accept the risks which, for Germany, were much higher in relation to her possible gains.[24] Yet the question was how far the Wilhelmstrasse actually decided foreign policy. Franco could not be allowed to lose, and thus other and potentially contradictory considerations also guided German decisions.

German hesitation was noted at once by Bernardo Attolico, the Italian ambassador in Berlin, who told Ciano on 30 December that he thought the Wehrmacht was holding Hitler back. Had he been able to read Von Hassell's views about letting Italy shoulder the responsibility for backing Franco he might have advised his master differently.

German concerns were more than political, however, for behind anti-Communism lay a policy of vital importance to the rearmament and economic development of the Fatherland: a guarantee of supplies of Spanish minerals.

Whatever Hitler's motives for agreeing to help Franco, the chance of assuring supplies of Spanish minerals loomed large in German calculations. The task of Minister-President Hermann Goering in carrying out the second Four Year Plan was to prepare the German economy for war within the next four years. A guaranteed and adequate supply of mineral ores was essential, for Germany was short of minerals. 66 per cent of her iron ore, 89 per cent of her copper ore and 70 per cent of the pyrites – sulphides of iron and copper – essential for the manufacture of sulphuric acid, had to be imported. A large proportion of these came from Spain. Half of Spain's iron-ore exports went to Germany, while most of the other went to feed Britain's steel-mills.

Arms shipment to Spain from Germany was placed under the aegis of a new company, the Hispano-Marroquí de Transportes SA, known by the acronym of HISMA. Constituted in Morocco on 31 July 1936, it was headed by the same Johannes Bernhardt who had explained Franco's needs to Hitler on 25 July in Bayreuth.

Franco's debt to Germany mounted quickly. He could not pay in cash, for the Spanish Nationalists needed all the foreign currency they could earn, while the gold reserve was in the Republican Government's hands. So the Germans began to press for increased exports of mineral ores. A central office for handling imports of raw materials from Spain was set up under Goering on 7 October 1936. This was the Röhstoffe und Waren Einkaufgesellschaft, or ROWAK.

HISMA and ROWAK enjoyed the monopoly of access to finance for bilateral trade between Nationalist Spain and Germany. Bernhardt began to build a commercial empire. The monopoly was often complained about, particularly by Germans who wanted a slice of Spanish trade and also by exporters from Spain, who had to pay sizeable commissions to HISMA and ROWAK. Nevertheless, the German Government thought that a single agency would better serve its aim to force Spain to increase exports of raw materials to Germany. As nazification of the German ministries increased, Goering obtained greater control over trade with Spain. On 16 October 1936, the Economics Ministry complained of HISMA and ROWAK, their monopolies and fat commissions, and the protection they enjoyed, for ROWAK had naval protection for its ships and a credit of three million marks.[25]

The Spanish insurgents did not have the gold or the industrial resources of the Republic, but they did have the inestimable advantage of a single command which could impose decisions *manu militari*. All foreign currency derived from exports had to be handed over to the authorities. As far as minerals were concerned, a decree of 27 August 1936, issued by the Junta de Defensa Nacional, the first Government of Franco's Spain, seized all ores. These came from the Spanish Riff Mines Company in Morocco and three British firms, Rio Tinto, the Orconera Iron Ore Company and the Tharsis Company. This was a critical matter for Britain, for Spain supplied two-thirds of the pyrites which were vital for its explosives, steel and refining industries. While these companies complained mightily to London about the compulsory redirection of their stocks to Germany, they realised that it was better than what might have happened had the insurgents not captured the mining areas. The mining companies had suffered from the legislation of the Popular Front and the obligatory re-employment of one thousand workers who had been dismissed. Rio Tinto was happy at the re-establishment of labour discipline and the 'removal' of rebellious workers. Nevertheless, whatever the threats of takeover from the Popular Front Government had been, it was the insurgents who were now sequestrating stocks of ore and compulsorily redirecting them to Germany. In addition, so short of foreign currency were the insurgents that they forced Rio Tinto to hand over its sterling balances.[26]

HISMA flourished as a result of the decree seizing mineral ores. At the end of October, this company contracted with the Riff mines to take 840 000 tons during the next fourteen months. A Spaniard who escaped from Spanish Morocco reported on 5 January 1937 that he had seen 14 German ships loading iron ore at Melilla. This was confirmed by *The Times* of London on the 12th which reported that 23 cargo-ships had arrived at the port between 11 and 23 December 1936. Figures from *The Economist* of 15 May 1937 indicate that Germany imported a third of a million tons of iron ore from Spain over the winter of 1936–37.

General Faupel was instructed by Hitler himself to develop commercial relations, to encourage Spanish purchases from Germany and to ensure that 'England ... would not take the market away from us at a later stage'. The prewar German–Spanish trade treaty was extended on 31 December on most-favoured-nation terms. Faupel pushed strongly for a new agreement, particularly since Italian influence was increasing. The delaying tactics of the Spaniards irritated the Germans, and Faupel was told to make sure that the Spanish negotiators would be available for discussions on a full-time basis.

Relations between HISMA and Franco were strained when in January 1937 Bernhardt arrogantly demanded control of all the foreign currency generated by exports from Franco's zone. Franco, of course, refused. The German authorities were informed that Bernhardt was making himself unpopular. To be fair, the Germans saw themselves as supplying enormous quantities of military aid virtually *gratis*, while Franco was buying goods in other countries with the foreign currency that his exporters were forced to surrender. Still, given Franco's armament problems, the Germans knew that he would have to give in or lose the supply of German war material.

This was the rather tense situation as negotiations began in March 1937 for an economic agreement. The ground was prepared by a conference of German experts held in Berlin on 23 February. The HISMA–ROWAK arrangement was conveniently obliging Franco to send his raw materials to Germany rather than to other countries in exchange for foreign currency. Despite opposition from more conservative economists, who would have preferred to allow other firms to participate in the Spanish market without paying commissions to HISMA and ROWAK, it was decided not to make any substantial changes. The 20 March 1937 agreement dealt mostly with political matters, agreeing that neither country would join in any alliances which might harm the other. On economic matters, the wording was extremely vague: economic relations would be 'intensified'. Spain and Germany would 'cooperate with and supplement one another'. A German delegation continued to negotiate with the Spaniards. Some members of the Franco Government realised that HISMA and ROWAK existed for German convenience and wanted to keep traditional trading channels open. The Germans, however, insisted that the big transactions in raw materials would be reserved for the two monopolies. German resources were not unlimited and supplies of war material to Franco would have to be dependent on regular imports of ores from Spain. On 20 May 1937, Franco told Faupel that he was happy to sign some agreements with Germany 'provided, of course, they complied with Spanish law'. This was a new element which would be the source of much ill-feeling in later months.[27]

Pressure on Franco by the British authorities was limited, perhaps because no permanent interference with the activity of the mining companies was feared. Rio Tinto sold ore to HISMA for a value of £2 million in the first two years of the war, but interference with traditional markets and HISMA's lower prices led to a £300 000 loss in 1936.

Spain, however, was declining as a source of British imports of iron ore. Furthermore, until Franco overran the mines in the Basque Country in June 1937, the majority of British supplies still came from the Government Zone and Franco gave private assurances that British factories would get their mineral ores.[28] So the British Government, already weary of the complaints of the mining companies, which it had considered exaggerated even in Popular Front days, was not over-energetic in pursuing their demands.

For Britain and the Non-Intervention Committee, this was seen as a side issue compared with the dangers created by the pouring-in of Italian troops.

Chapter 8

EDEN REACTS TO ITALIAN REINFORCEMENTS

Britain genuinely wanted to improve relations with Italy, but Eden insisted on giving nothing away, at least until 'Count Rossi' had left Majorca. Dino Grandi, who understood the British attitude well, cabled Rome on 20 December, 'Non è certo nel nostro interesse fornire ... sussidi a Rossi per sedurre Majorca (It is certainly not in our interest to provide ... subsidies to Rossi to seduce Majorca)'.[1] The impetuous young Fascist was removed soon afterwards.

In early January 1937, Eden learned of further large arrivals of Italian forces in Spain. He now thought it pointless to negotiate with a Mussolini who did not keep his word. For Eden, Mussolini was a gangster. It was hard for British policymakers to know what they should do. The Chiefs of Staff had warned that the country could not fight in the Mediterranean and the Far East simultaneously. There was also the pervasive anti-Communism which admired Fascist Italy. On the other hand, Eden held that, if Franco won in Spain with Italian and German aid, it would be more dangerous than the spread of Communism. At a Cabinet meeting on 8 January 1937, Eden proposed a Royal Navy blockade of Spanish coasts. If we did not stand up to the Dictators, said Eden, the risk of war would come nearer. Sir Samuel Hoare repeated his view that Britain ought not to adopt a policy of preventing General Franco from winning. Aside from Hoare's obvious partiality, a naval blockade would be very difficult. The Spanish coast was long. There were many harbours and inlets. Ships could not be thoroughly searched at sea and they would have to be taken into port. The blockade would occupy two British fleets and require mobilisation. So the Cabinet received Eden's suggestion with little enthusiasm.[2]

Naturally the Italian Government was asked to explain why it was sending troops to Spain. On 11 January Ciano admitted to the British Ambassador, Sir Eric Drummond, that Italian 'volunteers' had landed, but he insisted that Italy could not prevent them going unless the French blocked their own frontier. His evidence was that 45 000 men had entered Spain recently and were in the process of being trained and formed into

International Brigades. The entire question of limiting external support for both sides in Spain, which was the purpose of the Non-Intervention Committee, was unsolved and growing ever more serious.

On 12 November, the Committee had given preliminary approval to a plan for land and sea control of arms imports into Spain. Inspectors were to be stationed at the main entry-points. They would have unrestricted access to docks and railway yards, and could ask for relevant documents such as waybills or bills of lading. The full Committee met on 2 December 1936 to decide whether to ask the two warring parties in Spain to agree to have observers stationed in their territory. It was agreed to send the plan to Spain for approval, though many had reservations about the cost. The British estimate for this had been one million pounds per year, eighty per cent of which would be paid by the five most important powers: Britain, France, Germany, Italy and the USSR. The Foreign Office thought the plan too expensive and elaborate. Sir Robert Vansittart minuted that he thought the plan 'quite fantastic'. As for the scheme, put up by a technical sub-committee, for supervision of aircraft flying to Spain, the Foreign Office said that it 'was conceived in a mood of fantasy', for it required 158 observers to be scattered in countries up to 1500 miles from Spain. Since it did not cover the supervision of military aerodromes, which of course no country would accept, the plan would be ineffective in those countries which were in fact dispatching aircraft to the conflict, Sir Alexander Cadogan, the Deputy Under-Secretary, wrote that the whole thing seemed unreal. 'But of course we must not be caught killing it.' Since Britain could be reasonably sure that the Spaniards would not accept the scheme to supervise their frontiers, 'we should disingenuously give it our (mildest possible) blessing in principle... in point of efficacity... [the scheme] ... can be compared only to that under discussion between the Walrus and the Carpenter.'[3]

On 1 January 1937 the detailed plan was sent to both sides. The belligerents were not too impressed. The Spanish government in Valencia did not believe in the impartiality of the Non-Intervention Committee. In any case, to be expected to accept hundreds of agents with the right to ferret here and there under the protection of diplomatic immunity was intolerable. Still, the Republican Government accepted the plan in principle, but stressed the need to control Italian troop movements. Franco's reply on 15 January 1937 said the plan was pointless. The Reds were untrustworthy, the French were supplying them with arms. No international observer would be safe in Red ports. In fact, given the undeniable passage of thousands of volunteers over the French frontier into Catalonia, Nationalist suspicions had some justification. For Franco, however, there were purely pragmatic considerations for not wanting international inspection of his ports. Only a day after receiving the terms of the plan from London, Franco sent a note to persuade Ciano that it would be unfair to stop sending him arms since the Reds were getting large shipments of war material from the USSR. The caudillo – this was the medieval title which Franco assumed – thought it best to use all possible delaying tactics – 'cuantos trámites dilatorios sean posibles' – before giving a negative response to the Non-Intervention Committee's plan.[4]

As the British Government had predicted, this control plan for armaments was a non-starter. However, London had decided to bring the question of foreign personnel, already under debate with Italy, into the wider forum of the Non-Intervention Committee.

At the thirteenth meeting of the Committee, at 5 p.m. on Wednesday 9 December 1936, the German ambassador, the Nazi Joachim Von Ribbentrop, made a detailed statement on the numbers of French and Russian volunteers in the armies of the Spanish Republic. Ribbentrop and Maiskii exchanged heated words. Maiskii was able to speak from an assured position because there were no Russians in Spain, apart from pilots and advisers. Ribbentrop laboured under the general unpopularity brought about by his rudeness, his overbearing nature and the tactlessness which had led the diplomatic community to nickname him 'Brickendrop'. Maiskii held the stage as he said that Ribbentrop appeared to think that Russian troops 'with the aid of some magic carpet seemed able in a flash to travel from one side of Europe to another'.

The Soviet representative had been able to seize the diplomatic initiative by proposing that Non-Intervention should cover volunteers as well as armaments. The 9 December meeting suggested asking governments to make an effort to stop men going to Spain to fight. Italy had to delay this decision, for 4000 Blackshirts were about to sail for Spain. Twelve thousand more would be ready at the end of the month. The Italians returned to their original criticisms, which were that financial aid and propaganda would also have to be brought under control. In any case, as a German official told the French Ambassador on 26 December, France and Britain had not wanted to include volunteers in the Non-Intervention scheme before, so it was hardly reasonable to expect Germany to cooperate now, 'when the Red portion of Spain was entirely controlled by foreign Communist and Anarchist elements'.

The diplomatic fencing came to a sharp end, however, when Von Neurath called the British and French ambassadors to the Wilhelmstrasse on the morning of 31 December and told them that Germany would under no circumstances allow a Soviet Government in Spain and would even prevent this by force.

Count Ciano spoke to Britain in similar terms. The Italians were genuine volunteers, he said. Italian youth would continue to fight Bolshevism until other countries stopped the flow of men to the International Brigades.

These aggressive replies from Berlin and Rome showed that Nazis and Fascists had got the measure of the toothless Non-Intervention Committee. Could Britain and France strengthen it?

The problems of volunteers for the International Brigades was becoming thorny for the Democracies themselves. Local prefects had been told to close recruitment offices in Southern French towns. Decrees of 21 January and 18 February, 1937 forbade all passage to Spain through France.[5] This seems to have led to a reduction in the recruitment of French volunteers. In Britain, Conservative members of Parliament wondered why the Government did not do something to prevent men going to Spain. On 9 January, spurred on by press reports of young lads lured to Spain by unscrupulous Communist agents – and there certainly were cases of adventurous boys, dissatisfied sailors and desperate unemployed workers being encouraged to go to Spain for other than idealistic reasons – the Cabinet decided to activate an act of 1870 which forbade enlistment in foreign armies, though legal opinion doubted if courts would be able to use it in a civil war. Several cases were referred to the Director of Public Prosecutions but no action was taken.[6] Passports could, of course, be marked 'not valid for Spain' (though even the legality of telling a British subject that he could not go where he wanted was doubtful) but most men went to Spain on a no-passport trip across the Channel.

Calculations of the number of men in the International Brigades is difficult and varies greatly according to the sources employed, but by January 1937 there may well have been close on 35 000. This number was higher than the number of Italian Fascist troops in Spain in January, though not February, 1937, but if the German and Italian fliers, ground crews and special experts are added, together with the several thousand men recruited in French Morocco – Moroccans from the Spanish Zone, Franco would later argue, were Spanish – the figures may perhaps be equated. Of course, the International Brigades were untrained and not organised by their native countries, so the comparison with the German and Italian 'volunteers' cannot be supported.

Despite Italian and German obstruction, on 16 February the Committee extended the Non-Intervention agreement to include volunteers. It was hoped that this would at least gravely impede the passage of men to take service in Spain. This agreement would be even less effective than the ban on arms traffic had been. Yet it might have been successful, for, by now, Italy and Germany were beginning to think that they had done enough to help Franco.

After Franco had signed his agreement with Italy at the end of November 1936, Germany policy was to avoid diplomatic entanglement over Spain as far as possible and to leave the dispatch of army divisions to Italy. On 6 and 7 December, Admiral Canaris was again in Rome, where he stressed that Germany would not send troops. Nevertheless, the Condor Legion was reinforced by the newer Dornier-17 and Heinkel-111 bombers. Hitler was ready to send heavy reinforcements to try to win the war soon, as Hermann Goering's talks with the Italians show.

Goering arrived in Italy on 13 January. He stayed in the Italian capital for four days, the high point of which was a semi-public 20-minute sabre duel with the Duce.[7] He then spent five days on Capri, returning to Rome for a final long conversation with Mussolini and Ciano on the 23rd. If no satisfactory agreement on volunteers was reached in London, said Goering, Germany would go as far as she could without risking general war. The greatest peril was provoking the USSR into a massive intervention. In the meantime they agreed on the terms of a letter to Franco. The generalísimo had to make one final effort. After the end of January Germany and Italy would be forced to agree with the British plans for a naval blockade.[8] Franco replied on the evening of 25 January that he was doing his best but was chronically short of war material.

On 20 January, Rome announced that no more volunteers for Spain would be accepted. On the 25th, Italy and Germany replied to a British memorandum of 26 December. Both countries would support any proposal of genuine non-intervention provided it was rigorously applied, effective and complete.

On 12 February 1937, Franco was told that all Italian shipments had been completed. Mussolini had said that the Spanish insurgents now had enough men and arms to win the war on their own.

The Axis powers had prevaricated as long as they could. They had gained time to pour enough troops and aircraft into Spain to win the war. They were well aware of the weakness of the Soviet Union, which could not compete with Germany and Italy, and which in any case had no wish to be seen to intervene in Spain. Though French tolerance of the passage of thousands of volunteers for the International Brigades was an irritation, it was also useful, for until real control of volunteers was agreed by France and the Spanish Republican Government, Germany and Italy were not obliged to cease aiding Franco. What is demonstrably clear from the

German and Italian evidence is that a resolute attitude by Britain and France would certainly have led these powers to restrict their aid to the Spanish general.

THE LEAGUE, MOROCCO AND MEXICO

There were few diplomatic options open to the Spanish Republic. It had shipped the Spanish gold reserve to the Soviet Union in October 1936, which tended to confirm the international view that the Republic was under Soviet control. Little could be done to overcome the almost innate pre-judice against the Republic. Only three possibilities remained. One was the League of Nations; another was to inspire the Democracies, especially France, with a fear of Germany so great that it might stimulate real support for the Republic. The third possibility was to obtain its war material from countries which were not parties to Non-Intervention.

On 27 November 1936, Alvarez del Vayo requested a special session of the League under Article XI of the Covenant. He wanted to persuade the League that the armed intervention of Germany and Italy constituted 'war, or the threat of war'.

He spoke with passion to the League's Council on 11 December. But Eden and Delbos did not attend. They insisted that the Non-Intervention Committee, on which Germany and Italy were represented, was the proper forum to discuss the Spanish war, for it was essential to appease the Dictators, not to make them think that the international community was ganging up on them. The Soviet Union feared a British agreement with Germany and Italy over Spain and was unwilling to antagonise London. So Litvinov did not attend the League meeting. The other members of the League Council, often strongly anti-Communist and thus unfriendly to the Republic, voted to close the discussion and to leave Spain to the care of the Non-Intervention Committee.[9]

Rather more concern was created about German activity in Spanish Morocco. While in July 1936, the international administration of Tangiers had expelled the Republican fleet from the harbour, a decision which had denied the Republic any port nearer than Málaga, Franco had built up Morocco as a base for his entire military effort, securing the territory with the help of the able Colonel Beigbeder, an Arabist of high distinction with a profound understanding of the indigenous mentality and who was soon to be appointed High Commissioner in the Spanish Zone. Beigbeder tolerated limited activity on the part of Moroccan independence movements, and lavished money on mosques, schools and hospitals. The annual pilgrimage to Mecca was subsidised and escorted by Franco warships. Sheep were donated for festivals; missionary activity by Catholic priests was stopped. The authority of the Caliph and the chieftains was maintained.[10]

Reports of German landings in Morocco created alarm in Paris. Britain was asked for support in case the rumours proved correct. The rumours were false, as Nazi ambassador Faupel reported to Berlin on 9 January. Von Neurath minuted in the margin of Faupel's dispatch that the French, who had concentrated troops along their frontier with Spanish Morocco, should be reassured that there were no German volunteers in Morocco. Hitler also stressed to André François-Poncet, the French ambassador in Berlin, that Germany had no aims in Morocco. This calmed what Von Neurath called French 'hysterical nervousness'. Yet the speed of the German denial shows just how successful such a scare would have been in changing the French attitude towards Non-Intervention and how wary the Germans were of going too far in Spain.

The rumours of a German build-up in Morocco were almost certainly manufactured at the instigation of the Spanish ambassador in Paris, Luis Araquistain, and his brother-in-law, the Republican Foreign Minister Alvarez del Vayo.[11] There had been a proposal to create incidents in Morocco and thus stir up local indigenous sentiments against the Francoist authorities. However, Largo Caballero, the Spanish premier, feared to provoke the French by stirring up a hornet's nest in the Spanish protectorate, which might easily spread to the neighbouring French Zone.

The idea of provoking an uprising against Franco in Morocco persisted however, and del Vayo wrote to Araquistain on 2 January 1937, that the only way to do it was to persuade the French to free Abd-el-Krim, the Moroccan rebel who was now interned on the island of Réunion. Could the French be persuaded to let him return to Morocco and lead an independence movement?

At a higher level, plans had been laid to offer France territory in Spanish Morocco, which would allow France in turn to offer Germany a French African colony, in payment for which Hitler would withdraw support for Franco. Great Britain would, of course, be hostile to any such plan, both because she was not in favour of colonial concessions to Germany and because British policy required the Moroccan shores opposite Gibraltar to be occupied by a weak, but friendly, power such as Spain and not by France.[12]

This imaginative Spanish Republican plan to cede territory to France was leaked, almost certainly because Italian agents in London had access to the Spanish ambassador's documents. The Spanish Nationalists published it in full to demonstrate what they called the treachery and lack of patriotism of the Republic. It was an effective answer to those who claimed that Franco was handing over Majorca to Italy.

Scares about German activity in Morocco made for good newspaper headlines. The British public caught a real fright on 11 January 1937, when the London *Daily Telegraph*, not to be suspected of anti-Franco views, published an account of anti-aircraft and coastal artillery emplacements under construction on the Moroccan coast which might endanger freedom of shipping and the very Rock of Gibraltar. Spanish Republican Intelligence collected evidence and, aware that the Foreign Office would not use it for Spain's benefit, sent it to Lord Faringdon, a Labour peer of strong pro-Republican sentiments, who brought it up in the House of Lords. The Gibraltarian authorities were alarmed, and the British consul in Tetuán reported that security was so tight that he could not obtain information on the huge 305 mm cannon that Lord Faringdon claimed had been installed. Discussions went on throughout 1937 and into 1938, and internal documents reveal that the concern was far greater than the authorities cared to admit in Parliament, because a major scandal would have endangered the delicate diplomacy of Non-Intervention. In the end, apparently, the guns were removed. The whole story may, of course, have been propaganda. If so, it was quite effective in creating a scare, but not in changing the course of British policy.[13]

The Republic had not been entirely dependent on European countries for its military supplies. It had one major friend on the other side of the Atlantic. In Mexico, which was undergoing a process of revolutionary change, there were strong currents of sympathy for the Spanish Republicans and Socialists who had striven to carry out basic reforms from 1931 to 1933 and who had returned to power in 1936. The Spanish Right used Mexico, where anti-clericalism was even fiercer than in the mother country, as an example of the horrors of revolution, while the visits of Spanish intellectuals helped Mexicans to identify with a progressive Spain different from the traditional land of Church and bullfights. The Spanish Republic was looked on as a model to copy in tackling the issues of militarism and land reform. The leftism of the Mexican regime strained relations with the United States and many Latin American countries, so throwing Madrid's friendliness into greater relief, especially when Spain sponsored Mexico's membership of the League of Nations.

Mexican sympathy for Popular Front Spain was well-known. Therefore as early in the Spanish conflict as 20 August 1936, Britain refused to issue export licences for rifles, machine-guns and ammunition to Mexico in case this was a blind to re-export the arms to Spain.[14] Nevertheless, the Spanish ambassador to Mexico, Félix Gordón-Ordás, loyal to the Republic, explained the Spanish situation to Mexican President Lázaro Cárdenas, persuaded him to sell 3.5 million pesos' worth of arms, took over the Spanish Atlantic liner *Magallanes* at anchor in Vera Cruz and, aided by dockers who gave their time voluntarily, had it loaded with 20 000 rifles and twenty million cartridges. The ship sailed for Spain on 23 August. Cárdenas announced the shipment of the rifles on 1 September before the Mexican Parliament, which gave an ovation to Gordón-Ordás, who sat beaming in the gallery.[15]

Most of the Mexican rifles were lost in the routs of the Spanish militia that summer and autumn, Gordón-Ordás was also having problems getting funds. He did, however, manage to send three Lockheed aircraft to Spain in December 1936. Later the Spanish purchasing commission received an offer from an apparently well-known, but unfortunately unidentified, American gangster, for 50 Martin bombers and a wealth of other war material, for six million dollars. Again the funds did not arrive and the deal fell through.[16]

When the sterling equivalent of three million dollars was deposited in London in October for transfer to Mexico, the Midland Bank created difficulties over the spelling of the Spanish ambassador's name, which sometimes appeared as Ordax and not Ordás. Whether this was a deliberate delaying tactic or mere bureaucracy has never been established but, by the time the sum arrived on 25 November, Gordón-Ordás had lost the opportunity to buy up to 50 new aircraft as well as machine-guns, cannon and 20 000 Springfield rifles. Nevertheless, when transfers were made through the Banque Commerciale pour l'Europe du Nord, a Soviet-owned enterprise in Paris, which received the sums realised by the sales of Spanish gold, Gordón-Ordás found himself in charge of a credit of nine million dollars.

Sixteen aircraft were purchased at the end of 1936 and were waiting on the dockside at Vera Cruz to be loaded into the Spanish ship *Motomar*, when United States President Franklin D. Roosevelt, alarmed by American newspapers, pressed Cárdenas to cancel the sale. The Mexican leader agreed not to send arms to Spain unless the country where the material originated agreed.[17] Nevertheless, the Mexican embassy in Paris continued to buy arms for Spain from private dealers in various countries.

Mexican involvement in arms supplies to Spain must be seen in connection with United States policy. The United States was not concerned with European tensions and, had she supplied the Spanish Republic with arms, Britain and France might have reconsidered the Non-Intervention policy.

THE UNITED STATES

The United States wanted to defend American democracy and avoid involvement in European quarrels. She had not joined the League of Nations. She looked on as Hitler rejected the clauses of Versailles.

The US also disapproved of supplying other countries with weapons. This was echoed in the Neutrality Act of 31 August 1935, which obliged the President to impose an arms embargo on foreign wars. Isolationism was encouraged by the committee established under Senator Nye, which investigated the arms trade.

The USA refused to cooperate with the League's sanctions policy against Italy over Abyssinia, but nevertheless forbade United States ships to transport arms, and proclaimed a 'moral embargo' on the sale of raw materials which could be used for war. The Neutrality Act was extended into 1937.

Unwillingness to have anything to do with foreign wars, a desire to limit President Roosevelt's powers and to make him pay for congressional support for his New Deal policy: these were issues which would affect American actions during the Spanish conflict. Furthermore, Roosevelt depended on the largely Democratic Catholic vote, which had a great effect on policy towards Spain.

Roosevelt did not want to endanger his domestic policy by challenging Congress over foreign affairs, nor to tangle with Secretary of State Cordell Hull and the State Department, which was strongly neutralist. Ambassadors Bullitt in Paris and Joseph Kennedy in London exerted considerable influence on Roosevelt and were firm supporters of Non-Intervention. Both ambassadors had helped finance Roosevelt's campaigns, but they had little concept of the German threat or of the responsibility that the United States might have in Europe. Claude Bowers, an old-school liberal, sent personally to Madrid by Roosevelt, was largely ignored by Washington. The Popular Front Government in Spain was seen by many United States politicians and officials as a stalking-horse for the Soviet Union.

The United States had $80 million invested in Spain, mostly in the ITT telegraphs and telephones enterprise. ITT, together with the Spanish subsidiaries of Ford and General Motors, was taken over by trade-union militia at the outbreak of the war.[18] Though the Spanish Government agreed to compensate the owners, the State Department was unsympathetic to an administration which could not prevent these assaults on property. The Republic did not appear to represent American democratic values.

The USA had to take an early decision on helping one or other side in the civil war. The Vacuum Oil Company, which had stocks at Tangiers, was asked to deliver fuel to Spanish Government warships anchored in the port. The United States consul advised the company not to sell oil and Hull approved his action.[19] The US followed the example of other countries in refusing to recognise the Republican Navy's blockade of insurgent ports.

On 11 August, the United States announced its 'moral embargo' on arms supplies to Spain. It was not legally binding on US citizens but what it meant in practice was soon evident. On 10 August the Glenn L. Martin Company applied for licences to sell eight Martin bombers, ordered before the war, to Spain. Under-Secretary of State William Phillips answered, 'it seems reasonable to assume that the sale of aeroplanes...would not follow the spirit of the Government's policy'. Other firms received similar replies to their applications. Total neutrality over Spain gave Roosevelt political advantage with isolationists and internationalists alike. All were equally satisfied with the US Government's position and Roosevelt carried almost every State in the November 1936 elections. Nevertheless, the moral embargo was open to the same criticism as the Non-Intervention agreement, for it put the Spanish Government on the same footing as the insurgents, while Germany and Italy backed Franco.

Hull had already issued a statement of total non-interference in Spain while Roosevelt was on vacation. The President referred to Spain first in his Chautauqua (New York) speech on 14 August. War, said Roosevelt, might profit individual Americans who sold armaments, but it would be disastrous for the USA as a whole.[20]

A purchasing commission of Spanish Air Force officers arrived in the USA on 28 September. They bought 14 Vultee airliners, which could be converted into bombers, but were unable to pay for them because the funds did not arrive from Spain. There were various complicated negotiations to obtain export licences and finally 19 aircraft were shipped to Le Havre in December 1936, and six Vultees, three Lockheed Orions and two or three other aircraft at length reached Spain.[21]

The Republican purchasing commission came up against the unwillingness of the Spanish embassy to get involved in arms purchases, because American public opinion was so strongly neutral. In any case, the cyphers were insecure and Ambassador Gordón-Ordás in Mexico, who would be the ostensible purchaser of material obtained in the USA, could not get answers to his cables to Spain because of the chaos of the Republican ministries, where many officials had deserted or had been arrested. Luis Araquistain in Paris seems to have been reduced to sending his letters to

Washington and Spain in uncoded Spanish, somewhat pathetically trying to disguise the word 'Vultees' by *buitres* (vultures) and referring to French premier Blum as 'Señor Flor'.

Roosevelt's November 1936 election triumph might have swayed him to lift the embargo, but Soviet support for the Republic from October onward inclined him to leave things where they were. Harold Ickes, the Secretary of the Interior, recalled that when the Republic's ambassador, Fernando de los Ríos, told the newly-elected President that Madrid was successfully resisting Franco's onslaught. Roosevelt seemed relieved. Perhaps the good news swayed him against lifting the embargo.[22]

Nevertheless, the absence of a real, rather than a 'moral' embargo, meant that determined or unscrupulous dealers could sell armaments to Spain. Robert Cuse, president of the Vimalert Corporation in New Jersey, received large sums of money from the Soviet trade organisation Amtorg to buy aircraft and other arms for the Republic. He had been told in October that he could not sell planes to Spain through Mexico. On Christmas Eve, 1936, he applied for a licence to export nearly three million dollars' worth of aircraft and engine parts. The State Department said that to issue the licences would be against the interests of the USA. Roosevelt said at a press conference that it was quite legal but unpatriotic. The licences were issued on 28 December. Cuse's men worked at top-speed to dismount the aircraft for shipping. As a result, Roosevelt asked the Congress to extend the Neutrality Act to civil wars. The debate took place in the Congress on 6 January 1937. Senator Key Pittman of Nevada introduced the amendment, which would allow the President discretion to embargo arms shipments to civil wars if they 'threaten the neutrality or peace of the US'. In fact the embargo was made obligatory on the President. Penalties were heavy: a $10 000 fine and/or up to five years in gaol. It was a Congress strongly affected by the Nye Committee's exposure of excess profits made by arms dealers in the First World War.

A number of senators and representatives abstained. Only one voted against the resolution, though 31 others later said that they voted with misgivings.[23]

In Mexico, Gordón-Ordás was embarrassed and angry. Cuse had claimed that the Spanish Government had appointed him to acquire material. By openly applying for an export licence he had disturbed the State Department wasps' nest. Gordón-Ordás had paid for 15 aircraft, arranged for 41 more, was negotiating for 18 Martin bombers and four million dollars' worth of material. A subsequent cable to the Spanish Ministry of Marine and Air on 20 January 1937 said that he knew how to deal with American hypocrisy. Provided he went carefully he could do what he liked. He had a great deal of material in Los Angeles which he claimed he could get past American customs officers on the Mexican border. The Cuse scandal, he claimed, had spoiled everything.[24]

While the Congress was forbidding American citizens to sell material to Spain, part of the shipment left New York, taking advantage of a legal delay until the President signed the amendment on 8 January.

Hard work by dockers had stowed eight of Cuse's aircraft in the Spanish steamer *Mar Cantábrico* togéther with several hundred aero-engines. The ship docked at Vera Cruz, where it collected more cargo, leaving on 19 February. Secrecy was not maintained and the Nationalists had a good idea of the route of the ship, which the cruiser *Canarias* stopped and sequestered with its cargo on 8 March. Despite trying to pass itself off as a British steamer, and calling up a flotilla of British destroyers to protect itself, the true nationality of the *Mar Cantábrico* was evident.

Extending the embargo to civil wars was a disaster for the new Spanish ambassador to the United States, Fernando de los Ríos. But, as the American Socialist Norman Thomas cynically told a Spanish friend in 1938, the Republic should not have sent a professor like Don Fernando but a wheeler-dealer politician who would have persuaded the big aircraft and weapons manufacturers to exert pressure on the Congress.[25]

Following the embargo, the State Department marked United States passports 'not valid for Spain' and demanded that all citizens proposing to travel abroad furnish an affidavit that they were not bound for Spain. This did not stop the first American volunteers for the International Brigades from leaving at this time. They would soon become the Lincoln and Washington battalions. United States volunteers suffered, often for the rest of their lives, from suspicion of Communist disloyalty. In March 1937, the State Department refused passports to the second surgical unit of the American Friends of Spanish Democracy. The first unit had gone in January. After great protests and Roosevelt's intervention, the State Department changed its mind.

A new Neutrality Act became law on 1 May 1937. It continued the embargo which would last until the end of the Spanish Civil War.

Chapter 9

THE NAVAL PATROL

Every few days, the Non-Intervention sub-committees discussed the supervision of Spain's frontiers and coasts. There were many problems. The major drawback was that the Naval Patrol plan to watch the Spanish coasts covered neither Spanish ships nor vessels registered in non-participating countries. This was a get-out for Germany which painted names of Panamanian-registered vessels on its ships.[1]

Portugal agreed to accept British frontier inspectors only, while Grandi and Ribbentrop put a brave face on the matter and claimed that Germany and Italy had wanted this control all along. The USSR was supporting the control scheme, so Grandi and Ribbentrop were reduced to making difficulties about the Spanish gold reserve. This was now in Moscow and being sold on the international market to allow the Republic to pay cash for its supplies.

Smaller countries with merchant fleets hoped that the patrol scheme would protect their legitimate traffic, for Franco's navy was stopping vessels and confiscating the cargoes. For instance, by the end of April 1937, Franco had seized 26 Danish ships, not all bound for Spain, and had confiscated their cargoes. Danish, Norwegian, Finnish and Greek protests had been ignored. These were acts of piracy, given that Franco's belligerent status had not been recognised, but short of an international attack on his warships there was no way of stopping it.

After demanding the right to participate in the Naval Patrol, the Russians had chosen not to do so after all. The general view, according to the German chargé in London, was that the Soviet fleet was so inefficient that Moscow thought it better not to display it to international eyes. Nevertheless, Soviet warships would have been a very long way from home if they had been stationed off the northwest coast of Spain – and Italy had refused absolutely to tolerate them in the Mediterranean – so the difficulties and expense may have been too great.

Generally speaking, the ships which brought arms from Russia were Spanish and were escorted to Alicante, Cartagena or Valencia by the

Spanish Republican navy, so they would not be subject to any control. However, not all the 84 Russian merchant-ships that had been detained by Franco's navy were innocent. For example, the *Komsomol* was ostensibly carrying manganese ore to Belgium. However, its crew were specially selected for their mission of dodging Franco patrols and delivering arms to the Republic. The Franco navy had good reason to suspect the *Komsomol* of arms traffic. Officially, the cruiser *Canarias* sank the *Komsomol* with gunfire on 14 December 1936, but there is reason to believe that, following urgently radioed orders from the USSR, the crew scuttled the ship to avoid the discovery of a cargo of arms hidden beneath the manganese.[2] Though the *Komsomol* had almost been caught *in flagrante delicto*, Maiskii was very concerned that the Naval Patrol should work efficiently because he thought it would restrict Germany and Italy more.

Despite the drawbacks, the scheme was adopted and the date of midnight GMT on 19/20 April 1937 was set for the Naval Patrol to begin its task. Administrators were appointed for the Pyrenees and for the following harbours: The Downs (Dover), Cherbourg, Le Verdon (at the mouth of the Gironde), Brest, Lisbon, Madeira, Gibraltar, Oran, Sète, Marseille, and Palermo. All ships bound for Spain would be obliged to put in to one of these ports and take on one or two inspectors, who would sail with the vessels and observe their unloading in Spain. Ships carrying inspectors would fly the Non-Intervention pennant.

The hundreds of sea and land observers and inspectors came from almost all the countries which had agreed to Non-Intervention. Portuguese naval lieutenants, Estonian army captains, Norwegian lieutenant-colonels, Latvians, Dutchmen, Danes, Turks, Yugoslavs, Finns and Irishmen took up positions of authority on each other's territory. It was an example of smooth international cooperation, into which Germany and Italy were drawn, as the Foreign Office wanted. The Soviet Union kept out, partly because some countries were unwilling to have Soviet personnel on their territory, but also perhaps because the USSR recognised that the whole thing was largely meretricious and designed to put a cosmetic gloss of international agreement on what was fundamentally impractical, as indeed the Naval Patrol and the supervision schemes turned out to be.

At the end of March 1937, the major naval powers reported that they were ready to patrol off Spain. Britain and France would supervise the northern coast, Germany the southern part of the Mediterranean coast and Italy the northern stretch as far as the French frontier. Italy would also supervise the coast around the Republican-held island of Minorca; France would watch the Franco-held islands of Ibiza and Majorca, together with Spanish Morocco east of Gibraltar, while Great Britain would patrol west of Gibraltar. Arrangements were made for harbours for crew-leave and ships' revictualling and refuelling.

Everything appeared to be going smoothly, but it was unwise to assume that the Russians would be content to stay completely out of these arrangements. The opportunity to score points came soon, as a consequence of events hundreds of miles inside the high, wintry plateau of Spain.

Italy had supported the supervision schemes partly because she hoped that by the time they came into force the Italian expeditionary force, the CTV, would have enabled Franco to win the war. On 8 March, Italian armoured columns launched their drive towards Guadalajara. The plan was to be in Madrid by 15 March, thus bringing the war to a triumphant conclusion. However, by 20 March the Italian advance had been blocked and thrown back. Many men and much material had been lost. Even more significantly, from the political point of view, many Italian prisoners had been taken and the Republic made full use of the propaganda advantages that they provided. Prisoners were interrogated in public and appeared on newsreels. A full order of battle of the Italian forces was prepared and foreign countries were circulated with the information. The Republic's prestige was again high; Italy's plummeted.

On 23 March, at the morning meeting of the sub-committee, Maiskii noticed that Grandi seemed irritable.[3] Had he received a full account, without whitewash, of the defeat? Perhaps he could be nudged into a damaging statement. Maiskii began to ask questions about the working of the ban on 'volunteers', which had been agreed some time earlier. Grandi was needled by the news of the Italian débâcle and naturally opposed the establishment of a special commission to report on the number of foreign troops in Spain. Plymouth and Corbin asked pointed questions. Maiskii asked, 'Are we to understand the Italian ambassador as meaning that Italy and Germany, contrary to the decision of the Committee, are positively refusing to bring their volunteers out of Spain?' His trick worked. Grandi, furious at the wide reporting of the Italian defeat, lost his temper and retorted, 'If you want my opinion, I'll say this, not one single Italian volunteer will leave Spain until Franco is victorious!' Shocked silence settled over the conference table. Next day Maiskii dropped his second bomb. He announced that he had evidence that there were 60 000 Italians in Spain.

Lord Plymouth had been mentally rubbing his hands at his success in getting the supervision schemes agreed, so Maiskii's surprise speech angered and embarrassed him. All the time-consuming speechifying would start again, he feared. Ribbentrop called Maiskii's words 'an amazing exhibition of hypocrisy'. Grandi said, 'this provocative statement will get the answer it deserves'. However, Maiskii had made his point. Italy was on the defensive and this would affect her conduct over Spain from now on.

The Non-Intervention Committee did not meet again until 5 May. Delegates were fresh from their Easter holidays. There were twelve balmy spring days to go before the coronation of George VI, a happy ending to the constitutional crisis that had begun the previous autumn when the uncrowned Edward VIII had revealed his intention to marry the American divorcée, Wallis Simpson. Well might the British Government be proud of itself. The Frontier Supervision Scheme and the Naval Patrol had come into effect. There were 105 observers in place on the border of Spain and France. There were 330 observers of 17 different nationalities available to be taken on merchant-ships bound for Spain, and since 30 April every such ship had – if registered in one of the Non-Intervention countries – embarked two observers to examine the cargo, question the skipper and watch the unloading. Surely now the Spanish war could at last be isolated, as Britain had always wanted.

Unfortunately, the schemes were full of holes. They came too late to prevent the massive intervention that had already occurred. They were unlikely to decrease the tension between the countries involved in Spain. Many methods of smuggling arms had been evolved. German ships simply flew the Panamanian flag. Italian ships were closely escorted by warships, while Spanish ships were not liable to be checked. Methods of concealing arms from the eyes of perhaps none-too-vigilant observers had been perfected. Ships might fly the Non-Intervention pennant without having taken observers on board. Observers could be venal, drunkards or easily diverted by the pleasures available in Spanish ports.

The cynicism with which the supervision schemes were viewed was perhaps best expressed by a British Cabinet Foreign Policy Committee minute of 1 July 1937, in which Duff Cooper, who had replaced Hoare at the Admiralty, remarked that there was no essential reason why the patrol scheme *should* be effective, or should be useless if it were not *fully* effective.[4] The point was not that it should actually stop the arms traffic, but to show that there was active international cooperation in such a scheme.

If this was the aim, then the first report on the operation of the scheme, presented on 25 August 1937, could in fact boast of commendable results. In the first six weeks of operation, 323 ships belonging to the participating countries had entered Spanish waters. Only eight had failed to comply with the rules by not taking on observers. All the same, 79 ships had not been identified, while 415 ships registered with countries who were not signatories to the Non-Intervention agreement had sailed to Spain.

Would this, however, satisfy Franco, who was growing more and more agitated about the shipping which brought supplies, including fuel and foodstuffs, to the Republic? The answer to this question would be given at the very time that the Naval Patrol came into force. Paradoxically, it would be Britain, leading light of the supervision schemes, who would have to cope with a dissatisfied Franco.

WAR IN THE NORTH

By 20 April 1937, when the Naval Patrol began, Franco had drawn the lesson that the combination of a new Republican Army with Soviet aid and advisers and air cover, made further attempts to take Madrid impractical. He transferred his efforts to the conquest of the northern Republican Zone, which was composed of the autonomous Basque region (with its capital in Bilbao), Santander, and the coal-mining basin of the Asturias. These were areas with extensive industrial, shipbuilding and mining resources, but they were isolated from the main part of the Republic and depended heavily on supplies which arrived by sea, particularly Welsh coal for the furnaces of Bilbao. In turn, British steel industries depended on iron ore from northern Spain. Thus ships laden with coal and iron ore plied regularly between the ports of northern Spain and South Wales.

To prevent supplies reaching Spain, Nationalist ships patrolled the coast. The Republican warships were so demoralised by indiscipline and the unreliability of their commanders that they hardly left port.[5]

The Basques created their own auxiliary navy. One of their ships, the *Biskaia*, boldly arrested the German merchant-ship *Palos* on 23 December 1936, and took it to Bilbao. The Basques found war-material in the holds. Though the ship itself was immediately returned, the cargo was retained. The German authorities reacted fiercely. On 1 January 1937, German warships captured two Spanish cargo-boats and handed them over to the Nationalists.

The Germans seemed prepared to go a long way in insisting that the Spanish Republicans – 'Red pirates' in their view – had no right to touch their ships. How far were Britain and the Royal Navy, for their part, prepared to go to stop Franco interfering with British shipping? Would they be as firm as they had been at the beginning of the war when they refused to accept the Republican blockade and sent warships racing out of Gibraltar to protect British merchant ships? The question would soon have to be answered.

On 12 January 1937, a Franco warship had tried to detain a British merchant-ship, the *Bramhill*, which was suspected of arms-running for the Republic. A British cruiser warned the Spaniard off, inspected the *Bramhill*, but found no war-material in her hold. Another British merchant-ship, the *Hillfern*, belonging to Angel, Son and Company, a firm which had been under suspicion for some time, was stopped on 8 February, with the same result.

The Royal Navy had no great sympathy for British merchant-ships, which it suspected of gun-running and profiteering. There were also suspicions that many ships which had been purchased by British firms and had gone on to the British maritime register, had done so in order to be entitled to Royal Navy protection or because the Nationalists would believe that they had been properly checked. Certainly some British-registered ships had brought material from the USSR at the end of 1936 and the beginning of 1937. The Stanhope Company, owned by Jack Billmeir, was a case in point. Billmeir's operations would expand enormously during the Spanish war. His crews risked arrest and often bombing, while they supplied goods to the Republic at the inflated freight-rates which that traffic attracted. Beginning with two ships, by 1937 Billmeir owned twelve, all trading with Spain. They would become daily news. The Conservative press and the Royal Navy complained that many of these ships had nothing British about them but their names.[6] In spite of these doubts and despite frequent Nationalist protests to the British authorities, it was difficult to find concrete evidence of ships smuggling arms.

Public opinion and political activity was becoming more intense in early 1937. In January the Unity Campaign was set up. It brought together the Independent Labour Party, the Communist Party, and the Socialist League under Stafford Cripps, a later Labour Chancellor of the Exchequer. Cripps's policy on Spain led to his expulsion from the Labour Party, for Labour believed that any approach to the further Left would ruin its electoral chances.

The Unity campaign urged the rejection of the Non-Intervention policy. While it was unreal to expect the Government to do this, the Unity Campaign did have some effect as a ginger group within Labour. All the same, public opinion surveys suggested that large numbers of Labour voters were convinced that Non-Intervention was the safest policy.

Inside the Labour Party a group called Labour Spain was established at a meeting in London's Conway Hall on 13 March 1937.[7] It clashed with

Clement Attlee, the Party leader, and Ernest Bevin, the powerful head of the Transport and General Workers' Union. Labour Spain failed to persuade the movement as a whole to become militant over Non-Intervention. In spite of much pressure, on 6 May 1937 the Party Secretary wrote to Labour Spain that Party policy was to keep Non-Intervention but to try to make it effective. Therefore when, on 18 March 1937, the Labour Opposition decided to support the bill which would require British merchant-ships to take on Non-Intervention observers, only 16 Labour members of Parliament voted against. Given the apparent toughening of the Non-Intervention policy by the supervision schemes, the National Executive Committee of the Party and the Right-wingers, such as Bevin and Dalton, were even less inclined to be pushed in the direction of the fringe Leftists and the Communists and to attack the Government over its Spanish policy. Labour policy could be summed up in this quotation attributed to Ernest Bevin: 'we are willing to give you money. We are willing to give you food and medical supplies. But arms? No! Abandonment of the Non-Intervention policy? No! For any other policy would lead to a world war.'[8]

Only a few days later, on 22 March 1937, Eden told Bevin and Walter Citrine, General Secretary of the TUC, that threats against Mussolini were useless, unless Britain was willing to go to war. He did not seem to consider whether Mussolini would in fact fight and, if so, whether or not his navy could be dealt with by the Royal Navy. A week later, Eden's private secretary noted that Eden definitely wanted the Spanish Government to win. Just as Mussolini had been sending thousands of Blackshirts to Spain while he was signing the Gentlemen's Agreement in January, so he had launched his drive on Guadalajara and Madrid just as the supervision schemes were being completed in March. Eden saw that a Franco victory with the aid of Germany and Italy would be a menace to peace. As he wrote: 'From the early months of 1937, if I had to choose, I would have preferred a Government victory.'[9]

THE BLOCKADE OF BILBAO

On 29 March, Franco informed London that British merchant-ships approaching Spanish ports should obey signals to stop from his warships. London replied that ships on the high seas would not obey any such instruction because the Nationalists had not been recognised as belligerents and had no rights over neutral shipping. Parliament was irritated, since several of the British ships that had recently been stopped, at

Franco's request, had been found innocent of arms-carrying. Public opinion was particularly angry because two British destroyers, HMS *Havoc* and HMS *Gipsy*, had been bombed, albeit in error.

There had been business and personal contacts between Britain and the northern port of Bilbao for decades. The Basques were devout Catholics, but also enterprising seamen and businessmen, whose society was orderly, conservative and socially just. British public opinion could empathise with the Basques, who seemed unlike the Spaniards, who were seen as brutal and fanatical whether fighting for or against the Church. There had been few outrages in the Basque country, unlike other parts of Spain. Churches were open and crowded. It was hard to recognise in this nation the Bolshevik Antichrist against whom Franco claimed to be leading his Fascist, Nazi and Moorish crusaders. Thus the British public was very sympathetic to the cause of the Basque people, whom it saw as resembling themselves – conservative seamen, farmers, miners and steelmen – and fighting for their ancestral liberties.

British sea captains were the heroes of the hour as they braved Franco's navy to bring essential supplies to Bilbao. The Basque Government chartered 48 ships, many of them British, to bring in their supplies. Whether some of them risked carrying occasional quantities of arms cannot be said for certain, though pro-Franco authors have always insisted that this was so. Yet it is unlikely, for arms-smuggling would have been risky for a British-registered ship because it was subject not only to the Non-Intervention control scheme but also to the British law of December 1936 which allowed Royal Navy ships to search any British merchantmen making for a Spanish port.

Four British destroyers had been escorting boatloads of women and children, fleeing from the air-raids over Bilbao, through the choppy waters of the Bay of Biscay to safety in France. This in itself was an irritation for Franco, who insisted that he could provide a safe area for refugees and that, by escorting ships full of women and children, the Royal Navy was freeing food for soldiers and thus compromising its neutrality.

Late on 5 April, the *Brazen*, patrolling off Bilbao, hailed the British merchant-ship *Thorpehall*, whose skipper told the captain that he intended to defy the Nationalist blockade and enter Bilbao next day. The *Thorpehall* was a test case, for the Nationalists had reported her earlier for arms-smuggling. Nothing had been found, however, when she was searched at Gibraltar.

The crisis came at dawn on 6 April. At 5.56 a.m. the *Thorpehall* radioed that she was being fired on by the Nationalist armed trawler *Galerna* at about ten miles from the coast. The *Brazen* signalled to the *Galerna* to cease firing. At this moment the Nationalist cruiser *Almirante Cervera* was seen approaching at high speed. Captain Taylor of the *Brazen* ordered the decks cleared for action and placed his ship between the British merchant ship and the Spanish cruiser. The situation was tense, for the *Almirante Cervera* had far greater fire-power than the British destroyer. The Spanish warships responded by placing themselves between the *Thorpehall* and the coast.

Whose bluff would prevail? As the crews of the four ships waited tensely, two British destroyers raced to the scene. Then the German battleship *Graf Spee*, in the area as a warning to the Basques should they try to repeat their exploit with the *Palos*, steamed up. Possibly some quiet advice was given to the captain of the *Almirante Cervera*. Messages flashed back and forth. The British insisted that the *Thorpehall* was on the high seas, that she had been cleared earlier of arms-smuggling and that Franco had no right to interfere with neutral shipping.

Four anxious hours later, the *Almirante Cervera* and the *Galerna* steamed off. Then the *Almirante Cervera* received another order to stop the merchant-ship, returned to the scene and challenged her. The British destroyers adopted an attack position. However, before the *Thorpehall* had reached the three-mile line, the Franco cruiser steamed off again, unwilling to risk being hit by a salvo from the Basque coastal artillery.

The commander of the destroyer flotilla reported that the Nationalist blockade was 'effective', a word which gave it a certain legality and made the Admiralty very unwilling to escort British merchant-ships through to Bilbao. In reality, the Franco blockade did not have enough ships for a full blockade and, in any case, they had to stand several miles offshore because of the coastal batteries. Yet the Admiralty was only too willing to believe that the blockade was effective. British naval officers were often very sympathetic to Franco's commanders. So, early on 7 April, the Admiralty ordered its destroyer captains to tell the merchant skippers that the Navy could not protect them.

This was the subject of an acrimonious debate in the Cabinet that day. Some thought it was a clear case of illegal blockade. Sir Samuel Hoare reflected both the caution of the Royal Navy and his own dislike of the Republic when he insisted that the blockade was effective and that British ships could not be escorted individually. Some of the Cabinet were unwilling to risk British relations with a future Franco Government for the sake of, as they saw it, the profits of a few owners of ships which had only recently been registered in Britain.[10]

The Basque issue and the Franco blockade became headline news. How dared the 'dagoes' try to stop British seamen about their legitimate business? Yet, Franco's Nationalists, who had great respect for the Royal Navy, could not understand how the British Government could wish to provide food, the equivalent of guns, for the besieged city of Bilbao, a nest of 'Red Separatists', who had supported the atheistic Bolsheviks of Madrid, Barcelona and Valencia because they wanted to break away from Spain, when, as Catholics, they had a clear duty to fight with Franco. There was no compromise between these views. For the supporters of Franco, the Foreign Office and the British press were hypocrites. It was high freight rates and not principle that impelled them to act as they did.

The Cabinet decided to continue to protect merchant-ships. However, British merchant skippers were warned of the dangers and advised to wait in St Jean de Luz.[11] Very soon there were several merchant-ships at anchor in the French port. Wisely enough, the Admiralty realised that this was a temporary situation, and that a clash might well occur when the merchants did in fact leave, so the cruiser *Shropshire* and the most powerful ship in the world, the battle-cruiser *Hood*, came steaming up from Gibraltar flying a vice-admiral's flag.[12] Decisions were to be taken at the highest level.

British ministers came back to London early from their weekends and assembled around the long table at 10 Downing Street on Sunday evening, 11 April. It was a long and difficult meeting.[13] Hoare and Eden clashed, Hoare wanting to classify foodstuffs as war-materials and to forbid the ships to go to Bilbao, while Eden wanted to order the Navy to escort them. Hoare's Admiralty information suggested that Franco's navy was stronger than it was. He also overstated the danger of mines laid in the approaches to Bilbao, which were actually being swept by the Basques.

The Cabinet decided to maintain its policy. Ships were advised to stay in St Jean de Luz, and Franco was warned not to interfere with any British ships that did decide to risk the journey to Bilbao.

Next day the Government had a hard time from the Opposition in Parliament. Baldwin gave evasive answers about the dangers that British ships might face if they went to Bilbao. Clement Attlee insisted that the mines had been swept, that the Basque coastal batteries could easily protect any ship within the three-mile limit and that therefore the Royal Navy should be ordered to do its duty and protect British merchantmen on the high seas. In the end, the Opposition put down a motion of censure for 14 April.

At the debate on the censure motion deploring 'the failure of His Majesty's Government to give protection to British merchant ships on their lawful occasions', Conservatives demanded that Franco be granted belligerent rights. Eden explained that belligerent rights would have to be given to both sides and this would mean giving both Franco and the

Republic the right to stop and search British ships. Surely members did not want that. He told the Opposition that British ships would be protected up to the three-mile limit.

The motion of censure was lost, given the large Government majority. Apparently Franco was very satisfied and communicated his pleasure through Sir Henry Chilton on 17 April.[14] Obviously he misunderstood. If ships were advised to stay out of Bilbao, this was, in his view, as good as an order. The Franco authorities did not understand that the British Government could not issue orders to merchant skippers. It was the classic difference between an undemocratic and a free system. Franco understood that the British Government had to save face by insisting that it would protect ships which did try to reach Bilbao, but he could not believe that they really meant it.

British pro-Basque feeling reached its apogee. On 19 April, Hoare admitted in the Commons that ships were leaving Bilbao without difficulties. Mr Attlee rose to enquire, with heavy sarcasm, the nature of the problem which affected ships arriving at Bilbao but not leaving it.

Several ships were now at anchor in St Jean de Luz. Captain 'Potato' Jones, who commanded the *Marie Llewellyn*, made belligerent statements to the press. He claimed to have heard nothing of the Spanish Navy since the Armada of 1588. 'It makes me sick, thinking of these Spanish Dons strutting about the quarter-decks of their miserable ships intimidating the British Navy and interfering with British shipping.'[15]

Who would call Franco's bluff? As time wore on and the cargoes began to deteriorate, the skippers became to wonder just how risky it would be to dash overnight to Bilbao. On 15 April, 'Potato' Jones took the *Marie Llewellyn* out to sea. He was turned back by a British destroyer. Since he was heading directly towards the battleship *España*, his chance to defy the Dons might have come sooner than he thought. Eventually, 'Potato' Jones set sail but never arrived at any port in the north of Spain. Some days later he discharged his now elderly potatoes in Alicante on the Mediterranean coast.

Also lying in St Jean de Luz was the *Seven Seas Spray*, commanded by Captain Roberts. On the evening of Monday 19 April, he quickly raised anchor and sailed all night, docking at Bilbao next morning to a tumultuous welcome. Cheering crowds lined the miles of wharves. Captain Roberts and his daughter were nobly entertained by the Basque Government, for they had brought four thousand tons of food to a hungry population.[16]

Late on 22 April, three more foodships left St Jean de Luz. The Franco navy was determined to stop them. The Royal Navy was resolved that it should not. The 42 000-ton battle-cruiser *Hood*, with its eight 203 mm guns, accompanied by destroyers, waited off Bilbao. At 6.35 a.m. on 23 April, the *Almirante Cervera* ordered the *MacGregor*, under Captain 'Corncob' Jones, to heave to. The *Hood* told the Spanish ship to cease interfering. Messages flashed back and forth between Captain Moreu on the *Almirante Cervera* and Vice-Admiral Blake. The armed Spanish trawler *Galerna* actually fired a warning shot at the *MacGregor*. The destroyer *Firedrake* brought her guns to bear. The *Almirante Cervera* sailed straight at the *Firedrake*. Would the powerful guns of the Spanish cruiser sink the destroyer before the massive barrage of the *Hood* sent her blazing to the bottom? As Vice-Admiral Blake kept the conversation going, the merchantmen approached the three-mile limit. Then the coastal batteries fired. Captain Moreu, now relieved of the decision to risk his ship, retired.

Over the next ten days twelve more merchant ships arrived with foodstuffs and fuel. Thereafter Nationalist attempts to stop British ships would be directed more to other ports on the north coast, and British public opinion would be more concerned with the protection of Basque refugees, for the Basque struggle attracted general humanitarian concern, as opposed to political propaganda and pressure, and this took on an international dimension.[17]

Chapter 10

GUERNICA

In the midst of the Bilbao crisis, an event occurred which created a wave of outrage and, over 50 years later, still symbolises the Spanish Civil War. On the afternoon of Monday 26 April 1937, German aircraft destroyed Guernica, the spiritual centre of Basque nationalism. Other towns in the Basque country had been bombed, but none was so completely destroyed as Guernica. It was the use of incendiary bombs (rather than the high explosive which would have been appropriate for demolishing bridges, the ostensible reason for the bombing) which demonstrated the intention to obliterate Guernica as part of the war against the Basque nation itself.

The Nationalist authorities denied that aircraft under their command had bombed Guernica and insisted that the retreating Basques had destroyed the town themselves. This was believed by pro-Francoists for decades until even Franco spokesmen began to admit the facts and to try to lay the blame on the Condor Legion rather than on Franco's headquarters, from where the request, if not the precise orders, for the bombing had come.

The destruction of Guernica led to an intense journalistic and propagandistic war. A freelance journalist, George L. Steer, went to Guernica at 2 a.m. next morning, wrote his dispatch, returned to Bilbao and cabled it. Steer's famous report appeared in *The Times* and the *New York Times* on 28 April. He described the bombing, the machine-gunning, and the dropping of incendiary bombs and gave his view that Guernica was bombed for terror purposes.[1]

On 29 April, three days after the bombing, Guernica was in the hands of the advancing Franco forces. No impartial report was possible now. The Nationalists at once published a statement.

Guernica was destroyed by incendiaries and petrol. It was set afire and reduced to ruins by the Red hordes in the criminal service of Aguirre, the President of the Basque Republic.[2]

Newspapermen with the Nationalists, happily or under duress, published their own pro-Nationalist versions. Steer's dispatch in the *New York Times* was contradicted by the pro-Franco reporter, William Carney.

Eden learned, through the British consul in Bilbao, that Guernica had been destroyed by German aircraft, but it was not an appropriate moment to attack Germany. The patrol of Spanish coasts had just begun and it looked as though the Spanish war really could be isolated if nobody rocked the boat. In the Commons on 3 May, Eden replied as evasively as he could to MPs' accusations against Germany.

Britain now suggested appealing to both sides not to bomb open towns. Since refusal to back the appeal would look bad, Germany agreed to it on condition that Guernica should not be mentioned, and nobody uttered the name of the martyred town. There were, insisted Von Ribbentrop, other examples of inhuman behaviour in the Spanish war and other towns had been bombed. The Spanish Government's request for an international enquiry on Guernica was ignored.

Whether Guernica was destroyed in order to crush the spirit of the Basque nation or whether it was a purely tactical measure which went wrong, the episode created such a wave of emotion in Western Europe and the United States that large numbers of refugees were given shelter overseas, including even Britain, which received four thousand Basque children, and Catholic organisations helped in this work, for the Basques were fervent Catholics. The tragedy of the Basque people, however, aroused controversies within the Catholic world itself.

THE CATHOLIC CHURCH AND THE SPANISH WAR

For the Catholic Church the greatest challenge of the twentieth century had been revolutionary socialism, together with liberal agnosticism. Naturally the Church tended to approve of conservative regimes, which promised protection against the atheistic Left.

The Vatican, advised by its Nunzio in Madrid, Mgr Tedeschini, considered the Spanish Church, which had always been identified with conservative and reactionary views, as undesirably backward.[3] It saw the Spanish Republic of April 1931 as a challenge. However, a provocative pastoral letter by the Spanish Primate, Cardinal Segura, on 1 May, led to his expulsion from Spain. On 11 and 12 May, tactless behaviour by young Monarchists in Madrid provoked riots which, faithful to the Spanish revolutionary tradition, led to two days of church-burning. Before the June elections the Spanish bishops urged Catholics to unite to defend the interests of religion. This, together with Article 26 of the new Constitution, which forbade the religious orders to teach the young, ended compulsory religious education, removed crucifixes from classroom walls and dissolved the Society of Jesus – the Jesuits, influential teachers of the young – in Spain, put an end to the *modus vivendi* which the Vatican had hoped to reach with the Spanish Republic.

The aggressive anti-clericalism of the Left, for which the Republic symbolised a new and progressive Spain, faced the fierce reaction of the Right, which saw the Republic as incurably sectarian and intending to bring about a Bolshevist revolution. Religion and politics were indissoluble at both extremes of the spectrum.

For Spanish Catholics the battle was between stark alternatives: godless Bolshevism on the one side, Eternal Spain and the Church on the other. By 1936 Catholic Right-wingers were beginning to justify armed rebellion.

In contrast, Spanish liberalism and working-class movements were strongly anti-clerical. As a result, the military uprising of July 1936 was met by vindictive anti-clerical outrages. Clergy were hunted down and murdered, often with extreme brutality. Thirteen bishops, 4184 priests, 2365 monks and friars and 283 nuns perished in this way, mainly in the opening weeks of the war. The wearing of religious emblems and even the possession of religious articles became dangerous. Around female necks, medallions of the Communist leader Dolores Ibárurri – 'La Pasionaria'– replaced images of the Virgin. Churches were destroyed, statues hacked to pieces, and the mummified bodies of nuns disinterred and exposed to public gaze.[4]

The atrocities caused so much damage to the Republic's reputation that in September 1936 the Catholic Basque Manuel de Irujo was made Minister without Portfolio. On 9 January 1937, he submitted a memorandum proposing that priests should be freed and allowed to hold services in public. Churches should not be used for secular purposes. These suggestions were, however, rejected by the Government, most of whom were strongly resentful of the history of Catholic hostility towards the Republic, of the hierarchy's support for the insurgents and the Vatican's refusal to condemn the rebellion.[5]

In the Catholic Basque country, however, the Church was strongly entrenched in all classes. The loyalty of the Basques was an important factor in the international presentation of the Republic's case. It was also an embarrassment for General Franco in his relations with the Holy See and with Catholics in other countries, particularly France.

Questions of Catholic moral attitudes arose. What was the true duty of a Catholic in the circumstances? On 6 August 1936, the Cardinal Primate of

Spain, Mgr Gomà, condemned the Basques for making common cause with the enemies of the Church. National autonomy might be a justifiable aim, he wrote, but the means were not. Mgr Olaechea, Bishop of Pamplona, capital of the equally Catholic Navarre which had rallied to Franco, declared on 23 August that the war was a 'crusade'. The term was to be the subject of much passionate analysis in later months.

In Britain, scandal was aroused by two visits of Anglicans and Methodists to Republican Spain in early 1937. Their reports said little about the destruction of religious life. Traditional British anti-Catholicism was still strong enough for the reports to suggest that the Spanish Church had brought its sufferings on itself. After all, for most Britons, Spain was still the land of the Inquisition and the Armada of 1588. The Dean of Canterbury, the Rev. Hewlett Johnson, known as the 'Red Dean', enlivened the polemic. On returning from Spain, he insisted in a Canterbury sermon that the Republic's social concern was in itself a religious act of brotherly love. It was wrong, said the Dean, to say that Spaniards of the Left were irreligious even if they did not believe in God. The sermon caused such outrage that the Archbishop of Canterbury reproved the Dean for having brought the Church into the political arena. Vague approval for the Republic was as far as Anglicans wanted to go.

The popular Catholic press in England, as well as the intellectual journal *The Tablet* and the Jesuit *The Month*, had been hostile to the Republic once the anti-clerical outrages had been reported. Catholic newspapers saw the Spanish war as a fight to the death between Good and Evil. Though most English Catholics were working-class Labour voters, the intellectual minority which brilliantly edited the three Catholic weekly newspapers, together with the Church hierarchy, prevented any questioning of support for the Nationalists.

The twenty million American Catholics mostly supported Franco. American Catholics, who were an influential bloc of Northern voters, successfully lobbied to refuse to allow Basque refugee children to enter the US. In contrast, American Protestants tended to be anti-Catholic and, for that reason alone, anti-Franco.

Irish Catholics admired Franco. By late October 1936 the Irish Christian Front had sent £37 000 to help rebuild churches and to purchase medical supplies. General Eoin O'Duffy brought a few hundred Irish Fascists, known as Blueshirts, though they now wore green, to Spain in December 1936. They arrived after considerable difficulties in chartering ships to take them off remote Irish beaches. The unsuitable nature of some of the volunteers, together with lack of experience among O'Duffy's officers, led to a disaster on 18 February 1937, when they were taken for the enemy by Franco soldiers. The Irish force, depressed and decimated by illness, was repatriated in June 1937.

In France Catholic views were similar but not, however, monolithic. A minority opinion favoured mutual approaches between Catholics and the Left. In 1936, the Communist *main tendue* policy had struck a friendly note which attracted the younger generation of French Catholic intellectuals such as Jacques Maritain, the novelist François Mauriac and Emmanuel Mounier, founder of the *Esprit* movement which accepted, in Christian terms, the possibility of cooperating with Communists. On 25 July 1936, in *Le Figaro*, Mauriac had attacked Léon Blum fiercely for proposing to send arms to the Spanish Republic. Only one month later, he was criticising the Nationalists for the harshness of their repression. After the mass executions at Badajoz on 16 August, Assumption Day, he wrote in *Le Figaro* that the victory was stained by the atrocities which had been perpetrated. On that holy day, wrote Mauriac:

Should they not have been able to begin the task of reconciliation and pardon at once, in the name of she whose feast it was that day?

In February 1937, Maritain and other Catholic intellectuals signed a manifesto putting the blame for the Spanish war squarely on the military rebels. The outrage of Guernica, against one of the most Catholic peoples in the world, made some Catholic opinion cynical about Franco's claims to be leading a Crusade and fighting a Holy War. The Dominican journal *Sept* discussed how harsh a tyranny had to be before Catholics might licitly rise against it. Had all other means of non-violent resistance and of conciliation been exhausted? Was the remedy not worse than the sickness? Would it not be better for Catholics to endure persecution like the early Christians, rather than advance the triumph of the Cross with machine-guns?

The war against the Basques allowed progressive French Catholics to express their views without being accused of defending Communism. French prelates served on committees to aid the Basques. Five thousand children were given refuge in France. *Esprit* condemned the executions of Basque priests. On 8 May 1937, Mauriac, Maritain, Mounier and Georges Bidault, a later Christian-Democrat Prime Minister, published a manifesto protesting against the bombing of Guernica. On 1 July, Maritain published 'On Holy Wars', a long article in *La Nouvelle Revue Française*. In it Maritain attacked the insurgents for behaving as badly as the Republic anticlericals. To kill a priest was inexcusable, but so was shooting a

Communist; for the Republican air force to bomb a cathedral was no worse than for Franco to request the Luftwaffe to bomb Guernica.

François Mauriac wrote that, while he had attacked Blum for proposing to send arms to church-burners and priest-killers, he could now see that Franco was using religion as a cover for atrocities committed against Spaniards by Nazis, Fascists and Moors.[6]

Naturally, many French Catholic circles were appalled by Maritain's arguments. Vice-Admiral Joubert wrote a pamphlet, *La Guerre d'Espagne et le Catholicisme*, in which he accused Maritain of compromise with evil and of academic detachment. He defended the use of Moorish troops by Franco. They were, after all, very religious in their way and respected Jesus Christ. Cardinal Verdier's support of the Spanish Bishops' Collective Letter defending the Crusade and Paul Claudel's inspired poem lauding the murdered Spanish clergy as martyrs were, in their way, more representative of most French Catholic opinion than the small group of intellectuals around Maritain.

For Spain itself, however, it was the attitude of the Vatican that counted.

THE VATICAN

On 31 July 1936, the Vatican Secretary of State, Cardinal Pacelli, protested to the Republican ambassador about the murders and church-burnings. He was told that the Spanish Government was striving to control the situation but people had been enraged by priests firing from churches. It would hardly have been appropriate to reply that anti-clerical outrages had been a concomitant of Spanish revolutions for a century and to point out that the firing from churches might well have come from Catholics trying to defend them against incendiary mobs. There was no official break in relations with the Vatican but they ceased. The Nunzio, due to retire, had left Madrid. The Republic's ambassador left the Vatican in which he could no longer function because of the dissidence of most of his colleagues. Neither would be replaced.

The Vatican's *L'Osservatore Romano* was the first Italian newspaper to attack the Spanish government. On 23 and 26 July 1936 it referred to 'Carnage and frightful devastation created by Communists'. In August, it attacked the concept of Non-Intervention. Something should be done about the atrocities taking place in Spain. Naturally, this article was quoted approvingly by the Fascist newspaper *Popolo d'Italia*, for it seemed to give ecclesiastical licence for Italy to intervene in Spain.

At first, the Spanish military rebels seemed indifferent to the position of the Church. The first *Instruction* of the major planner of the uprising, General Mola, on 5 June 1936, had even spoken of freedom of religion. Other leading rebel generals were Freemasons. It was the anti-clerical outrages and the association of the politics of the Right with religion, which brought Army and Church together.

Cardinal Gomà, the Spanish Primate, became the Holy See's major source of information from Spain. He wrote that the future form of the State and its relations with the Church were uncertain. Many military men were indifferent to religion and the *Falange* believed in separation of Church and State. All that could be said was that the rebels were respectful to the Church. This was, however, no small matter. Spain was fighting Anti-Spain; religion struggled with anti-religion: Christian civilisation with barbarity, wrote Gomà to Rome on 13 August 1936. This was the information that the Pope had when on 4 September he received five hundred Spaniards fleeing from the anti-clerical outrages.

The Pope's speech was carefully phrased so as not to make things even worse for Catholics in Spain. The Pope said:

Above any secular and political considerations, our blessing goes especially to those who have accepted the difficult task of defending and restoring the rights and honours of God and religion, which means the rights and dignities of the conscience....

This would appear to give approval to the rebellion, but the Pope added,

A task, as We said, which is difficult and dangerous, precisely because, only too easily... selfish interests or mere party feeling may easily enter, cloud and change the entire morality of the action....

The speech ended with a call to those who had escaped the massacres to help their misguided persecutors:

We cannot doubt for a single instant what we have to do: to love them with a special love born of pity and compassion.[7]

The parts of the Pope's address which warned against selfish interests undermining the purity of the Spanish rebellion and called for love and compassion for the enemy were censored in Spain.

L'Osservatore Romano commented on the Pope's address in a way which could not be misunderstood:

Here is the justification and the limit of Catholic action. The right to
defend oneself... has limits which must be respected so that such
defence may be blameless.

The first opportunity for the Vatican to oppose the wishes of the rebel
generals concerned the embarrassingly Catholic Basques and their loyalty
to the Republic. Gomà wrote a pastoral instruction telling the Basques that
to ally themselves with the enemies of the Church was wrong.[8] The document was broadcast but the Basque clergy, doubting whether their two
local bishops, who were in Nationalist territory, had signed the Instruction
in full knowledge of the situation, advised their leaders to continue to
support the Republic. The episode led to a certain coolness of the Holy
See towards Franco.

The Spanish hierarchy saw the situation in far simpler terms than the
more worldly Vatican prelates. The slogan of the rebels was 'For God and
Country'. They speedily adopted the term 'Crusade'. Even though the
rebels were of diverse ideologies, including agnostics and certainly anticlericals, they insisted that their ideals of social order and the defence of
property were Christian or 'Catholic' in the political sense, and they could
bring even atheists under the umbrella of the 'Defence of Christian civilisation.' Cardinal Gomà's reports to the Vatican indicated that, whatever
its various hues, the uprising would be good for the Church.

Gomà protested to Franco on 26 October 1936 about the shooting of a
number of Basque priests. Franco claimed ignorance and had the
executions stopped at once. In return for this, Gomà advised Pacelli not to
protest officially. This would become a bitter issue in correspondence
between Gomà and the Basque leader, José Antonio de Aguirre, who
would accuse the Cardinal of silence over the shootings.

Rome delayed its *de facto* recognition of Franco until 19 December
1936, when Gomà was appointed official representative of the Holy See,
the nearest thing to a nunzio. It was not *de jure* recognition, but this was as
far as the Holy See would go.

However sincere Franco's protestations of submission to the Church
were, the Vatican would not easily put all its eggs in his basket. There
were still too many doubts. Would he be able to win the war? Would he
interfere with the rights of the Church in Spain? Was his barbarity worth
defending when it cast such a bad light on the Church? More than anything else, to recognise Franco at that moment would imply tilting the
balance towards Germany and Italy. This explains the low level of diplomatic recognition reflected in Gomà's appointment. As Gomà himself
confided to his diary, the conduct of the Vatican was 'delicate and

somewhat distrustful'.[9] By maintaining Gomà as a 'representative' rather than a nunzio to Nationalist Spain, the Vatican was not obliged to cut its connections with the Republic, however tenuous these were.

In 1936–37 the main issue in Franco's relations with the Vatican was to persuade Rome to declare that the Basques were bad Catholics if they kept on supporting the Republic. In December 1936 Franco asked the Holy See to condemn the actions of the Basque Nationalist Party. In return for this the Vatican wanted Franco to give some concessions to Basque rights. Aguirre broadcast a Christmas message accusing the Spanish Catholic hierarchy of ignoring the executions of Basque priests and turning their backs on their obligation to defend the legally-constituted order. Did a people not have the right of self-defence?

The answer was an open letter from Gomà to Aguirre. Ignoring the regionalist issue, he concentrated on the profound significance of the uprising. For the Cardinal, Catholic unity, the protection of the Church and the unity of Spain came before Basque national liberation, but he failed to answer the specific questions that Aguirre had put to him.[10]

Nothing came of Franco's attempts to get the Vatican to delegitimise the Basque struggle. The Vatican did not want to compromise itself with either side. Attempts at mediation failed. Neither side would give in. After the fall of Bilbao on 19 June 1937, the Vatican tried hard to moderate the inevitable repression. It sent Mgr Ildebrando Antoniutti to negotiate the return of Basque Catholic children who had taken refuge in France, Belgium and Britain. In Britain, the Catholic clergy, who had collaborated with the Basque Children's Committee, now withdrew their support, insisting that the danger had passed and the children should be repatriated. A certain number returned while the others were looked after during the war and often afterwards by local committees.

Thus relations between Franco and the Vatican were uneven. The General was particularly resentful that while he was fighting the godless Reds to protect the Church, the Vatican was talking to Basques and to the exiled Cardinal Archbishop of Tarragona, Mgr Vidal, who did not approve of the Franco rebellion. Worse still, the Holy See still maintained relations of some sort with the Republic. By 1937, the Vatican's original fear of revolution in Spain had abated. More worrying were developments in Nazi Germany; and Hitler was aiding Franco.

The Nazis glorified pagan values and persecuted Catholics who spoke against them. On Palm Sunday, 21 March 1937, the Pope's encyclical *Mit Brennender Sorge* ('With burning anxiety') was read in German Catholic churches. It was a strong attack on Nazi theories and behaviour, culminating in criticisms of Hitler's *widerliche Hochmut* ('repulsive arrogance').

This was not a moment to embitter relations with Germany over Spain, however, and Cardinal Gomà cancelled his plans to have the encyclical widely published in Spain when Faupel explained to Franco that the encyclical was an intolerable interference in German internal affairs. He reminded the caudillo that the most Catholic monarchs of Spain had often rejected papal interference.

The Vatican was not pleased. German influence in Spain was increasing. On 17 April 1937 Franco merged the Catholic Carlists and the Fascist Falange to form the amorphous National Movement, with himself as head. Franco's power was supreme. He was head of the Army, the Government, the State and the National Movement. His rivals had perished in one way or another. The space for diplomatic manoeuvring by the Vatican was small.

This was the background to the most important Catholic document on the Spanish Civil War: the *Carta Colectiva* or Collective Letter from the Spanish bishops to the bishops of the world. The Letter, justifying the 'Crusade', was signed by 48 of the surviving bishops and their replacements. Cardinal Vidal refused to sign it because he thought it would harm Catholics in the Republican Zone. So did the exiled Basque bishop Múgica.

The Letter was addressed to the whole world. It defended the military uprising as the only way to save the values of Catholic Spain. The Vatican realised that this was a propaganda letter and accepted it in silence. *L'Osservatore Romano* published only a summary and the Pope refused publication in the *Actae Apostolicae Sedis*.[11]

Nevertheless, the letter was widely published. One hundred thousand copies were distributed in the USA, 15 000 in France and substantial numbers elsewhere. It was the major statement of the Spanish Church on the civil war and compromised it with the Franco regime for over thirty years.

By summer 1937 some international problems over Spain appeared to have been solved. Principally, the frontier control and the naval blockade were working. The conquest of most of the North meant that the blockade issue there was about to disappear.

The withdrawal of foreign troops now became a key concern. Guadalajara was a watershed, for the Non-Intervention Committee could no longer hide behind procedural bureaucracy. Everybody knew there was an Italian army in Spain.

For the Spanish Republic, still hoping to persuade the Democracies to sell it arms, it was vital to win a victory somewhere to prove that it could now defend itself and that Franco could not win. For Franco, who refused every suggestion of mediation that was put to him, the important thing was to press on slowly.

For his allies, Germany and Italy, Spain was a tiresome business. They needed Franco, not only because their long-term aim was to weaken France by defeating the Popular Front in Spain, but also because Germany wanted Spanish minerals and Italy wanted to maintain her challenge to British hegemony in the Mediterranean. This allowed Franco to take an independent attitude to Italy and to be very obstructive towards German demands.

Part Three

Chapter 11

AFTER GUADALAJARA

Franco had proved a disappointment to Italy, who had received no rights in the Balearics. Internally, Spain appeared to be sliding back into feudalist clericalism, rather than adopting a Fascist social programme.

Spain, Ciano told Randolfo Cantalupo, Italy's first ambassador to Franco, was the cause of serious friction between Italy and Britain. Franco understood only repression, not how to win his enemies over.[1]

In early March 1937, Mussolini sent his own messenger, Roberto Farinacci, an aggressive Fascist, who was both anti-British and anti-Catholic. He was hardly a wise choice for Catholic Spain.

In a letter to Franco, Mussolini said he was sending Farinacci to familiarise himself with the situation and to talk to the Spanish leader about the Duce's ideas for the future. Mussolini advised Franco to prepare a programme including a single, powerful State party and press. The policy should include Fascist-style social reforms. Farinacci was not the most tactful person to speak to the touchy Spaniards. Franco gave a cold answer to Farinacci's suggestions for appointments and to his criticisms of mass executions. Farinacci in turn told the Duce that Franco was 'rather timid and his appearance is certainly not that of a *condottiero*'.[2]

Farinacci also met Manuel Hedilla, José Antonio's successor at the head of the Falange. The two discussed organising the movement, but Farinacci was not very impressed by Hedilla and nothing came of this. Italian loss of prestige at Guadalajara and Franco's takeover of the Falange and imprisonment of Hedilla in April 1937 put an end to possible Italian Fascist political influence in Spain. Cantalupo's disagreements with his hosts also precipitated his departure in the same month.

In the meantime, Mussolini was gathering his thoughts. On 23 March, he proclaimed that Guadalajara had led to a torrent of ink, paper and words, but the defeat would be avenged. Mussolini could not withdraw now from his costly Spanish adventure in the face of the international jeers and the encouragement given to the Italian opposition. Victory in Spain was psychologically essential for Mussolini, for Fascism was based on invincibility. The Duce informed Von Hassell that he had told his commanders that none would return home alive except in triumph.

Despite all the evidence of Italian involvement in Spain, Guadalajara did not have serious international consequences for Italy. The Non-Intervention policy continued, with all its disadvantages for the Spanish Republic. Seeing this, Mussolini grew confident and thought no more about withdrawal. He wrote an article in *Popolo d'Italia* on 17 June, on the reasons for the defeat: the weather, unexpected strength and air superiority of the enemy, and confusion of orders. Guadalajara, wrote the Duce, was a 'non-event', swollen by the press to raise the morale of the 'Bolshevik hordes'. It was not a defeat, merely a victory which the Italian Army could not fully exploit.

Though Italy and Germany had accepted the Non-Intervention Committee's control system because they thought they had enough troops and armament in Spain to give Franco victory, they would now have to impede it. For the time being, Italy would be careful not to lay herself open to accusations of evading the naval control system. Spanish, rather than Italian, vessels should be used to ship arms.

New commanders were appointed for the CTV, Italy sent more aircraft, reaching a total of 418 by September 1937. Mussolini ceased to tell Franco that he should conduct the war in a Fascist style. He now accepted that, as Franco said to Roberto Cantalupo at the latter's farewell audience on 18 April, Franco was in no hurry. He had to make a 'spiritual' as well as a material conquest of Red Spain.

THE *DEUTSCHLAND* AND THE *LEIPZIG* INCIDENTS; THE END OF THE NAVAL PATROL

By the end of June 1937, the Naval Control powers, Britain, France, Germany and Italy, had 52 warships off Spain. Accidents happened, especially since Spanish airmen were not skilled in recognising ships from high altitudes and Spanish mines sometimes slipped their moorings. The British battleship *Royal Oak* and the destroyers *Havoc*, *Gipsy* and *Hunter* all suffered casualties and damage.

The risks were recognised by the Royal Navy. Not so by the Germans, for, when in May 1937 the Republic's new Russian 'Katiuska' bombers began to make low-level attacks on Franco's important base at Palma, the local German admiral threatened to fire on any aircraft which flew too low over his ships. At 7.12 p.m. on 29 May, two bombers swept out of the setting sun over the German battleship *Deutschland* at anchor in Ibiza. Their pilots, who were newly-arrived Russians,[3] scored a hit on the crew's quarters which caused over one hundred casualties.

The Spanish Government claimed that the aircraft had been fired on, which the Germans denied. Yet, since the Germans had threatened to do just that, their denial was suspect. Furthermore, the Spanish Government argued that the *Deutschland* was not on patrol duties at the time and that Ibiza was in the war zone and a legitimate target. The government's Air Force could reasonably suppose that the warship was one of Franco's.

Von Neurath told Ribbentrop to protest at the Non-Intervention Committee, to withdraw Germany from the Naval Patrol and to insist on guarantees before she returned. Probably the *Deutschland* incident was to be used as a weapon to reduce what must have been a heavy burden on Germany. In any case, the event was to be the pretext for a ferocious reprisal. Hitler was enraged that 'Red pirates' had killed German sailors. He ordered his ships to bombard Cartagena or Valencia. With difficulty, his admirals persuaded him that these harbours were heavily mined and that Almería, a smaller port, would be a better target. The German commanders were embarrassed at what their Royal Navy colleagues on the Naval Patrol would think of their shelling an undefended town, but they were terrified of the Fuehrer's rage. Consequently, early on 31 May they fired 275 shells at Almería, causing 74 casualties. The commander of a British destroyer who watched the events commented acidly in his report, that the German ships could not be accused of bombarding an undefended port, as the press proclaimed, since the small-calibre coastal battery had indeed fired sixty ineffectual shots.[4]

Later that morning in Valencia, the Minister of National Defence, Indalecio Prieto, suggested declaring war on Germany and a mass air raid on all German ships in the area, which would, he hoped, either make Germany decide to withdraw from Spain, or provoke a major European war which would save the Republic. The Spanish cabinet balked at the implications of Prieto's proposal. The Communist ministers referred to their advisers, who consulted Moscow by radio. The answer was immediate: at all costs they had to prevent Prieto's 'provocation'.[5] No other piece of advice could have been expected. The USSR was not ready for war.

Later that day in London, Italy's and Germany's seats were empty at the Non-Intervention Committee. After a letter from Ribbentrop had been read out, there was a sepulchral silence. It seemed as though the whole house of cards was collapsing. Corbin remarked that the Committee had to be saved and wondered what guarantees could be offered to Italy and Germany. While Eden delicately told German diplomats that the reprisal had been rather harsh, Corbin said that France had not retaliated when the insurgents had attacked an Air-France aircraft. At last, by 12 June, a text was agreed. Both Spanish parties would be asked for a guarantee. If there were another incident, the four naval powers would decide on the measures to be taken. Thus the Germans were vindicated and rejoined the Naval Patrol. However, the solution was to be of short duration.

On 15 and 18 June, the German cruiser *Leipzig*, sailing off Oran, reported torpedo attacks from unseen submarines. The Germans accused the Spanish Republic, which strongly denied the charge. Neither British nor French naval authorities suspected Republican submarines. Spanish Government secret intelligence reported that the episode was faked.[6] Another possibility is that the Germans manufactured an incident out of a genuine attack made on the *Leipzig* by one of Franco's new Italian submarines which mistook the German ship for a Republican cruiser.

Whatever the facts, it seemed that Germany and Italy wanted to leave the Naval Patrol or to discredit it. Perhaps it was proving too effective and, sooner or later, the regular sailings from Germany to Franco's ports with arms and men would be impossible to conceal.

When Britain and France refused a German request for an international naval demonstration outside Valencia, Germany withdrew from the Naval Patrol.

Britain and France offered to take on the Patrol themselves, a move which was opposed by Germany and Italy. The alternative was to recognise the belligerent status of both Spanish parties, which would allow Franco's navy to stop neutral shipping and thus remove the need for supervision of Spanish coasts. But it had always been British policy to deny these rights to both sides, so there was now stalemate.

NYON

On 29 June, Britain proposed withdrawing an equal number of volunteers from both sides. Quite cynically, Ciano told Von Hassell that, though Italy could not simply reject the British proposal, 'we had to entrench ourselves under cover of delaying and obstructionist tactics'.[7] These would consist in stalling and claiming that the 'Reds' were too untrustworthy to abide by an agreement to withdraw their International Brigades.

Germany and Italy now demanded belligerent rights for Franco. But Eden refused to grant them until some progress had been made in withdrawing foreigners. The British Government issued a revised proposal on 14 July 1937. The Naval Patrol would end and belligerent rights would be granted, but only when 'substantial' progress had been made on withdrawal. Germany and Italy accepted this proposal as a basis for discussion but Grandi used it as an opportunity to filibuster.

Maiskii thought the Democracies mad even to consider granting belligerent rights to Franco. On 2 August, the Maiskiis spent the Bank holiday at a house rented for the summer by the Spanish ambassador, Pablo de Azcárate. That night, Azcárate wrote in his diary that the USSR had given the Non-Intervention Committee up as a bad job. It might be best if it wound up, allowing the Republic to buy arms where it liked, even if this meant giving Franco what he wanted.[8] In a sense, he was right. The Republican fleet was strong enough to protect convoys of ships coming into Mediterranean ports with war-material. For the USSR, however, Spain was probably a lost cause.

Attitudes were changing also in Britain, for Stanley Baldwin, who took little interest in foreign affairs, had been replaced on 28 May by Neville Chamberlain, who wanted to take an active part. In his view, Britain could not afford to antagonise Italy over Spain and risk letting her fall into the arms of Hitler. Britain was heavily outweighed by Italy in the Eastern Mediterranean. Air defences were inadequate and even the Royal Navy was none-too-confident of its ability to meet an Italian threat. As a senior Foreign Office official wrote on 4 October:

> it does not matter two straws what happens in Spain unless the Chiefs of Staff say that the presence of the Italians... is of real strategic danger.

Most of the Cabinet shared this view. Nor did the Chiefs of Staff think there were strong strategic reasons to force Italy out of the Balearics.[9]

The astute Grandi was well aware of Chamberlain's views and began to work on him at once. At a dinner party on 15 June, Grandi had a long *tête-à-tête* with Chamberlain. He claimed to have received a letter from Mussolini referring to his 'sincere liking' for the British Premier.[10] From then on, Grandi 'massaged' the British premier, using as a contact a counsellor to the Italian embassy named Dingli, who was an acquaintance of Sir Joseph Ball, Head of the Conservative Party's Research department. In a letter to Ciano of 12 July, Grandi said that he was trying to widen the 'incipient split' between Chamberlain and Eden.[11] The result was an exchange of friendly letters between Chamberlain and Mussolini. Eden learnt of the letters and insisted that the Premier should show them to him first. In his view, Italy would have to leave Majorca before Britain could even think of recognising the Italian empire in Abyssinia. Two further episodes put the cause of Anglo-Italian understanding back again.

When Santander fell to Franco and the CTV at the end of August 1937, Mussolini publicised his congratulatory telegram to Franco, referring to the Italian contribution and the 'comradeship of arms' between Franco Spain and Fascist Italy. In London this was seen as discourtesy to the Non-Intervention countries, especially as it came amid intolerable Italian behaviour at sea.

In early August 1937, Franco learned of massive and imminent Russian supplies to the Republic. Reports spoke of 2600 tanks, 3000 self-propelled machine-guns and 300 aircraft. While the reports were probably exaggerated, there was no doubt at Franco's headquarters that a lot of material was on its way. Ciano was pressed by Franco. The Russian arms must be stopped *en route*. Italy should either give Franco the means – that is, more submarines – to do so or do the job herself. She could do this openly (*descaradamente* or 'brazenly' was the word used in the Spanish messages) or with Italian submarines. On 22 August, García Conde cabled from Rome that 18 Italian submarines were on watch.[12]

The manipulation of Chamberlain and the new British conciliatory attitude were to have their first result. While suspected British ships had earlier been left alone and reported to the Royal Navy, Franco now asked Italy to torpedo any suspected ship going to Spanish Mediterranean ports.

On 6 August, three merchantmen were attacked off the Algerian coast by aircraft. The next week, eight more vessels were attacked, mostly by torpedo. The next week another five ships and, in the last week of August, eight, including six British vessels, were attacked. On 2 September four British ships were victims of submarines. In all, at least thirty ships had been attacked, of which eight had been sunk. In the first fortnight, the victims had mostly been Spanish, but towards the end of the period, most were British.

The press hinted that the unknown attackers were Italian, but the diplomacy of appeasement required Italy not to be mentioned by name. In Paris, the Boulevard des Italiens was ironically nicknamed the 'Boulevard des Inconnus'. As Ciano noted in his *Diary*, when the British chargé, Mr Ingram, approached him about the attacks on shipping he lied 'quite brazenly'. The supine British attitude noted by Ciano encouraged such a reply. In Ciano's words:

> Mr Ingram was anxious to inform me that the British Government did not wish to make the least protest to us.... It merely wished to inform us of its earnest desire that the atmosphere between Great Britain and Italy, which had so fortunately been cleared, should not be troubled by unforeseen and deplorable complications.

France, who had also lost some ships, pressed an unwilling Britain to react. No attack on Italy could be made at the Non-Intervention Committee in case she resigned and the Committee collapsed. The only solution could be to hunt what were being called 'unidentified pirate' submarines, though the Royal Navy, which had broken the Italian naval codes, was aware of their nationality.[13] Ample information about Italian naval movements came from the British consul in Palma, Commander Hillgarth, who saw the submarine *Iride* in dock, badly mauled by the depth-charges of the destroyer *Havoc*, which the submarine had mistakenly tried to torpedo. (A friend of Winston Churchill, Hillgarth was one of London's best sources of information on naval movements in the Spanish War. He would be Naval attaché in the British Embassy in Madrid during the early part of the Second World War, ending his war career as Director of Naval Intelligence in the Far East).

An international conference was rapidly convened. Eden travelled to Paris and dined with Chautemps and Delbos on the evening of 9 September. They quickly settled details. Later, sleeping-cars sped Eden to Geneva, from where he motored a few miles to Nyon.

Britain took a firm attitude, but she already knew, through Naval Intelligence, that Italy, fearing a reaction, had decided to stop the attacks. Agreement was soon reached to patrol the Mediterranean with French and British destroyers and to sink unidentified submarines. Eden wanted to be firm with Italy but to avoid threatening her with an Anglo-French bloc. In particular, he wanted to keep Russia out of the Mediterranean. Litvinov openly accused Italy of sinking three Russian ships, which was embarrassing because the whole point was to show firmness without naming the culprit. So Britain and France refused the Russian demand to attack Italian surface ships or aircraft, and Russia was not invited into the Mediterranean to share in the patrol. To save appearances, even Italy would have to be invited to join the patrol and guard against her own submarines. Ciano crowed that the Italian pirate was now a policeman, while the Russians, whose ships Italy had sunk, were excluded.

No 'pirate' submarines were found. However, Italian tactics had to change. Italy now gave Franco four submarines for use in Spanish waters. Italian aircraft based on Majorca flew with Spanish markings. 'In future', wrote Ciano to Grandi, 'life will be made impossible in Valencia, Barcelona, Tarragona, Alicante and Almería. Bombing will be very severe and continuous.' Attacks from the air on merchant-ships increased, usually against vessels lying in harbour or in territorial waters. Since Spain claimed a six- rather than a three-mile limit, and given that the exact position of a ship was often disputed, bombing of cargo ships bound for Republican Spain would lead, for the rest of the Spanish Civil War, to repeated and fruitless diplomatic protests.

Chapter 12

THE SPANISH REVOLUTION CRUSHED

The Spanish Republic, in its attempts to persuade Britain and France to stop Italy and Germany aiding Franco, claimed to have checked the assassinations, church-burnings and revolutionary acts that had taken place. This was, of course, the aim of the Soviet Union, which wanted to persuade the Democracies that it no longer, if ever, represented a revolutionary threat.

Russia's determination to aid Spain had never been absolute.[1] From the end of 1936, rumours had suggested that the USSR feared being isolated by Western pacts with Hitler and Mussolini. Despite Maiskii's defiant statements, the USSR could not afford to isolate itself by leaving the Non-Intervention Committee.

Meanwhile, the Soviet Union would do its best to curb the excesses of the Spanish revolution. NKVD chief Alexander Orlov went to Spain at the end of August 1936 with the major task of purging the revolutionary Marxist party, the Partido Obrero de Unificación Marxista or POUM.[2]

The largest section of the Spanish working-class movement was Anarchist. Events in the USSR confirmed their belief that State Socialism was counter-revolutionary. Anarchist ministers were now in the Government, so Stalin sent a timely letter to the Spanish Premier on 21 December 1936, advising him not to antagonise the landowning peasants or the petty bourgeoisie of the cities.[3]

For revolutionaries who threatened the new Soviet image there was to be no mercy. On 17 December, 1936, *Pravda* wrote that in Catalonia 'the cleaning-up of the Trotskyist and Anarcho-Syndicalist elements ... will be carried out with the same energy as in the USSR'.[4] A few days later, the Comintern Executive wrote to the Spanish Communist Party that 'whatever happens, the final destruction of the Trotskyists must be achieved...'.[5]

By December 1936 things appeared to be going well. The Anarchists were cooperating in the war effort, Madrid had been saved and the POUM was expelled from the Catalan Government. However, Largo Caballero and the Minister of Navy and Air, the moderate Socialist Indalecio Prieto, resented what they saw as Communist domination of the corps of political commissars, while Anarchist commanders quarrelled with Soviet officers. In March 1937, therefore, the Comintern advisers insisted that Largo Caballero should be ousted.[6]

The method used was to take advantage of the crisis of May 1937. This was the bullet-and-gun manifestation of the ideological conflict and the power-struggle between the revolutionary views held by Anarchists, left-wing Socialists and dissident Communists, on the one hand, and Spaniards of the Centre and Right who feared revolution, on the other, supported by the Spanish Communist Party and its Catalan associate, the PSUC (Partido Socialista Unificado de Cataluña), swollen by the entrance of thousands of the middle class and enjoying prestige because of the support received by the Republic from Soviet Russia.

The physical battle began when a prominent Barcelona Communist was found dead, presumably executed by a self-appointed Anarchist public order patrol. After a battle between Government customs-guards and local Anarchists at the frontier town of Puigcerdà, both sides began to gather forces. When Anarchist telephone-controllers interrupted a call from Prieto, the Navy and Air Force Minister, and another one between President Azaña and the President of Catalonia, Lluis Companys, the Barcelona Chief of Police went to establish order in the Barcelona central telephone exchange. Shots were fired by the Anarchist telephone workers. They demanded the resignations of the Chief of Police and the Councillor of Public Order. Firing continued. Bands of Anarchists and members of the POUM fought with Republican police forces. Government ministers and Anarchist leaders strove to calm passions and to persuade the newly-militarised Anarchist columns to stay at the front. Both Franco and the Italians claimed that their *agents provocateurs* had had a hand in creating the crisis. After a brief truce, fighting began again on 6 May. That evening, warships brought Government Assault Guards to the Catalan capital and by 8 May, the miniature civil war was over. There were several hundred dead.

For the Communists and all save the Anarchist CNT and the POUM, the revolution was over. Republican order was restored. Caballero then refused to dissolve the POUM as the Communist Ministers demanded, so they left the Cabinet on 15 May. Fearing that the USSR would abandon Spain, the other ministers supported the Communists. Caballero resigned and was succeeded by Juan Negrín, a Socialist who would cooperate with the Communists by holding down the revolutionaries. Negrín was selected because Azaña admired him as a brilliant, internationally-recognised physiologist and a competent Minister of Finance under Largo Caballero, while fellow-Socialist Prieto was probably unacceptable to either Azaña or the Communists, who doubted they could influence him. The Anarchist public order patrols were dissolved as were their public safety committees in the Catalan towns. The Catalan Government, the *Generalitat*, was now composed only of PSUC members and the Catalan Republican Party, the Esquerra. Local defence and police now came under national control.

Negrín was a realist. Russian support was indispensable. The price was the crushing of the POUM, which was hunted down, its leaders arrested and its Secretary, Andrés Nin, kidnapped and tortured to death in an unsuccessful attempt to make him confess treason. So desperate were the Comintern advisers to crush the revolution in Spain and gain the approval of Stalin that they kept Nin hidden from the Spanish authorities. This was in the context of the execution in Russia of eight senior generals, accused of intriguing with Germany, and the recall and later disappearance of the Soviet consul-general in Barcelona, Antonov-Ovseenko, of Berzin, head of the military mission and of Stashevsky, the economic counsellor.

At the League of Nations Council on 24 May, Litvinov stressed that the USSR had no interest in Spain as such. There had been no Russians in Spain at the outset of the war. He did not say, though his listeners were meant to infer it, that the Spanish revolution had not been encouraged from Moscow and, in any case, it was now over.

The crushing of the POUM led to the disillusion of many Communists and, for those who understood what was going on in Spain, to a loss of Soviet prestige, low in any case because of the show-trials and executions. Yet it was seen as the price to be paid for the restoration of public order and the end of revolution, as well as for Soviet support, the only way Franco could be defeated.

Since October 1936, the USSR had made a huge effort to supply the Republic with war-material. Official figures up to the end of March 1937 refer to 333 aircraft, 256 tanks, 60 armoured cars, 7277 machine-guns, 189 000 rifles, $1\frac{1}{2}$ million shells and 376 million cartridges.[7] Nevertheless, interest in Spain was waning. Litvinov told the British ambassador that a Franco regime in Spain was acceptable provided it did not become a German or Italian satellite.[8] Togliatti, the Italian Communist and leading member of the Comintern, reported that work in Spain would not be successful while the Communist and Socialist Parties were separate. The Comintern's advisers, he added, were incapable of dealing with the difficulties to unity posed by the powerful Anarchist movement. Togliatti's report may have conditioned attitudes in Moscow.[9] The Communists also had to contend with the hostility of Prieto, now Minister of National

Defence, who got rid of several Communist nominees in high military positions. While the USSR still stood by the Spanish Republic, policies became less resolute. Resistance, rather than victory, became the slogan.

This veering-away from Spain also reflected the internal political scene in Moscow, where there was a reaction against the liberal hope and idealism associated with the Republic which, in September 1936, had triumphed over Stalin's caution. The Republic was not going to win, but Stalin wanted the Spanish war to continue to tie Germany and Italy down. So long as the West was assured that Moscow was not a threat to them in Spain, there was always the chance that the Democracies might wake up to the Nazi–Fascist danger.[10]

The Soviet Union was also increasingly preoccupied with the war in China, whose international repercussions were beginning to overshadow Spain.

PROGRESS AT GENEVA AND IN THE WITHDRAWAL OF VOLUNTEERS

Britain pressed hard for an Italian withdrawal in Spain, but Franco rejected the British plan of 14 July and Italy had said that her troops would remain in Spain until Franco won. Alarmed by the friendlier British attitude towards Italy since Chamberlain's accession, Hitler invited the Duce to Germany. On 28 September 1937, he received a triumphal welcome. The Berlin–Rome Axis was reaffirmed. Mussolini stressed that Fascism and Nazism were fighting – with arms if necessary, as in Spain – the same enemies.

Mussolini could now afford to take a strong line. The next month the CTV was reinforced and given a new commander, at Franco's request. General Berti's orders required him to act 'like any other general under Franco's command'.[11] Ciano recommended Grandi to take a firm attitude at the Non-Intervention Committee, while Mussolini threateningly dispatched three divisions to the Libyan border with Egypt.

Negrín's resolution at the League of Nations on 18 September, that foreigners should withdraw from Spain or Non-Intervention should come to an end, was approved, but with many abstentions from Latin American and anti-Communist European countries. It remained a mere proposal. The League on the whole, as well as Mussolini, preferred to leave Spain to the Non-Intervention Committee, where Germany, now out of the League, was present.

By halfway through October, however, Grandi's warnings had impressed Ciano and on 21 October he ordered Grandi to agree to the dispatch of an investigatory commission to Spain and an immediate partial withdrawal of troops. The German and Italian delegates kept discussions going until 4 November 1937, when the Non-Intervention Committee agreed to submit a plan to both Spanish sides. If it were accepted, belligerent rights would be granted. On 26 October, Maiskii conceded that the USSR might not object to granting both sides belligerent rights when the bulk of foreign combatants had left Spain. Not to do so would have isolated the USSR from the Democracies. Given the lessening Soviet interest in Spain, this would have not been advisable.

Eden himself urgently wanted to check Mussolini's aggression by encouraging France to open the frontier. In his Llandudno speech on 15 October 1937, he said he would not criticise any nation which felt obliged to recover its freedom of action. The French Cabinet was, as always, deeply divided on the Spanish issue. From Paris it seemed as if Italy were taking over the Mediterranean. This led to a reconsideration of French foreign policy and pressure to open the frontier to allow arms to enter Spain.

In the Chautemps Government, which took office on 22 June 1937, Blum had agreed to be vice-premier only on condition that *la non-intervention relâchée* should continue. On 27 September, Spanish President Azaña wrote in his *Diary* that the transit of material through France was secure and that Daladier was allowing reserve officers to volunteer for the International Brigades. Before the fall of Bilbao, 20 Spanish aircraft had been allowed to fly across French territory to northern Spain.[12] President Azaña, however, noted only what his friends and aides told him. Much of it reflected occasional French cooperation rather than the normal state of affairs.

The French Government, however, tolerated France-Navégation, a company set up by the French Communist Party on 15 April 1937. The ships of France-Navégation, 23 at their maximum, carried arms from Baltic ports to Bordeaux, Sète and Marseille for transfer to Spain. Ostensibly not bound for Spain, they had no need to take an Non-Intervention observer on board. In all, 272 journeys were made and only two cargoes were lost.[12a]

Because the Republic's foreign volunteers were of no great importance by this time, the Non-Intervention Committee proposals for the withdrawal of volunteers were acceptable to her. They could only be prejudicial to Franco who had about 50 000 Italians. So the Republican Government accepted the plan but Franco refused. He did not believe that the French frontier would be closed to replacements. His view was justified for, despite the ban on volunteers, they were generally unimpeded, though the

French police occasionally made arrests. It was reported that the Spanish consul at Perpignan issued Spanish passports freely to volunteers, who could thus not be legally turned back at the frontier.

Franco delayed until June 1938 when he replied that he would send three thousand to five thousand Italians home but then he wanted belligerent rights. In the meantime, he sent a note to the German Embassy on the subject of the Inspecting Commissions which were to count foreign troops and supervise their withdrawal. It betrays his true attitude: one of the phrases reads, 'If it were necessary to hinder (*entorpecer*) the work of the Committee...'. Such delaying tactics would go on for months. On 16 July 1938, Von Mackensen, the German Ambassador in Rome, cabled Berlin that 'The London plan offers every opportunity for objections and questions.'

Italian views seemed resolute. On 6 November 1937, Mussolini told Ciano and Ribbentrop that Italy intended to stay in the Balearics so that 'not one negro will be able to cross from Africa to France;[13] that is, France would not be able to bring her African troops to Europe in case of war. This was, of course, really to alter the *status quo*, which Mussolini had promised, in the Gentlemen's Agreement of December 1936, to observe. Six days later, Italy left the League of Nations. Yet Italian attitudes were not as firm as they seemed. When the Republic launched its attack at Teruel on 15 December 1937, Ciano wrote in his *Diary* that 'Franco has no idea of synthesis in war. His operations are those of a magnificent battalion commander. His objective is always ground, never the enemy.' Ciano wondered whether withdrawing now would look like betrayal. 'This Spanish business', he wrote, 'is long and burdensome.' There were no signs of a quick victory and, when Mussolini sent a letter to Franco suggesting a joint Spanish–Italian–German general staff, Franco replied late and negatively.[14]

Chapter 13

TERUEL

On 15 December 1937, Republican forces launched an attack on the Teruel salient in eastern Spain. A victory might persuade Franco to accept the compromise peace which he so frequently rejected. It would also convince the Democracies of the Republic's military efficiency and make them hesitate about getting closer to Franco. It would also strengthen the Spanish Government and especially its Minister of National Defence, Indalecio Prieto, still at loggerheads with the Communists in the armed services.

Teruel was taken by the Republic in the New Year. It was reoccupied by Franco forces on 20 February 1938. In a letter of 2 February 1938, Mussolini threatened to withdraw unless his CTV was fully used. Mussolini's urgency was probably due to the imminent arrival of Non-Intervention Committee inspectors to count foreign troops. The Italian leader wanted one big victory before withdrawing. Franco's tardy answer was wordy and vaporous, taking for granted that the CTV would want to stay in Spain if only for reasons of solidarity.[1]

It was at this point that Neville Chamberlain's intrigues behind Eden's back came to a head. On 12 February 1938 the Austrian Chancellor, Schuschnigg, was forced to agree to the nazification of Austria, which made Chamberlain even more desperate to gain a rapprochement with Italy. In contrast, Eden thought that Mussolini's apparent anxiety over a German move into Austria made this a good moment to press him to abandon Franco. Both were wrong, for Mussolini had probably accepted the Anschluss already.

Eden could not shake Chamberlain's views, and a tense situation arose between the two over the next few weeks. Chamberlain's sister-in-law, the widow of Sir Austen Chamberlain, brought a letter from Mussolini, suggesting formal conversations with a view to British recognition of Italy's Abyssinian empire. Chamberlain proposed a meeting with Grandi and Eden. At this stage Eden wanted to delay a settlement with Italy until bombing of civilian targets in Spain and of merchant-ships ceased, and until Italy stopped reinforcing the CTV. He thought that the Italian leaders understood this, as well as that public opinion in Britain was against any settlement until Italy complied. Eden was aware also that many of his Cabinet colleagues wanted an agreement with Italy without conditions. At this point also, Sir Joseph Ball, Director of the Conservative Research Department, undermined Eden by spreading rumours in the press to suggest that agreement with Italy was close.

Grandi agreed to a meeting with Eden and Chamberlain at 10 Downing Street on 18 February. There Grandi complained bitterly about British hostility to Italy. He threatened that, if an Anglo-Italian settlement were not at once reached, Italy would adopt a permanently hostile position. Eden said that there was no point in any discussions until Italian intervention in Spain ceased. Grandi spoke at length about the Non-Intervention Committee's tolerance of contraband traffic and volunteers for the 'Reds'. Chamberlain, reported Grandi the next day to Ciano, was showing signs of visible annoyance with Eden. Eden recorded that, as Grandi made his points, Chamberlain nodded approvingly.

Next, Chamberlain said he would discuss an Anglo-Italian agreement if Rome agreed to the British formula now before the Non-Intervention Committee for withdrawal of volunteers. Grandi promised to consult Ciano but pointed out that he could not bind Italy to an agreement where 'Red' bad faith might lead to imbalance in withdrawals. Italy would certainly not give an advantage to Russia and France merely to gain an agreement with Britain.

Grandi concluded his report to Ciano by saying that the meeting was one of the most extraordinary he had ever attended. The British Prime Minister and the Foreign Secretary were less like statesmen, than 'two cocks in true fighting posture'. Grandi saw that Chamberlain's questions were put precisely to elicit answers which would give him a weapon against Eden, so he gave the required answers. He understood the issues because of his information from Sir Joseph Ball. That evening, in fact, Grandi had a secret meeting in a London taxicab with a messenger from Chamberlain who conveyed the Prime Minister's gratitude.[2]

Chamberlain's view, as he confided to his diary, was different.[3] He saw Mussolini as desperate to reach an agreement with Britain given the imminence of the Anschluss. This was the chance to force Italy to give way on some points. Chamberlain was determined to agree to Anglo-Italian talks even if this meant losing Eden. He reproached Eden for his doubts about Italian honesty in accepting a formula for the withdrawal of volunteers. 'I told AE that he had missed one opportunity after another for advancing towards peace', he wrote. This is confirmed by Eden's notes.[4] Yet Grandi wrote the next day to Ciano that he had not guaranteed anything about withdrawal from Spain. It seems that Chamberlain heard what he wanted Grandi to say rather than what the Italian ambassador actually uttered.

That Saturday afternoon, 19 February 1938, a small crowd gathered in Downing Street, for rumours of the Eden–Chamberlain split had got about. At the Cabinet, no formula to keep Eden at the Foreign Office was satisfactory to him and he resigned the next day.

Later revelations of Italian intentions would show that Chamberlain was mistaken in believing that he could sway Mussolini over Austria. The Duce was ready for the Anschluss. Grandi lied when he told Chamberlain that there was no Italo-German understanding over Austria. If there had been a real desire by Rome to reach an understanding with Britain, Mussolini would have found a way to make a concession on Spain.[4a]

Ciano was at a party when the news of Eden's resignation came through. Everybody cheered. The way was open now for an Anglo-Italian agreement giving Mussolini what he wanted without requiring him to leave Spain. The Spanish Republic had no more hope, save to resist and hope to wear Franco down.

THE COLLAPSE OF SPRING 1938

Following his victory at Teruel, on 7 March 1938, Franco launched an attack on the whole eastern front. He reached the frontiers of Catalonia in the north and, on 15 April 1938, the Mediterranean on the coast just north of Valencia, thus splitting the Republican Zone into two parts. The events would have a serious effect on French policy.

After Eden had resigned, Chamberlain made a speech in which he said that the League of Nations could not protect small states against aggression.[5] The effect was to make France doubt whether Britain would stand by her if she ever had to honour her guarantees to the Eastern European countries.

France and Britain did nothing about Hitler's incorporation of Austria into the Greater Reich. The French had wanted a strong common front with Britain. The British, especially Chamberlain, were concerned to come to an agreement with Germany. The Chautemps Government resigned on 10 March. As its last deed, it opened the frontier to allow arms through to Spain. On 13 March, Léon Blum became Premier again, much to the distaste of the Foreign Office. Between 12 and 14 March, Spanish premier Negrín visited Paris to ask for aid, but the French Government, though sympathetic, could do nothing for Spain in the face of British hostility.

On the afternoon of 15 March 1938 the French Permanent National Defence Committee met to discuss the situation.[6] Blum suggested sending an ultimatum to Hitler to withdraw from Spain. General Gamelin, the Chief of Staff, said France could not risk war with Germany. The French military leaders were aware of the consequences of a Franco victory but fearful of having to call for general mobilisation. They were unprepared for the risk of war. They considered launching operations in Morocco but accepted that this would also mean a war where British support was doubtful. Gamelin said that the Spanish Republican forces were too inept to make use of large supplies of arms. Alexis Léger, Secretary-General at the Quai D'Orsay, warned the meeting that large-scale intervention in Spain would be a *casus belli*. The Air Minister, Guy La Chambre, confirmed that French factories were producing only 40 aircraft per month.

Finally, they decided to concentrate two French divisions on the Catalan frontier, which probably halted Franco's offensive in that direction. This decision was known almost immediately in Franco Spain, probably through a leak in Paris.[7] In Berlin, fears were calmed by an accurate political analysis of French hesitations. German confidence transmitted itself to Franco's ambassador in Berlin who wrote that nothing was going to happen, though leaks in the French General Staff indicated that Blum was going to do as much as he could to aid the Republic.

The French were going to send 50 aircraft and facilitate the transfer of Russian machines. Military counsellors would be sent. It is difficult to know how much material actually went to Spain after this decision. Nationalist documents reported immense amounts which, even if exaggerated, indicate much traffic.[8] Azcárate, who seems to have conducted the negotiations, received contradictory information from French ministers.

Things were looking up for Italy in Spain. Though Franco had not used Italian ground troops during the Teruel battle, he had employed the air force. On 23 February, Mussolini cabled Franco, exhorting him to use Italian troops or send them home. Franco delayed his reply, but calmly argued that he was sure the Duce would leave his troops in Spain as an act of moral solidarity. Mussolini was convinced and confident that Franco would find a worthy task for his men.

On 31 January 1938, Franco had announced his first civilian government, whose most important member was his brother-in-law, Ramón Serrano Súñer, who appeared to prefer the Italian model of the New State. Italian Fascist advice contributed to Falange thinking about social legislation. The result was the Labour Charter, or Fuero del Trabajo of 9 March 1938, which included statements about the New State's determination to protect the working class against exploitation and to create 'vertical' unions of workers and employers in the service of the State. While the Fuero del Trabajo contains echoes of Catholic social thought, it strongly reflected the Italian Carta del Lavoro.

This was the limit of Italian activity in Spanish politics. At least it seemed that Italians were not dying for a completely reactionary regime of generals and landowners.[9]

Mussolini resumed sending troops to Spain as well as some warships. Franco now reacted to Mussolini's exhortations. The CTV was in the vanguard of the attack into Aragon on 9 March and by the 14th had taken its first objective, Alcañiz. On the 19th, the CTV occupied Tortosa on the Ebro river. The CTV faced some of the best Republican units and suffered relatively heavy losses. However, the disgrace of Guadalajara was purged. From 16 March till the 18th, Italian machines indiscriminately terror-bombed Barcelona, to the extent that even Franco asked them to desist because of the international repercussions. Ciano was also uncomfortable at the bombing though Mussolini said that the world had better get used to being horrified rather than charmed by Italy.

While the French were discussing what to do, Britain signed the Anglo-Italian Agreement on 15 April 1938. Ciano confirmed that Italy would leave Spain as soon as Franco won the war. Britain accepted the Italian conquest of Abyssinia. However, Italy was now anxious to capitalise on the new friendship with Britain and thus slowed down Franco's request for surface ships.[10]

Nevertheless, in June 1938, more reinforcements of Italian troops and a further two destroyers, as well as 44 bombers, went to Spain. The following month the CTV took an important part in the assault on the Republican capital of Valencia, though excellent Government fortifications blocked the attack. When newly-reorganised Republican forces attacked across the Ebro on 25 July, the CTV took part in the battle of the Ebro, the greatest in the whole war.

This was the battle which put Franco in most urgent need of German aircraft and heavy artillery. He would be forced to pay the price.

GERMAN ECONOMIC PENETRATION

Behind Germany's political reasons for helping Franco lay important economic considerations. Eighty per cent of Germany's iron ore was imported. Spanish Morocco produced some of the highest-grade ore in the world. Germany imported large proportions of her pyrites and mercury from Spain also. Her Four Year Plan required a guaranteed source of raw materials.

At first, HISMA and ROWAK, the companies set up in 1936 to run the traffic between Germany and Franco Spain, controlled all German–Spanish commerce. The Francoists had hoped to sell raw materials to earn foreign currency, but Germany insisted that they should be used to pay Franco's debts to her. Franco had little choice since he was dependent on Germany. His major problem was pressure from Spanish business sectors which had traditionally dealt with Britain, as well as from the British-owned Rio Tinto and Tharsis mining companies. At the beginning of the war, cargoes of minerals bound for Britain from these mines had been diverted to Germany. This was the price the British companies had to pay for the repression of their workforces by Franco's authorities. This loss of revenue was preferable to the confiscations which were taking place in the Republican Zone where, by the end of 1937, 35 British firms had been taken over by workers' committees.

However, Spanish mineral ores, mostly in Franco's territory, were vital for British industry and provided the finance for Spain to buy British coal. The cessation of copper-ore shipments to Wales caused considerable anxiety in the Commons. Under pressure from the mining companies, the British Government, having considered and rejected naval intervention, urged Franco to cease requisitioning ores. Franco's conquest of the mining regions of northern Spain in 1937, as well as the massive increase of shipments of ore to Germany from the Riff mines in Morocco, made it all the more essential to appoint a diplomatic agent in his zone to represent British interests.

This was a very delicate matter because the Labour and Liberal Opposition would attack any form of recognition of Franco, especially if the financial interests of Conservative politicians were seen to be involved. The British Government found a suitable moment when Franco released a number of captured British ships. On 16 November 1937, London announced the appointment of Sir Robert Hodgson as Agent in Burgos. This was a form of *de facto* recognition compelled by realism. Sir Robert's high ambassadorial rank and staff of embassy-size were needed to counteract German status in Spain. He was accorded full diplomatic privileges, even though Britain did not recognise the Franco Government, as was his Spanish equivalent in London, the Duke of Alba. For the Duke, already well-known in London society, diplomatic status ensured that his secretary would not have to take the British driving test. Sir Robert and his retinue were granted a special section of the beach at San Sebastián the following summer where he and his staff were not subject to the puritanical rules for bathing dress imposed by the new Spanish regime.[11]

On 16 July 1937, an agreement was signed between Franco Spain and Germany which required the repayment of the arms debt in Reichmarks at 4 per cent interest or by means of deliveries of raw materials. Furthermore, Spain would allow German-financed companies to have full control over the foreign currency they generated. Lastly, and this was to be the most significant point, Spain would allow the establishment of mining companies run by Germans, though only, as the Spaniards insisted, 'compatible with the general stipulations of Spanish law'.

This last phrase was a source of tension in following months, German firms had already acquired rights in 73 Spanish mines, which led to a decree on 9 October 1937 forbidding any further transfer of property or shares to foreign interests. This caused considerable anxiety in Germany where HISMA had been endeavouring to develop a plan known as the Montana project, whose aim was to bring several mining companies under German control. This, the Germans stated, was the 'whole aim and purpose of our assistance in Spain in the economic field'. The Germans wanted at least equal participation with Spaniards in their shareholdings, while the Franco authorities insisted on a 30 per cent maximum. The German report of their attempts to persuade Franco's Foreign Minister, General Jordana, reveal fundamental differences in attitude. While the Germans wanted clear and immediate answers, Jordana was evasive. He could not give a definite answer and he thought that Franco would want to take time to consider. The Germans said that 'it was tremendously important not to lose any time', while Jordana replied that 'setting the time was ... a matter for the Spaniards to decide'. In fact Spain was endeavouring with some success to equalise her ore-exports to Britain and Germany. Even the blandishments of the experienced diplomat Eberhardt Von Stohrer, who had replaced Von Faupel, could not penetrate the evasiveness of the generalísimo.

The Spanish mines issue created anxiety in Germany. To threaten to suspend military aid might provoke Franco, who was doing better, to defy Germany altogether. Von Stohrer urged conciliation. Several countries were courting Franco Spain with favourable trade agreements. The rigidity of the entire HISMA–ROWAK structure was questionable.

At the beginning of December 1937, Franco again assured the German ambassador of his friendship and that he would meet German wishes – always, of course, under the new Spanish law. In the midst of the battle of Teruel, on 20 December 1937, Franco received Von Stohrer and Johannes

Bernhardt, the German businessman who had gone to see Hitler on Franco's behalf over a year before and he had done very well out of the war. Bernhardt insisted on the concession of the Montana mining rights. This gave Franco the chance to stress that each of the 73 German claims would have to be considered. It would take a long time. Von Stohrer concluded that Franco was being obstructive, as indeed he was. Throughout early 1938 Von Stohrer struggled against Franco's delaying tactics. A special mining law was being prepared, but the terms were kept from Von Stohrer. The Foreign Minister, General Jordana, evidently had orders to keep Von Stohrer away from Franco. He explained to him that German participation in Spanish mines could go as high as 40 per cent. He hoped Germany would be satisfied. The irritated Von Stohrer grew intemperate. Jordana endeavoured to pacify him. Surely he did not want it to be said that new Spain was acting under pressure from Berlin? In fact, concluded Von Stohrer, the new law, which allowed controlling German interest in a number of mines, seemed acceptable. It was the Spanish attitude that was not.

Chapter 14

THE NEW NEGRÍN GOVERNMENT SEEKS HELP EVERYWHERE

The Republic's military débâcle of Spring 1938 and the division of its territory into two parts, led to a political crisis. The unity of the Popular Front had to be reinforced and foreign governments convinced that the disaster could be remedied by large-scale arms deliveries. The aim of the Spanish Communist Party and its advisers was to inspire resistance until the expected European war and to get rid of Indalecio Prieto, Minister of National Defence, whom they saw as a liability.

Negrín, fearing Prieto's pessimism, convinced that he could not afford to lose Soviet support, and determined to stress the policy of all-out resistance, asked for his resignation. Prieto saw this as proof of Communist hegemony. On 5 April 1938, Negrín formed his new Government, with himself in the Ministry of National Defence. A rapid and large-scale reorganisation of Republican forces was carried out to cope with the division of the Government zone into two sections: the Eastern or Catalan Zone and and the Central–South Zone bounded by the triangle of Madrid, Valencia and Cartagena.

The recovery of morale in Republican Spain profoundly impressed the French military attaché, Lt-Colonel Morel, who wrote from Barcelona on 12 April 1938 that extraordinary progress had been made in a week. The new Under-Secretary for War, the Communist Colonel Cordón, was working all-out to reorganise the Republican armies.[1]

Now the Republic's international diplomacy went on the attack. Spain was on the agenda of the League of Nations Council on 11 May. Del Vayo proposed a resolution to end Non-Intervention. He was opposed by Lord Halifax and Georges Bonnet, the new French Foreign Minister. Nobody, save Spain and the USSR, supported the motion. Evidently, Non-Intervention would stay.

Outside the League and the Non-Intervention Committee, hopes had been placed in the USA. However, the embargo imposed on arms shipments to Spain in January 1937 was extended and confirmed by the Neutrality Act of 1 May 1937. The Catholic vote, the State Department's firmness and the hesitation of Congress, corralled Roosevelt, in spite of strong pressure exerted to end the embargo.

However, the extremes of United States neutrality began to crumble. Gallup polls had reported 67 per cent neutrality among the public in early 1937, but by the end of 1938 this had fallen to 40 per cent and 46 per cent supported the Republic. Pro-Franco percentages had always been low. By late 1938 only 38 per cent of even Catholic respondents supported Franco.[2] However, this does not mean that they favoured sending arms to the Republic. Roosevelt may have been justified in his view that it was unwise to sacrifice his New Deal by abandoning the embargo. Catholic pressure to keep it remained strong. The 'Radio Priest', Father Charles Coughlin, spoke of '200 Loyalist–Communist' groups in Washington alone, working, as he put it, for the 'crimson cross of Communism'. Senator Nye's resolution of May 1938 to repeal the Embargo Act was indefinitely postponed by the Senate Foreign Relations Committee.

All the same, some war material was sent from the USA to Republican Spain. Félix Gordón-Ordás, Spanish ambassador in Mexico, bought commercial aircraft and tried to ship them through Mexico or even to bribe Latin American officials to invent orders from their Governments for the aircraft. The problem was that, when the aircraft reached Spain, they were often unsuitable and spare parts were unobtainable. In all, except for 34 Grumman fighters, which reached Spain as a result of a fake Turkish order organised through shady arms dealers and NKVD agents, only single-figure numbers of individual aircraft types and 29 in all were bought in the United States.[3]

On the other hand, Ford, Studebaker and General Motors supplied some 12 000 trucks, which were not on the embargo list, to Franco's forces, while Texaco supplied his oil. At the beginning of the Spanish Civil War, Captain Thorkild Rieber, President of Texaco and a Nazi sympathiser, diverted five tankers bound for Spanish Government-controlled refineries to rebel ports. Juan March, the Majorcan millionaire, guaranteed payment. Though Texaco was eventually fined for selling Franco 1.4 million tons of oil on credit, total US oil sales to Franco reached 3.4 million tons.[4]

Franco benefited more from United States oil and trucks than the Republic did from the extensive American pro-Republican propaganda campaigns, which were in any case matched, newspaper by newspaper and person by person, by supporters of Franco. Business naturally tended to be anti-Republican. Franco was fighting, in the view of American business, against the Spanish version of Roosevelt's New Deal. But Guernica and German and Italian participation worried the influential news magazines such as *Time*, *Newsweek* and *Life*. Well-known American writers, such as

Erskine Caldwell and Upton Sinclair, called for an effort against Spanish Fascism. The American Government was forced to reverse its decision to refuse passports to American medical personnel going to Spain. Most of the committees aiding the Republic would later be cited as Communist and subversive. This was particularly the case with the 3000 Volunteers for Liberty, the American International Brigaders, 900 of whom were killed. In Hollywood, a committee was set up to aid Spanish democracy, under Lewis Milestone, who had directed the famous film of Remarque's pacifist novel, *All Quiet on the Western Front*. Members included Sylvia Sidney, Paul Muni, James Cagney and Franchot Tone. Eddie Cantor, Bing Crosby and Rudi Vallee also performed in public at pro-Spanish Republic functions. Film stars such as Joan Crawford, Bette Davis, Miriam Hopkins, Ann Miller and others gave blood, money, and their signatures to appeals and petitions. Ernest Hemingway, author of *For Whom the Bell Tolls*, probably the most famous novel and film of the Spanish Civil War, and the Dutch film-maker Joris Ivens made the propaganda film *Spanish Earth*. It was screened first for President Roosevelt and then in Hollywood on 12 July 1937 at the house of the actor Fredric March. The screening raised thirteen thousand dollars for medical supplies.[5]

From Mexico, which had been supportive of the Republic, some 2.2 million US dollars' worth of arms were shipped to Spain in 1937. The Mexican ambassador in Washington tried unsuccessfully to persuade Cordell Hull to release planes which Mexico had bought in the United States. So, of the nine million US dollars that Gordón-Ordás had received, nearly half was unspent by 1938.

Some 330 Mexicans, of whom only a few survived, fought in Spain. Mexican sympathy for the Republic, particularly at international diplomatic level and at the League of Nations, effectively isolated Mexico, not only from the USA but also from most Latin American countries.

Fifteen of the Latin American republics were under military rule in July 1936, while the presidents of most of the others were conservative representatives of the social and economic oligarchies. The liberal Government of Colombia, for instance, was inhibited from expressing support for the Spanish Republic by the power of the Church. Attitudes to the Spanish Civil War were often conditioned by the domestic political needs of Latin American politicians. Admiration for the Nazi–Fascist model was widespread, which expressed itself in a large measure of tolerance for Francoist propaganda. Yet at the same time, Roosevelt's 'Good Neighbour' policy was increasing Latin American dependence on the United States, which inhibited support for Franco at international level.

The Negrín Government also made efforts to gain Vatican support, capitalising on the Catholicism of the Basques. Manuel de Irujo, the Basque Nationalist, was appointed Minister of Justice and so carried responsibility for church issues. The repression of revolutionaries by Negrín encouraged Irujo to demand that priests be released from prison.

The problem for the Republican Government in reinstating religious practice was the hostility of the populace and much of the Government itself. In addition, the Vatican was very chary even of reopening churches. Irujo prepared a legal text on freedom of religion but the Government decided that churches should stay closed though previously-approved private chapels could exist.[6] The first permitted mass in wartime Republican Spain was celebrated on 15 August 1937, at Irujo's residence in Valencia for his family and the Basque delegation.

Irujo sent out many feelers, principally in Paris through Cardinal Verdier, with the aim of re-establishing relations with the Vatican, trying to obtain the latter's permission to open churches in Catalonia and generally toning down Catholic support for Franco.[7]

The Spanish Government hoped that a senior cleric could be sent to verify the improved state of things in Spain. Unfortunately, Cardinal Verdier wrote to Cardinal Gomà in praise of the Spanish bishops' Collective Letter of July 1937, which supported Franco. It was 'truly illuminating', wrote Verdier, who also referred to the Christian struggle against Bolshevist atheism. As a result, Negrín told Irujo that the Republic could not entertain any official representative of Verdier.

Nevertheless, contacts at lower level were maintained but there was little favourable to be said. Soviet influence in Republican Spain was considerable and priests were still in jail. The anti-clerical outrages had isolated pro-Republican Catholics and the Negrín Government was suspicious. The Church authorities feared the insincerity of the Republican authorities, who were probably playing to the international gallery.[8] Indeed, the imprisonment of the Bishop of Teruel, Mgr Polanco, after the Republican capture of the city, did not help matters. The hoped-for visit of a prelate was delayed indefinitely.

Relations grew worse in 1938. There was justifiable suspicion about religious activities, for private masses sometimes concealed the activities of the Socorro Blanco or 'White Aid' which succoured pro-Franco fugitives.[9] On 17 April, the Holy See extended *de jure* recognition to Franco. From then on, despite further liberalisation permitting religious acts in the Republican Army, the Vatican kept its distance even more. The Vatican Secretary of State and next Pope, Eugenio Pacelli, was sceptical about the Republic's motives. Whether priests in clerical garb could walk freely about Barcelona, was the prime question and it could probably not be answered in the affirmative.[10]

Irujo left the Negrín Government in August 1938. Attitudes and repression were hardening as the Republic adopted the policy of resistance at all costs. As a last tragic paradox, Negrín's telegram of condolence on the death of Pope Pius XI reached Rome on the same day, 14 February 1939, that the body of the executed Bishop of Teruel was found by advancing Franco troops.[11] Mgr Polanco had been captured when Teruel was taken by Republican forces on 7 January 1938. The Government had given instructions that he was to be protected. He spent thirteen months imprisoned in Barcelona, where he was allowed to celebrate mass in his cell. He was tried for having signed the Collective Letter of July 1937. Since the documents were destroyed during the retreat towards France in 1939, the result of the case is unknown. Prisoners over 50 years of age were escorted to the frontier when Barcelona fell, either to protect them from extremist violence or perhaps to use them as hostages. On 6 February, orders came to transfer them to the still Government-controlled Central Zone. In the chaos of the moment, neither naval nor air forces were available or able to carry out the order. On the morning of 7 February, soldiers under an officer and political commissars arrived to transfer the prisoners to Rosas, presumably to embark them for Valencia. On the way, the prisoners were assassinated, presumably by the soldiers who were escorting them, in perhaps the last example of the anti-clerical hatred which possessed the Spanish Left.[12]

The Republican Government was being opportunist in its negotiations with the Vatican. That much is obvious. The Holy See was understandably opposed to establishing a *modus vivendi* with the Republic in the circumstances. Nevertheless, that is what diplomacy is about and, after the Second World War, the Vatican would negotiate with countries whose anti-clericalism and hostility to the Catholic Church were at least on a par with that of Republican Spain.

In its relations with the Nationalists, the Vatican was hesitant until the end of Basque resistance. Even then, relations remained tense, for the Vatican refused to allow Franco the traditional Spanish right of presenting the names of possible bishops. Nevertheless, religious life was being restored in Franco Spain by official decree. The crucifix was back on the classroom wall, mass was obligatory, as was religious education. Church marriage had full legal value.

On 16 May 1938, a nunzio was appointed. Important questions remained to be settled about church–state relations. Largely, this could be done by derogating the Republican anti-clerical legislation of 1931–33. The only real anxieties were the effect of irreligious Nazi–Fascist nationalistic ideas in Spain. The German–Spanish Cultural Agreement of 24 January 1939 was never ratified by Spain because of Church protests.

In addition to Germany, Italy and Portugal, friends of Franco from the beginning, the Vatican was now added to Japan and Hungary, as well as the sundry South American states and Albania, which had recognised Franco.

THE CZECH CRISIS

Léon Blum's Government, which had replaced the Chautemps administration on 14 March 1938, was brought down, in its turn, on 8 April. His Cabinet was not really a Popular Front one because the Right had refused to respond to Blum's appeal to their deputies to form a Government of National Unity. The new administration could not last. As in 1937, Blum could not persuade the Senate to accept the radical financial measures that he judged necessary and France was plagued by a series of strikes. He resigned on 22 June. International considerations also played a part. The Right, constantly vilifying Blum and his ministers, accused the Government of proposing to send French troops into Spain, even though the Permanent Committee of National Defence had been hesitant. Nor was it possible to get British guarantees of support in any conflict arising from French guarantees to Czechoslovakia,[13] which was coming under intense German pressure.

Edouard Daladier formed a Government on 10 April 1938, without the Socialists. Georges Bonnet, a Radical of conservative views, became Foreign Minister. He was unsympathetic to the Spanish Republic and determined to reconcile France with Italy. In this he was at one with Chamberlain and his new Foreign Secretary, Lord Halifax.

Bonnet began negotiations in Rome. At the same time an envoy from Daladier and Bonnet sought the urgent resumption of supplies of Spanish pyrites to French factories in exchange for the closure of the frontier with Republican Spain.

Franco refused to accept a French representative until the frontier with Government Spain was closed and Paris returned quantities of gold which had been deposited by the Spanish Government to cover arms purchases. At the end of April 1938 Daladier and Bonnet agreed with Chamberlain and Halifax to continue strict Non-Intervention when final agreement on the withdrawal of volunteers was reached. Intense British pressure, however, brought about the sealing of the frontier on 13 June 1938. Non-Intervention was a reality. Now that the Nationalist advance had appeared to have destroyed the Government forces, the war seemed close to an end. With the French frontier closed to reinforcements for the Republic, it might be possible, thought the Foreign Office, to lever Italy out of Spain.[14] All this took place against a serious crisis over the German-inhabited Sudetenland, part of Czechoslovakia. Already on 24 March, Chamberlain had said in Parliament that Britain could not issue a guarantee to Czechoslovakia. This was a disappointment to France, as ambassador François-Poncet cabled from Berlin to Paris on the 28th. If Britain gave an assurance, wrote the ambassador, who was in a position to know, Germany would think twice.[15] In the tense atmosphere, Britain and France were particularly concerned to conciliate Italy over Spain because they still thought they could separate Mussolini from Hitler.

At last something began to move at the Non-Intervention Committee. Two commissions were appointed to calculate the number of foreigners fighting in Spain. Both sides, of course, delayed. The Republic objected to the assumption that the numbers were equal; the Nationalists complained that International Brigade soldiers were being given Spanish nationality. Nevertheless, arrangements for withdrawal were accepted by the Republican Government on 26 July 1938. Franco temporised. Finally, Negrín announced to the League of Nations on 21 September that the Republic agreed to unilateral withdrawal. This was followed by the emotive farewell parade of the International Brigades on 1 November in Barcelona.

An international commission to supervise the complete withdrawal of the International Brigades, under the chairmanship of the Finnish General Jalander, aided by one British and two French senior officers, went to Barcelona on 16 October 1938 and issued a preliminary report on 15 January 1939, which calculated that the Republican Zone had a total of 12 208 foreign volunteers. The final number who left Spain was 12 688.[16]

Mussolini offered to reinforce the CTV but, despite the initially successful Republican offensive on the River Ebro at the end of July 1938, Franco was not too interested. The Duce seems to have lived in a world of his own. He wrote to General Berti on 7 September to say that he did not want Franco to think Italy was letting him down at a difficult time. 'My style is to stick by my friends till the end.' Ciano was more critical. On 21 August he wrote that Franco was a 'serene optimist'. On 29 August he wrote that Franco would be defeated because the Reds were fighters whereas he was not. It looks, therefore, as though the Italian withdrawal of 10 000 men in September came about not through international pressure, but because of annoyance with Franco. Aircraft, pilots and military hardware, of course, remained. Longest-serving troops were withdrawn, but the CTV still had 35 000 men in Spain. This token withdrawal brought the Anglo-

Italian agreement into force on 16 November 1938. The CTV stayed in Spain, however, till the end of the war.[17]

In the meantime, on the night of 25–6 July 1938, the elite units of the Republican Army of the Ebro had crossed the River Ebro and advanced swiftly against weakly-held Franco territory. The Republicans were held up by determined resistance and their own incapacity to manoeuvre, and the attack ground to a halt. Franco's immensely superior air force bombed Republican communications continually, while his efficient logistics ensured quick reinforcements of his armies from other parts of Nationalist Spain. The war became a fight to the death among the rocky crags of Aragon.

During the battle of the Ebro the Czech crisis came to a head. In September 1938 Hitler was demanding Home Rule for the Germans of the Sudetenland. On 23 September, Czechoslovakia mobilised its forces. The next day France followed suit partially, calling up about 600 000 men. The Royal Navy mobilised on the 27th. The German ultimatum to Czechoslovakia was due to expire at 2 p.m. on Wednesday, 28 September. Hitler invited Chamberlain, Daladier and Mussolini to meet him at Munich, where the Czechs were betrayed by their allies and forced to give in to Hitler's demands. Neither Britain nor France really wanted to go to war for the Czechs, while the French generals over-estimated German forces. The internal conflicts among the German generals as to the wisdom of risking war were kept secret.

The result of Munich was to destroy the confidence of the small countries of Eastern Europe in Britain and France. Finally, the Soviet Union, already in despair over the West's attitude towards German and Italian intervention in Spain, gave up any hope of collective security against Nazism and Fascism. As Litvinov told Coulondre, the French ambassador, 'You are handing Spain over to Franco to gain the approval of Mussolini.' The way was open for the Nazi–Soviet pact of August 1939.

The Czech crisis might have made a difference to Spain, had Britain and France stood firm against Hitler. Plans were reactivated for a French invasion of Minorca and to seize Mediterranean harbours. Franco was forced to a less arrogant stand, for he announced that if war came he would stay neutral.[17a] The alternative was to expect attack on the Pyrenees and in Morocco.

The French Chambre approved the Munich agreement on 4 October, by 535 against 75 votes. Some of the fiercest defenders of Franco, such as Henri de Kérillis, who had condemned Blum's plans to send arms to the Spanish Republic in 1936, now said that a Franco victory would be a catastrophe for France.[18]

15

At the End

Franco's need for arms during the critical battle of the Ebro in Autumn 1938 forced him to accept German conditions. When he asked for more material, the Germans presented a bill, asking at least for acknowledgement of their claims. Expenditure up till 31 October 1938 for the Condor Legion alone was 190 million Reichsmarks. The final claim would be 288.7 million Reichsmarks or £24.7 million.

Finally, on 11 November 1938, Franco promised to grant German mining demands. He had given in, but at the last moment and only when he received the armaments he needed to push the Republican armies back over the Ebro and begin the conquest of Catalonia.

Italy, in contrast, made no demands. In almost every letter from Rome García Conde wrote that Ciano was accommodating.[1] In early July 1938 he sent 4000 more troops and was about to make the total of replacements up to 12 000 with the necessary weapons. In January 1939 Ciano even threatened to send more men if France intervened as Franco approached the French frontier.[2]

The USSR had accepted the plans for withdrawal of volunteers only reluctantly, given that the counterpart would be the granting of belligerent rights, which would be profitable to Franco. During the summer of 1938, once Indalecio Prieto had left the Government and Negrín and his able Under-Secretary for Defence, Colonel Cordón, were rapidly reorganising the Republican armies with the help of Communist commanders, the USSR reinforced the Republic heavily, sending some 250 aircraft, paid for by a $70 million credit obtained by Negrín. But the abandonment of Czechoslovakia at Munich signified the end of Soviet hopes that Spain would awaken Britain and France to the dangers of Nazism and Fascism. However, some time in early December 1938, Negrín sent his Air Force Commander, General Ignacio Hidalgo de Cisneros, to Moscow to ask for 100 million dollars' worth of arms, even though the gold sent to Moscow had all been spent. A proportion of the arms reached Bordeaux, but a considerable amount was blocked in France,[3] while much of the rest reached Catalonia too late to be deployed. As Franco's forces neared the

French frontier, a debate in the Chambre produced a majority against intervention. Ships were unloading Russian supplies at Bordeaux while Franco's representatives pressed Bonnet not to aggravate the situation by letting the material through to Spain.[4]

The French Government was concerned about the security of its frontier as Franco's troops approached. Bonnet sent Senator Léon Bérard to get guarantees from Franco. Arriving at Burgos on 4 February 1939, as the Spanish Republican Government crossed into France, Bérard was received by General Jordana and made his demands. Foreign troops should leave, Spain should remain neutral in a European war and collaborate with France in Morocco. Jordana said that these guarantees had already been given. He wanted full *de jure* recognition. Bérard returned to Paris and was sent back again to begin formal negotiations. Within one week matters were settled, including the return of Spanish gold deposited in France as guarantee of payment, as well as arms and ships which the exiled Republicans would probably demand as their own.[5] On 24 February, the Chambre voted to recognise the Franco Government. On 2 March Marshal Pétain, the hero of Verdun, an admirer of Franco and future Head of the puppet Vichy State, was appointed ambassador. To send the distinguished Marshal of France as ambassador was a great compliment to Franco Spain, which responded ungraciously by keeping him waiting for a week at San Sebastián until the Spanish Government fleet, which had fled to Bizerta, was brought back by Nationalist crews.

The Nationalists' intransigence grew because they were aware that France urgently wanted to settle the Spanish question. There was also intense anger against France for what was seen as her favouritism towards the Republic.

It took until the end of June 1939 for Spanish demands to be met. Franco began to export pyrites again to France and gradually to take back a considerable number of the 400 000 Spanish refugees.

Great Britain had done its best to persuade France not to pass arms over the frontier in the summer of 1938, even though Franco was sinking British merchant-ships. The Government considered that no action it could take would be beneficial in the long run. 'I do not think', said Chamberlain in the Commons on 13 June 1938, 'any action we can take is practicable in stopping these attacks if they persist'.[6] There were campaigns to end Non-Intervention. A National Spain Weekend was held on 21–22 May 1938 and, on 23 April, a national emergency conference took place at the Queen's Hall in London, attended by leading figures in the pro-Republican Spain movement such as the Duchess of Atholl, Stafford Cripps, and the Communist leader Harry Pollitt. This was beginning to look like a Popular

Front and there were calls for strikes to force the Government to end Non-Intervention. But the official Labour Party would do nothing which hinted at Popular Fronts or collaboration with the Communists, and threats of expulsion were made. In the event, nothing came of the campaign except the collection of money to send a food ship.[7]

It was now time to settle outstanding grievances, expressed by General Jordana on 14 December in reply to a letter from the Duke of Alba, saying that he had had repeated assurances of British sympathy. Why did Britain allow the agitation on behalf of Red Spain? asked Jordana, unaware as always that there was nothing the British authorities could do about it. What about belligerent rights, never allowed to Franco?[8]

In this context, the bloodless surrender of Menorca, masterminded by the British Consul at Palma, Commander Hillgarth, was considered a skilful piece of diplomacy. Franco had agreed not to let Italian troops land on the island and to permit the British cruiser, HMS *Devonshire*, which had carried Franco's representative to Menorca, to take off Republican leaders. As the Negrín Government tried to establish itself in what was left of Republican Spain, and Franco refused terms for surrender, the British Government decided that it had no alternative but to recognise the Nationalist Government, which it did on 27 February.

Franco did not object to a British warship evacuating Colonel Casado, commander of the major Central Army of the Republic, who rebelled against the Negrín Government and negotiated surrender with Franco at the end of March 1939.

Though it has frequently been written that Colonel Casado was encouraged to mount his coup against Negrín by Denys Cowan, the agent of the Chetwode Commission, which was negotiating exchanges of prisoners, no convincing proof of this has been brought. It seems more likely that Cowan merely recommended favourable consideration for Casado and his entourage, who were allowed to come to Britain, because they had collaborated with the Chetwode Commission and prevented a last-minute massacre of prisoners.[9]

Aftermath

At a banquet in Berlin on 3 March 1939, Franco's ambassador thanked Hitler for his 'constant and efficient help'.[1] Spain had agreed to join Germany, Italy and Japan in the Anti-Comintern Pact, but Franco delayed official announcement until the end of the Civil War, for fear of upsetting delicate negotiations with France and Britain. The Pact was a mere statement, to be added to by future agreement. On 31 March Spain signed a Treaty of Friendship with Germany, which included a clause mutually promising not to give any advantage to an enemy.

The Condor Legion held a final parade on the airfield at León on 19 May before Franco and the senior Spanish and Italian generals. The debt to Germany was fixed at 288.7 million Reichmarks. A German mission was to go to Spain to discuss repayment. It was particularly not to suggest to the Spaniards that Germany was seeking payment for the shedding of German blood, which would probably have been counterproductive, for Franco believed he had given Germany the chance to fight against Bolshevism without committing herself to a major war. Negotiations took place between 12 June and 5 July 1939. The Germans noted the Spanish wish not to be rushed into allowing too much Germanisation of the Spanish economy. The debt would be settled by Spanish exports of raw materials to Germany over a number of years.

The CTV set sail for home on 31 May. They had left nearly 4000 dead in Spain. As for the debt of some 8.3 thousand million lire, agreement was reached to fix the sum at 5 thousand million lire (£56 million), to be paid over ten years by Spanish exports.[2]

Given Franco's failure to join the Axis in the Second World War, Italian and German contribution to his victory was very expensive. Italy sent over 70 000 men, 1801 cannon, 1426 mortars, 3436 machine-guns, 157 tanks and 6797 other vehicles, 320 million cartridges and 7.7 million shells, together with a total of 759 aircraft.[3] From Germany came some 840 aircraft.[4] Fourteen thousand Germans had served in Spain, of whom about 300 were killed; 200 tanks were sent, together with thirty anti-tank companies.

Soviet aid ended after Munich, save for the material sent in late 1938. According to Soviet figures, the USSR had shipped 806 planes, 482 tanks and armoured cars, 1555 cannon, 15 113 machine-guns, 862 million cartridges and $3\frac{1}{2}$ million bombs and shells.[5]

The anti-revolutionary role played in Spain by the Comintern created profound hostility towards Communism. Spanish Anarchists and Left-wing Socialists accused the Communists of suppressing the Spanish revolution, disillusioning its masses and so contributing to the defeat. Others attacked Russia for not fully supporting the Republic. These views were reinforced by the news of Stalin's execution of many Russians and others, suspected of critical views of Soviet policy in the Spanish Civil War, on their return from Spain. However, 59 became Heroes of the Soviet Union (19 posthumously).[6]

The policy of resistance, urged by the Communists, failed. The Spanish Central Committee and the advisers hastily abandoned Spain on 6 March 1939 when Colonel Casado, commander of the largest Republican Army, seized power with the intention of seeking terms from Franco, and claimed that Negrín's Government was now illegal, given that President Azaña and the Chief-of-Staff, General Rojo, had resigned and stayed in France. The very success of the coup proves the impotence of the Communist policy of resistance. The Spanish Civil War ended officially on 1 April 1939.

The Non-Intervention Committee held its last meeting on 20 April 1939, to wind up business. What had been its achievements?

Whether Non-Intervention prevented a general war breaking out over Spain depends on whether Germany and Italy would have helped Franco had Blum actually sent aid to the Spanish Republic. The dates and details of German and Italian decisions to help and, more importantly, to augment their help, would seem to indicate that neither Hitler nor Mussolini were ready to get into a war over Spain. Both countries knew that the USSR was not encouraging revolution in the West. Again, Non-Intervention was meant to dissuade foreign countries from sending arms to Spain, but this would only have worked had the consequences of doing so been serious. If even Britain's ally, France, continually permitted volunteers and weapons to pass over the frontier, why should Germany and Italy have worried? In any case, as early as August 1936, these two countries realised that Non-Intervention was only a face-saving device.

Could anything else have been done? Nothing, save to make a stand and apply the blockade properly, but this would have required a level of understanding and cooperation between France and Britain for which the latter was just not ready, given recent history, its present situation and the pervasive fear of revolution.

Once Non-Intervention was in place, Spain was seen as a side-issue. Italy's actions in Spain were not the central question for Britain: the Chiefs of Staff stressed that Britain could not afford a war with Italy given British imperial responsibilities. What Italy did in Spain was merely an example of behaviour which Eden would not tolerate but Chamberlain would put up with for the sake of appeasement over the bigger questions of Central Europe.

This, however, is the major question in the discussion of the importance of the Spanish Civil War in the international politics of the later 1930s. Of course, today it is easy to see that the behaviour of the Democracies over Spain could not have avoided sending a message to the Dictators that they would be able to do what they liked anywhere else. Is it misplaced to condemn the statesmen of the time for not having seen the truth of this? The answer can only be to examine whether, given their own preoccupations, they were justified in abandoning the Spanish Republic. Would they have protected a Spanish Right-wing regime against a Left-wing revolution? This is to enter into the realm of hypothesis, but, given the concern with avoiding involvement in Europe, the answer might be that they would not have defended such a regime. The other issue is why the British Government, in particular, did not see that Franco, put into power by Hitler, would be a danger. Indeed, Eden did see this, but Chamberlain and Halifax may have judged the future more soundly. The question was never discussed in these terms, but the reasons why Franco did not join the Axis powers – the threat of Royal Navy blockade and the unreliability of the Spanish generals themselves – may have been present, if inchoate, in British minds, while a victorious revolutionary or non-revolutionary and Communist-dominated Spain may have seemed far too incalculable a risk.

Major Actors

ALVAREZ DEL VAYO, Julio (1891–1974). Republican Foreign Minister 1936–37, 1938–39.

ARAQUISTAIN, Luis (1886–1959). Republican Ambassador to France.

AZANA, Manuel (1880–1940). President of the Second Republic, 1936–39.

AZCARATE, Pablo de (1890–1971). Republican Ambassador to Britain.

BERNHARDT, Johannes (1897–?). German businessman in Morocco. Took Franco's appeal for help to Hitler on 25 July 1936. Director of HISMA.

BLUM, Léon (1872–1950). Premier of France, 1936–37, March–April 1938.

BONNET, Georges (1889–1973). French Foreign Minister, 1938–40.

CABALLERO (see LARGO CABALLERO)

CHAMBERLAIN, Neville (1869–1940). British Prime Minister, May 1937–May 1940.

CIANO, Count Galeazzo (1903–44). Son-in-law of Mussolini. Italian Foreign Minister.

CORBIN, André (b. 1881). French ambassador in London.

COT, Pierre (b. 1895). French Minister of Aviation.

DALADIER, Edouard (1884–1970). French Minister of War, 1936–38; Premier, 1938–40.

DELBOS, Yvon (1885–1956). French Foreign Minister, 1936–37

DE LOS RIOS, Fernando (1879–1949). Interim Republican ambassador to France, Ambassador to USA, 1936–39

DEL VAYO (see ALVAREZ DEL VAYO)

EDEN, Anthony (1897–1977). British Foreign Secretary, December 1935–February 1938.

FAUPEL, General Wilhelm (1873–1945). German ambassador to Franco Spain, 1936–37.

FRANCO, General Francisco (1892–1975). Leader of Spanish insurgent Nationalists.

GARCIA CONDE, Pedro. Nationalist ambassador to Italy, 1937–39

GIRAL, José (1880–1962). Republican Prime Minister, 19 July-4 September 1936

GOERING, Marshal Hermann (1893–1946). Commander of Luftwaffe. Commissioner for Four-Year Plan.

GOMA, Cardinal Isidro (1869–1940). Primate of Spain.

GOMEZ JORDANA, General Francisco (1876–1944). Foreign Minister of Franco Government, 1938–39.

GORDON-ORDAS, Félix (?–1973). Republican ambassador to Mexico.

GRANDI, Count Dino (1895–1988). Italian ambassador in London.

HASSELL, Ulrich von (1881–1944). German ambassador to Italy.

HITLER, Adolf (1889–1945). Chancellor and Fuehrer of Nazi Germany.

HOARE, Sir Samuel (1880–1959). First Lord of the Admiralty, 1936–37.

JORDANA (See GOMEZ JORDANA).

174

KUZNETSOV, Captain Nicolai. Senior Soviet naval adviser in Spain.

LARGO CABALLERO, Francisco (1869–1946). Spanish Republican premier, 5 September 1936–17 May 1937.

LITVINOV, Maxim (1876–1951). Soviet Commissar for Foreign Affairs.

MAISKII, Ivan (b. 1884). Soviet ambassador in London.

MUSSOLINI, Benito (1883–1945). Head (Duce) of Italian Government.

NEGRIN, Dr Juan (1892–1956). Republican Premier, 18 May 1937–5 March 1939.

NEURATH, Constantin Von (1873–1956). German Minister of Foreign Affairs until 1938.

PRIETO, Indalecio (1883–1962). Republican Minister of Air and Marine, 1936–37; Minister of National Defence, May 1937–March 1938.

PLYMOUTH, Earl of (1889–1943). Chairman of Non-Intervention Committee.

RIBBENTROP, Joachim Von (1893–1945). German ambassador in London, 1936–38, Foreign Minister from 1938.

ROATTA (alias Mancini), General Mario (1887–1968). Commander of CTV.

SPERRLE, General Hugo Von (1885–1953). Commander of Condor Legion, 1936–37.

STALIN, Joseph (1879–1953). General Secretary, Central Committee of the Communist Party of the USSR.

STOHRER, Eberhardt von (1883–1944). German ambassador to Franco from 1938.

TOGLIATTI, Palmiro (1893–1964). Italian Communist. Comintern adviser in Spain.

WARLIMONT, Lt-Col Walter (b. 1893). Special German envoy to Franco, 1936.

References

Only essential references are noted here. Further sources are to be found in the Bibliographical essay. Full bibliographical details are given in the Bibliography.

Chapter 1

1. P. G. Edwards, 'The Foreign Office and Fascism 1924–1929'.
2. *Enciclopedia Italiana di Scritti Politici, Scienze, Lettere ed Arti*, XIV (1932), p. 267.
3. Anthony Eden, *The Eden Memoirs*, Vol. 1. *Facing the Dictators*, p. 318.
4. F. Walters, *A History of the League of Nations*, p. 653.
5. A. Dallin, 'The Use of International Movements', in *Russian Foreign Policy: Essays in Historical Perspective*; I. Deutscher, *Stalin, a Political Biography*, p. 392.
6. J. Haslam, *The USSR and the Struggle for Collective Security in Europe*, p. 29

Chapter 2

1. W. Shirer, *The Collapse of the Third Republic*, p. 216.
2. J. Lacouture, *Léon Blum*, p. 341.
3. R. Rémond, *Les Catholiques, le Communisme et les Crises 1929–1939*, p. 174.
4. A. Aldgate, *Cinema and History: British Newsreels and the Spanish Civil War*, pp. 100–1, 105–6, 117.
5. *Documents on British Foreign Policy 1919–1939 (DBFP)*, 2nd Series, Vol. XVII, Western Pact Negotiations; Outbreak of Spanish Civil War, June 1936– January 1937.
6. L. Bolín, *Spain, the Vital Years*, pp. 13–15, 50: D. Jerrold, *Georgian Adventure*, p. 371.
7. M. Alpert, 'Gibraltar y la Guerra Civil Española'.
8. *Rapport fait au nom de la Commission chargée d'enquêter sur les évènements survenus en France de 1933 à 1945*, pp. 215ff.
9. Thomas Jones, *A Diary with Letters 1931–1954*, p. 231.
10. P. Renouvin, 'La politique extérieure du premier gouvernement Léon Blum', in *Léon Blum, Chef du Gouvernement 1936–1939*, p. 332.
11. A. Viñas, 'Blum traicionó a la República'.
12. I thank Gerald Howson for much patient explanation of the details of these events.
13. Cable from the Italian consul in Marseille, cit. in I. Saz, 'Antecedentes y primera ayuda material de la Italia fascista a los sublevados en España en julio de 1936', in *Italia y la guerra civil española*.

Chapter 3

1. *Documents on German Foreign Policy*, No. 2.
2. Information from Herr Peter Emmerich, of the Bayreuther Festspiele. According to an eyewitness, however, Hitler saw *Die Wälkurie*. (My thanks to Professor Paul Preston for this information.)
3. E. Von Weizsaecker, *Memoirs*, p. 107.
4. W. Shirer, *Berlin Diary*, pp. 58, 60.
5. *Archivo del Ministerio de Asuntos Exteriores (AMAE)*, Madrid (Azaña Papers RE144, C5 and C6: RE64 C88).
6. A. Galland, *The First and the Last*, p. 23.
7. A. Koestler, *Spanish Testament*, p. 37.
8. J. Coverdale, *La intervención fascista en la guerra civil española*, p. 107.
9. J. Tusell and I. Saz, 'Mussolini y Primo de Rivera: las relaciones politicas y diplomáticas de dos dictaduras mediterráneas', in *Italia y la guerra civil española*.
10. Papers of Luis Araquistain (Archivo Histórico Nacional, Madrid) L70/40, p. 5.
11. I. Saz, *Mussolini contra la Segunda República Española*, pp. 139–141.
12. Ibid., p. 153.
13. The texts of the cables are in ibid., Appendix 5.
14. P. Sainz Rodriguez, *Testimonio y recuerdos*, p. 233.
15. G. Ciano, *Ciano's Diplomatic Papers*, pp. 21–2.
16. G. Ciano, *Ciano's Diary 1939–1943*, p. 33.

Chapter 4

1. E. Moradiellos, *Neutralidad benévola; el Gobierno británico y la insurrección militar española de 1936*, pp. 222–4.
2. Eden, pp. 401–2.
3. Cit. Moradiellos, p. 224.
4. J. Moch, *Rencontres avec Léon Blum*, p. 195.
5. P. Renouvin, in *Léon Blum, chef de gouvernement*, p. 334.
6. For many otherwise unrecorded details of the French aircraft I have been greatly helped by Gerald Howson's as-yet-unpublished manuscript on arms traffic in the Spanish Civil War, which considers all existing evidence.
7. J. Duroselle, *La Décadence 1932–1939*, p. 302.
8. J. Coverdale, *La intervención fascista en la guerra civil española*, p. 94.
9. R. Quatrefages, 'La politique française de non-intervention et le soutien matériel à la République pendant la guerre civile (1936–1939)'.
10. Clerk-Delbos interview in *DBFP*, No. 67, 7 August 1936.
11. Churchill's letter to Blum in M. Gilbert. *Winston Churchill* Vol. 5, (London: Heinemann, 1976), pp. 781–2, cit. in Moradiellos, p. 224.
12. C. Serrano, *L'enjeu espagnol: PCF et la guerre d'Espagne*, p. 42.
13. Blum's Luna Park speech is quoted by Lacouture, pp. 375ff.
14. E. H. Carr, *The Comintern and the Spanish Civil War*, p. 16.
15. M. T. Meshcheryatov, 'The Soviet Union and the Antifascist struggle of the Spanish people'.

16. DBFP, No. 32.
17. Henderson (US Chargé d'Affaires in Moscow) to Washington 4 August 1936 in *Foreign Relations of the United States (FRUS)*, ii, p. 461.
18. P. Spriano, *Storia del partito communista italiano*, Vol. iii, 'I fronti populari, Stalin, la guerra', p. 86.
19. Haslam, p. 114: R. M. Slusser, 'The role of the Foreign Ministry', in *Russian Foreign Policy*, pp. 219–20.
19a. P. Broué 'La Non-Intervention de l'URSS en Espagne'.
20. 'Soviet Shipping in the Spanish Civil War'.
21. C. Oliveira, *Salazar e a Guerra Civil de Espanha*, p. 149.
22. Ibid., p. 184.
23. H. Kay, *Salazar and Modern Portugal*, p. 95.

Chapter 5

1. Lacouture, p. 370.
2. A. Boyle, *The Climate of Treason*, p. 98.
3. Eden, p. 408.
4. *Foreign Intervention in Spain* (Ed. 'Hispanicus'), Chapter 7.
5. H. Dalton, *The Fateful Years*, p. 102.
6. Heather Errock, 'The Attitude of the Labour Party to the Spanish Civil War', p. 50.
7. Michael Foot, *Aneurin Bevan*, i, p. 230.
8. Eden, p. 443.
9. G. Howson, *Aircraft of the Spanish Civil War*, pp. 134–5, 201.
10. Coverdale, p. 110.
11. DBFP. No. 265, 3 October 1936.
12. Public Record Office (PRO), AIR 40, 221.
13. PRO CAB 57/36.

Chapter 6

1. S. Krivoshein, 'Los tanquistas voluntarios en los combates por Madrid' in *Bajo la bandera de la España Republicana*, pp. 319–41.
2. Quoted by H. Thomas, *The Spanish Civil War*, pp. 533–4.
3. Araquistain Papers L23/A, 113 and L23/A 1158.
4. AMAE L1460 C16.
5. This diplomatic correspondence is in PRO, F0371 W14793/9549/41.
6. PRO FO 371 W15074/9549/41.
7. N. Kuznetsov, 'Con los marinos españoles en su guerra nacional-revolucionaria' in *Bajo la bandera de la España Republicana*, p. 178.
8. M. Alpert, *La guerra civil española en el mar*, pp. 179–81.
9. R. De Felice, *Mussolini il Duce*, Vol. 2, *Lo Stato totalitario 1936–1940*, pp. 386–8.
10. Aircraft figures in Howson, p. 26.
11. Technical details in Howson under names of aircraft.
12. Alpert, *La Guerra Civil en el mar*, pp. 166–7.
13. R. Whealey, *Hitler and Spain: the Nazi Role in the Spanish Civil War*, p. 45.

14. R. Proctor, Hitler's Luftwaffe in the Spanish Civil War, pp. 412–43.
15. De Felice, p. 381 and A. Aquarone, 'La guerra di Spagna e l'opinione pubblica italiana': Coverdale, pp. 245–6.
16. Proctor, p. 57.
17. I. Maiskii, *Spanish Notebooks*, pp. 57, 63, 81–2.
18. Eden, p. 412.
19. Whealey, p. 48–9.
20. Proctor, p. 57–69.

Chapter 7

1. DBFP No. 357.
2. Araquistain Papers L70/54a and 55a.
3. Eden, pp. 413–14.
4. Maclean's note in DBFP No. 369.
5. PRO FO 371 W 16391 and W1543/9549/41.
6. *Ciano's Diplomatic Papers*, pp. 75–6.
7. G. Ward Price, *I Know these Dictators*, p. 245.
8. Coverdale, p. 155.
9. De Felice, p. 385: S. Attanasio, *Gli italiani en la guerra di Spagna*, p. 107.
10. DGFP. No. 148.
11. O. Conforti, *Guadalajara, la primera derrota del fascismo*, pp. 33–6.
12. De Felice, p. 388, note.
13. Conforti, p. 39, note.
14. Charles A. Burdick, 'The American Military Attachés in the Spanish Civil War'.
15. AMAE R1459 C1.
16. Troop figures in Coverdale pp. 108ff. Tables 4 and 6.
17. Italian naval activity in Alpert, *La guerra civil en el mar*, pp. 167–73.
18. Ibid., pp. 174–6.
19. British details on Faupel in PRO FO371 W16585/340/41.
20. DGFP Nos 128, 144 and 145.
21. *La Guerra y su Preparación* (Madrid, September 1928).
22. Proctor, pp. 74–6.
23. DGFP No. 157.
24. Von Weizsaecker, p. 113.
25. Details on HISMA and ROWAK in DGFP Nos. 80, 101.
26. Whealey, p. 75.
27. For the agreement of 20 March 1937, see DGFP No. 234.
28. Edwards, p. 94.

Chapter 8

1. R. Quartararo, *Roma tra Londra e Berlino: la politica estera fascista dal 1930 al 1940*, p. 310.
2. PRO CAB 23/87.
3. DBFP, No. 370.
4. Spanish Government reply in P. de Azcárate, *Mi embajada en Londres*

durante la guerra civil española, p. 142: Franco's reply in AMAE R1060 C206 and C207.
5. Serrano, p. 80.
6. Edwards, p. 252, note 68.
7. R. Garriga, *Guadalajara y sus consecuencias*, pp. 42–8.
8. Coverdale, pp. 165–7: De Felice, p. 390.
9. F. Schwarz, *La internacionalización de la guerra civil española*, p. 235; Manuel Azaña, 'La República española y la Sociedad de Naciones', in *Obras Completas*, iv, p. 81ff.
10. Charles R. Halstead, 'A "somewhat Machiavellian" face: Colonel Juan Beigbeder as High Commissioner in Spanish Morocco 1937–1939'.
11. Araquistain Papers L70 C74a: AMAE RE4 C1 and C2.
12. Azcárate, p. 73.
13. PRO FO371 W4564, W4730, W6222, W8619/95/41.
14. PRO FO 371W9883/9549/41.
15. F. Gordón-Ordás, *Mi política fuera de España*, pp. 720ff.
16. F. Olaya, *El oro de Negrín*, Appendix 5.
17. Raymond L. Buell, *United States Neutrality in the Spanish Conflict*.
18. *Franklin D. Roosevelt and Foreign Affairs*, p. 473.
19. FRUS 1936, ii, pp. 444 and 445.
20. *FDR and Foreign Affairs* iii, pp. 377–83.
21. Howson (under headings of aircraft types).
22. Harold L. Ickes, *The Secret Diary of Harold L. Ickes*, Vol. 2, *The Inside Struggle 1936–1939*, p. 5
23. For Cuse and the Pittman amendment, see R. P. Traina, *American Diplomacy and the Spanish Civil War*, pp. 81–2, 86–7.
24. Gordón-Ordás, p. 701.
25. S. Vidarte, *Todos fuimos culpables*, p. 817.

Chapter 9

1. S. Tanner, 'German Naval Intervention in the Spanish Civil War as reflected in the German Records'.
2. *Soviet Shipping in the Spanish Civil War*.
3. Maiskii, pp. 124–6.
4. Edwards, p. 62.
5. Alpert, *La guerra civil en el mar*, pp. 231–4.
6. For Billmeir, see Edwards, p. 18.
7. Labour Spain papers in Churchill College, Cambridge.
8. *Tribune*, 19 March 1937, quoted in D. Lancien, 'British Left-wing attitudes to the Spanish Civil War'.
9. Eden, p. 441 and *The Diplomatic Diaries of Oliver Harvey*, pp. 31, 35.
10. Edwards, pp. 114ff.; PRO FO 371 W6481, W6684 and W6725/23/41; J. Cable, *The Royal Navy and the Siege of Bilbao*, pp. 55ff.
11. PRO FO 371 W7726/23/41.
12. PRO FO 371 W6908/23/41.
13. CAB 23/88.

14. PRO FO 371 W7418/23/41.
15. P. M. Heaton, *Welsh Blockade Runners in the Spanish Civil War*, p. 39.
16. G. Steer, *The Tree of Gernika*, pp. 203–5.
17. Alpert, *La Guerra civil en el mar*, pp. 255–7.

Chapter 10

1. Steer, Chapter XX.
2. *ABC* (Seville) 29 April 1937.
3. V. Cárcel, *Historia de la Iglesia en España*, v, pp. 47–8.
4. Details of the anti-clerical outrages in A. Montero, *La persecución religiosa en España 1936–1939*;
5. S. A. Manent and J. Raventós, L'Església clandestina a Catalunya durant la guerra civil: els intents de restablir el culte pùblic, pp. 22–4.
6. Rémond, pp. 177,181,182.
7. D. Binchy, *Church and State in Fascist Italy*, pp. 653–4.
8. M. Rodríguez Aisa, *El cardinal Gomá y la Guerra de España: aspectos de la gestión pública del Primado 1936–1939*, pp. 102–7.
9. Ibid., p. 93.
10. Ibid., pp. 191–205.
11. *The Collective Letter* was published by the Catholic Truth Society (London, 1937) and is in Montero, pp. 726–41. For the Vatican attitude, see G. Hermet, *Los católicos en la España franquista*, ii, pp. 49–50.

Chapter 11

1. De Felice, p. 378, note.
2. For Farinacci, see Coverdale, pp. 178–1853. AMAE R1459 C9 and C12 of 24 and 25 March 1937.
3. N. Kuznetsov, *Na Dalyokom Meridiane*, pp. 205–9; Alpert, *La guerra civil en el mar*, pp. 275–84: M. Merkes, *Die Deutscher Politik gegenüber dem Spanischen Bürgerkrieg*, pp. 114–15.
4. P. Gretton, *El factor olvidado: la marina británica y la guerra civil española*, pp. 260–1.
5. J. Hernández, *Yo fui un ministro de Stalin*, p. 165.
6. Spanish Intelligence on the *Leipzig* is in AMAE *Archivo* Azaña RE134 C2, Document 7, 7 August 1937.
7. *Ciano's Diplomatic Papers*, p. 126.
8. Azcárate, pp. 186–7.
9. Edwards, p. 158 and Chiefs of Staff's Report Of 21 September 1937, quoted in L. Pratt, *East of Malta: West of Suez. Britain's Mediterranean Crisis 1936–1939*, p. 87.
10. Grandi, p. 429.
11. De Felice, p. 424, Appendix 9; Eden, p. 453.
12. AMAE R1459 C2 and C12, Sangróniz (Head of Franco's Diplomatic Cabinet) to García Conde, ambassador in Rome.

13. D. Dilks, 'Diplomacy and Appeasement' in *Studies in British Foreign Policy of the Twentieth Century*, Vol. 1, 1916–1939, p. 145.

Chapter 12

1. Haslam, pp. 124–5.
2. B. Bolloten, *The Spanish Revolution: the Left and the Struggle for Power during the Spanish Civil War*, Chapter XIV and p. 141, note 33.
3. Carr, *The Comintern and Spanish Civil War*, Note A.
4. Beloff, ii, p. 31.
5. Haslam, p. 116.
6. Bolloten, p. 342ff.
7. Haslam, pp. 145–6, quoting Soviet Defence Ministry records.
8. Haslam, p. 143.
9. P. Spriano, *Togliatti, Segretario dell'Internazionale*, pp. 86ff.
10. Carr, p. 51; G. Kennan, *Russia and the West under Lenin and Stalin*, pp. 310–11.
11. AMAE R1459 C12.
12. Azaña, *Obras Completas*, iv, pp. 804–6; Araquistain papers L71 C25.
12a. Serrano, *L' Enjeu espagnot*, pp. 104–16; Eden, p. 577.
13. *Ciano's Diplomatic Papers*, p. 145.
14. *De Felice*, p. 444.

Chapter 13

1. Coverdale, pp. 300–2.
2. *Ciano's Diplomatic Papers*, p. 183; Eden, Appendix D.
3. Carlton, p. 127.
4. Eden, p. 582.
4a. *Ciano's Diplomatic Papers*, p. 161.
5. N. Chamberlain, *The Struggle for Peace*, p. 173.
6. General G. Gamelin, *Servir*, ii, pp. 322–8 gives the *procès-verbale* of the meeting.
7. AMAE R832 C19, 24 March, 1938.
8. AMAE R1047, various files.
9. Coverdale, pp. 304–5.
10. AMAE R1458 C2.
11. Edwards, p. 193. Sir R. Hodgson, *Spain Resurgent*, pp. 79–80.

Chapter 14

1. *Documents Diplomatiques Français* (DDF), 2nd Series, Vol. IX 12 April 1938.
2. F. Jay Taylor, *The United States and the Spanish Civil War*, p. 137.
3. Howson, pp. 161–3, 303.
4. Ickes, ii, p. 194,: A. Dixon, *Señor Monopolio; la asombrosa vida de March*, p. 1445; PRO FO 371 W21773/7/41 and W10773/9/41.
5. E. Sanz de Soto, 'Hollywood y la guerra civil de España'.

References

6. A. de Lizarra, *Los vascos y la República Española: contribución a la historia de la guerra civil*, pp. 201ff.
7. Hermet, ii, p. 81.
8. V. Palacio Atard, 'Intentos del Gobierno republicano de restablecer relaciones con la Santa Sede durante la guerra civil', in *Cinco historias de la República y de la guerra civil.*.
9. Manent and Raventós, pp. 171–3.
10. Hermet, ii, p. 85.
11. Ibid, ii, p. 87.
12. Montero, pp. 424–7.
13. Adamthwaite, p. 85.
14. Edwards, p. 173.
15. DDF, 2nd Series, Vol. IX, nos 65 and 497.
16. Report of Commission on Withdrawal of Volunteers in Azcárate, pp. 245–7.
17. G. Ciano, *Ciano's Diary, 1937–1938*, pp. 145, 147–8, 159.
17a. Documents on German Foreign Policy, no. 666.
18. Kérillis in *L'Epoque* of 23 January 1939, quoted by D. Pike, *Les Français et la guerre d'Espagne*, p. 328.

Chapter 15   At the End

1. See, for example, AMAE R1459 of 12 July 1938.
2. Coverdale, p. 335, note.
3. I. Hidalgo de Cisneros, *Cambio de Rumbo*, ii. Chapter 13; L. Romero, *El final de la guerra*, pp. 58–69; Grisoni and Herzog, *Les brigades de la mer*, p. 218; PRO F0371 W1990/8/41 of 31 January 1939: A Viñas, *El oro de Moscú* pp. 361ff., 418–19.
4. AMAE R832 C7.
5. Bonnet, ii, pp. 83–87: Pike, pp. 351–2: J. Borrás, *Francia ante la guerra civil española: burguesía interés nacional e interés de clase*, p. 294; J. Martínez Parrilla, *Las fuerzas armadas francesas y la guerra civil española*, pp. 355–8.
6. Alpert, *La guerra civil en el mar*, pp. 331–2.
7. Errock, pp. 134–5.
8. AMAE R832 C7 and R833 C18.
9. Alpert, *La guerra civil en el mar* and M. Alpert, 'Gran Bretaña, el coronel Casado y el final de la guerra civil'.

Aftermath

1. AMAE R832 C7.
2. AMAE R2065 C13: Coverdale, pp. 341–2: A. Viñas *et al.*, *Política Comercial Española*, i, pp. 24, 164, 179.
3. Coverdale, p. 347.
4. Howson, p. 304.
5. Academy of Sciences of the USSR, *International Solidarity with the Spanish Republic 1936–1939*, pp. 329–30.
6. Meshcheryatov, article cit.

Bibliographical Note

Full references will be found in the Bibliography.

GENERAL PRIMARY SOURCES

A very useful selection of diplomatic and other official papers was produced by Sevillano Carvajal in Spanish in 1969.

GENERAL INTERNATIONAL BACKGROUND

Hugh Thomas (1961) offers the most stimulating and complete account of the whole war in English, weaving the international repercussions in with the internal politics of the struggle and the military action. Van der Esch (1951) and Puzzo (1962) produced pioneering works with stimulating ideas on the international aspects of the Spanish war, but the opening of documentary sources has rendered them largely out-of-date. Schwarz (1972) is a valuable work which uses the documents of the Non-Intervention Committee, but takes the story up to March 1937 only.

France and Great Britain

There is a rich bibliography on the political, economic and social background to the Spanish war. On France, the works of Shirer (1969), Adamthwaite (1977) and Duroselle (1979) can be added to British works such as the stimulating Kennedy (1981), and the collection of essays called *Paths to War...*(1989). Essential in any study of the period is Anthony Eden's autobiography (1962), though its lacunae are often more informative than its content. British strategic problems are dealt with by Pratt (1975).

Italy and Germany

On Italy, Lowe and Marzari (1975) can be added to the works of Renzo de Felice (1981) and Quartararo (1980), while Weinberg (1970) and Hildebrandt (1973) give the German foreign policy background.

The Soviet Union

The USSR was the subject of many academic studies in the years of the Cold War. There are many useful essays in *Russian Foreign Policy* (1962). Wesson (1969) and Brown and Macdonald (1981) can be added to Deutscher's biography of Stalin (1967) and Beloff's work on foreign policy (1949). More recent books have concentrated on the origins and conduct of the Popular Front policy as a defence against Nazism and Fascism, notably *The Popular Front in Europe* (1987) and J. Haslam (1984).

Spain

The opening of the Spanish archives has led to the publications of works on pre-Civil War Spanish foreign policy, notably Egido León (1987).

THE SPANISH CIVIL WAR

For France there is a published selection of the documents of the Quai D'Orsay *in Documents Diplomatiques Français* (1966). The only work on France and the Civil War as a whole is still D. Pike's *Les Français et la guerre d'Espagne* (1975), though to a large extent this is an account of the French press and the war. Borrás Llop's work (1981) is restricted and gives predictable conclusions, though its detail is interesting. Martin Alexander's essay on the French military officers in *The French and Spanish Popular Fronts* (1989) and Martinez Parrilla (1987) put a different light on the policies of French governments. There is an analysis by Dreifort of Delbos's role at the Quai D'Orsay (1973) while Bonnet's memoirs (1946–48) are useful on the end of the war.

Detailed reaction in France to the outbreak of war in Spain is to be found in the collection of papers entitled *Léon Blum, Chef de Gouvernement* (1967), and in the recollections of Jules Moch (1970 and 1971) and Pierre Cot (1944). Blum's evidence is recorded in the Assemblée Nationale's *Rapport fait au nom... sur les événements survenus* (1951). Viñas's essay on Blum (1978) is a necessary corrective to these accounts. Needless to say, on particular subjects such as the supply of aircraft to Spain, these works need to be contrasted with more specialised studies. While J. Salas (1974) is enlightening on military aid to both sides, he is also *parti pris* on the supply of French aircraft, while Howson (1990) possesses the originality of using quite different sources from those normally handled by the historian. Hilary Footitt's cogent thesis on the French Right (1972) is enlightening. For the Left, Serrano's work on the Communists (1987) can be added to the intriguing book on France-Navégation by Grisoni and Herzog (1979).

The major work on Britain and the Spanish war is Edwards (1979), which replaced Kleine-Ahlbrandt (1961) and Watkins (1963), written before the Public Record Office documents were open for scrutiny. Moradiellos's (1992) fine volume is a very close analysis of British policy during the first few months of the war. British documents on the early months of the war were published as *Documents on British Foreign Policy* (1979) and can be supplemented by the vast corpus of material in the F0371 series in the Public Record Office, where the records of some of the other ministries, such as the Board of Trade, can be searched. The PRO also holds the minutes of the meetings of the Non-Intervention Committee. Two unpublished theses, Errock (1980) and Lancien (1965), deal with the British Left, while propagandistic, humanitarian and religious aspects are examined by

M. Alpert (1984 and 1991). Naval questions from the British point of view are analysed by Gretton (1984) and Chatfield (1942). On the particular role of Eden in dissuading Blum from sending war material to Spain there has been a scholarly conflict in the works of Carlton (1971), Gallagher (1971), Stone (1978) and Warner (1962). Carlton's biography of Eden (1986) and Oliver Harvey's *Diaries* (1970) are necessary reading for understanding the period. Aldgate (1979) is a fascinating view of the way the Spanish war was portrayed in cinema newsreels. On the months before July 1936, Little (1985) supplements Moradiellos, while Bolín (1967), Jerrold (1937) and Sainz Rodríguez (1978) give valuable information about Franco's flight from the Canaries to Morocco. Hodgson (1953) gives some interesting details on Franco Spain in 1938 and 1939, while M. Alpert (1991) attempts to disentangle Britain's role at the end of the war.

The Spanish Foreign Ministry archives are now available. The Franco side is still disorganised and filed under very broad categories, while the Republican Government's *Archivo Recuperado*, also known as the *Archivo de Barcelona*, awaits examination by scholars. Some material can be found in the memoirs of Azcárate (1976), the Republican ambassador in London, while Gordón-Ordás's memoirs (1965) are very useful on his negotiations in Mexico. The papers of the ambassador to France, Luis Araquistain, are to be found in the *Archivo Histórico Nacional*. They appear to deal more with his secret negotiations with an Italian agent and with his attempts to suborn the Moroccan leaders than with normal ambassadorial negotiations.

Italian Foreign Minister Ciano's *Diplomatic Papers* (1948) and his 1937–38 *Diary* (1952) are indispensable, but they can be supplemented and seen in a broader light by Coverdale (1979), and De Felice (1981), who uses Grandi's papers, while Grandi's own work (1985) is less informative on Spain. Quartararo (1980), Montanelli and Cervi (1984), the collection of essays called *Italia y la guerra civil española* (1986), and Saz (1986) offer valuable information and insights. Aquarone's article on Italian public opinion (1966), Garosci's book on the exiled Rosselli (1948) and Spriano's works on the PCI and Togliatti (1970 and 1988) display Italian intervention in Spain in a different context. Ambassador Guariglia (1950) illustrates Mussolini's views on the Second Republic, while Cantalupo (1949) gives the views of an ambassador in Franco Spain. Conforti (1967) and Garriga (1974) discuss Guadalajara and its causes and consequences.

On Germany, one of the finest historiographical works is Viñas's study (1977), to be supplemented by Smyth's stimulating essay (1984). The indispensable collection of *Documents on German Foreign Policy* contains some eight hundred items. Two more recent American works, Proctor (1983) on the Luftwaffe in Spain and Whealey (1989) are valuable, while Merkes (1961) remains a standard work in German which ought to have found a translator. On the question of German economic interests in Spain, the authoritative study is Harper (1967), to be supplemented by Viñas *et al.* (1979) on Spanish external trading. Tanner's thesis (1976) on the German navy is invaluable on this specific aspect. Calculations of German arms supplies to Franco made by Hidalgo Salazar (1975) and Salas (1974) must be contrasted with Howson's researches (1990).

On the Church, Lannon (1987) and Hermet (1986) are essential, while Rhodes (1973) and Binchy (1970) should be consulted for the general background in the age of the Dictators. On the reaction of the Vatican to the Spanish war, Marquina (1983) offers a complete study, to be supplemented by Rodríguez Aisa on Cardinal

Goma. A number of works, including Lizarra (1944), Margenat (1983) and Manent and Raventós (1984), show how the Church kept its distance from Franco and that there were Catholics who strove to restore relations with the Holy See, while Montero (1961) remains the authority on the anti-clerical murders and church-burnings (1981). An overall view in English is Sánchez (1987), and there is a useful article by Kent (1986). The religious question is closely related to the Basque issue. The major authoritative work here is F. de Meer (1992). On the destruction of Guernica, Southworth (1977) is the authoritative work and can be supplemented usefully by Viñas (1979). President Aguirre's official report on the collapse of the northern front (1978) gives a full picture, while for the issue of sea-supplies and blockade-running, Gretton (1984), Alpert (1987) and Heaton (1985) provide substantial data between them.

On the USSR there is no work on the Spanish war which quotes original material. The best-known work is the Spanish translation of the memoirs of Marshal Malinovski and other survivors of Stalin's purges who fought in Spain, published as *Bajo la bandera de la España Republicana* (undated but probably about 1967). Very valuable material, however, can be obtained from Kuznetsov (1966). On arms supply, Salas (1974) and Howson (1990) can be contrasted with the Academy of Sciences' widely translated work *International Solidarity with the Spanish Republic* (1974). On the political actions of the USSR and the Comintern in Spain the two works by Cattell (1955 and 1957), and Bolloten's (1979 and various re-editings) justly-famed book must be consulted. Of the many works on the International Brigades, Castells (1974) is still the most useful, but one should consult Luigi Paselli's article (1982). Maisky (1966) discusses the Soviet view of the Non-Intervention Committee with a great deal of humour. The pamphlet called *Soviet Shipping in the Spanish Civil War* (1954) gives information on the subject not available elsewhere.

The works of Cattell and Bolloten were prepared in the Cold War period and relied partly on the account of Krivitsky (1939) and other Soviet fugitives, together with the anti-Soviet and anti-Communist literature produced in exile by the Spanish Anarchists and by the Spanish dissident Jesús Hernández (1974, but first published much earlier). It has to be remembered that there has been much discussion about the value of these accounts. During the Cold War, writers sought to prove that the Soviets intervened seriously at a very early stage in the Spanish Civil War. More recent investigations such as E. H. Carr (1984), Haslam (1984), Broué's important article (1986) and Haigh and others' collection (1986) have put Soviet reactions to the war in Spain in a different light.

The United States probably offers the fullest accounts. Apart from the ample primary sources available in *Foreign Relations of the United States* (1954) and *Franklin D. Roosevelt and Foreign Affairs* (1969), the works of ambassador to Spain Bowers (1954), Secretary of State Cordell Hull (1948) and Harold Ickes, Secretary of the Interior (1955), together with the scholarly studies of Taylor (1956), Little (1985), Fee's Oxford thesis (1959), Traina (1968), Dallek (1979) and Guttman (1963) give a full picture. Conley and Sanz (both 1985) provide an important view of Hollywood and the Spanish war.

On Mexico Powell (1980) is the standard work, though Gordón-Ordás (1965–67) and Olaya (1990) should be consulted. The latter's sources, however, are obscure. On the rest of Latin America see *The Spanish Civil War: American Hemisphere Perspectives* (ed. Falcoff and Pike, 1982).

The League of Nations can be studied in Walters (1960) and Veatch's article on the League and the Spanish war (1990), while there is a study of the Non-Intervention Committee by Watters (1971).

Portugal is best studied in the official papers, *Dez Anos de Política Externa* (1964), Delgado (undated), Oliveira (1987) and H. de la Torre (undated), who sets the scene. Kay (1970), the only work in English, has occasional references to the Spanish Civil War.

Bibliography

PRIMARY SOURCES

Unpublished Documents in Public Record Office (PRO).
Unpublished Documents in Ministry of Foreign Affairs, Madrid (AMAE).
Documents on British Foreign Policy 1919–1939 (DBFP): Second Series, Vol. XVII (London: HMSO, 1979).
Documents on German Foreign Policy 1918–1945 (DGFP), Series D, Vol. III (London: HMSO, 1951).
Documents Diplomatiques Français 1932–1939 (DDF) 2nd Series, (Paris: Ministère des Affaires Etrangères, 1966).
Dez Anos de Politica Externa 1936–47, A Naçao Portuguesa e la segunda Guerra Mundial, Vol. III (Lisbon, Imprenta Nacional, 1964).
Assemblée Nationale, *Rapport fait au nom de la commission chargée d'enquêter sur les évènements survenus en France de 1933 à 1945* (Paris: Imprimerie Nationale, 1951).
Foreign Relations of the United States 1936 (FRUS), Vol. II, *Europe* (Washington: US Government Printing Office, 1954).
Franklin D. Roosevelt and Foreign Affairs (Ed. E. Nixon), Vol. III (Cambridge, Mass.: The Belknap Press of Harvard University Press, 1969).
F. Sevillano Carbajal, *La diplomacia mundial ante la guerra civil española* (Madrid: Editora Nacional, 1969).
Papers of Luis Araquistain (Archivo Histórico Nacional, Madrid).
G. Ciano, *Ciano's Diplomatic Papers* (London: Odham's Press, 1948).
G. Ciano, *Ciano's Hidden Diary 1937–8* (London: Methuen, 1952).

SECONDARY SOURCES

A cinquanta anni dalla Guerra di Spagna (ed. Natoli and Rapone) (Milan: Angeli, 1987).
Academy of Sciences of the USSR, *International Solidarity with the Spanish Republic 1936–1939* (Moscow: Progress, 1974).
A. Adamthwaite, *France and the Coming of the Second World War* (London: Frank Cass, 1977).
The Agony of Spain. Socialist Appeal to British Democracy. Spanish Envoys tell the Facts (speeches of Jiménez de Asúa and Isabel de Palencia at 1936 Labour Party Congress) (London: Labour Party, 1936).

J. M. Aguirre, *El informe del presidente Aguirre al Gobierno de la República sobre los hechos que determinaron el derrumbamiento del frente del norte, 1937* (Bilbao: La Gran Enciclopedia Vasca, 1978).

A. Aldgate, *British Newsreels and the Spanish Civil War* (London: Scolar Press 1979).

M. Alexander, 'Soldiers and Socialists: the French Officer Corps and Leftist Government 1935–37' in *The French and Spanish Popular Fronts: Comparative Perspectives* (Ed. Alexander and Graham) (Cambridge: Cambridge University Press, 1989).

M. Alpert, *El ejército republicano en la guerra civil* (Madrid: Siglo XXI, 1989).

M. Alpert, *La guerra civil española en el mar* (Madrid: Siglo XXI, 1987).

M. Alpert, 'Humanitarianism and Politics in the British Response to the Spanish Civil War', *European History Quarterly* (XIV), (1984), pp. 423–40.

M. Alpert, 'Gibraltar y la guerra civil española' (Salamanca, *Studia Historica*, IV (1985), pp. 91–101.

M. Alpert, 'Las iglesias inglesas y la guerra civil española' in *Homenaje a la profesora Dolores Gómez Molleda* (Salamanca: 1991).

M. Alpert, 'Gran Bretaña, el coronel Casado y el final de la Guerra Civil', (Madrid: *Historia* 16, September 1991).

J. Alvarez del Vayo, *Freedom's Battle* (London: Heinemann, 1940).

J. Alvarez del Vayo, *The Last Optimist* (London: Putnam, 1950).

J. A. Ansaldo, ¿Para qué? (De Alfonso XIII a Juan III) (Buenos Aires: Vasca Ekin, 1951).

A. Aquarone, 'La Guerra di Spagna e l'opinione pubblica italiana', *Il Cannocchiale* (IV), 6 (1966), pp. 3–36.

S. Attanasio, *Gli italiani e la guerra di Spagna* (Milan: Mursia, 1974)

M Azaña, *Obras Completas* (Mexico City: Oasis, 1966–8).

P. de Azcárate, *Mi embajada en Londres durante la guerra civil española* (Barcelona: Ariel, 1976).

Bajo la bandera de la España Republicana (Moscow: Progreso, n.d).

F. Belforte, *La guerra civile in Spagna* (Milan: Istituto per gli studi della politica internazionale, 1938–39).

M. Beloff, *The Foreign Policy of Soviet Russia 1929–41* (Oxford: Oxford University Press, 1949).

D. Binchy, *Church and State in Fascist Italy* (Oxford: Oxford University Press, 1970).

L. Bolín, *Spain, the Vital Years* (London: Cassell, 1967).

B. Bolloten, *The Spanish Revolution: the Left and the Struggle for Power during the Civil War* (Chapel Hill: University of North Carolina Press, 1979).

E. Bonnefous, *Histoire Politique de la Troisiéme République*, Vols 6 and 7 (Paris: PUF, 1965–67).

G. Bonnet, *Défence de la Paix* (Geneva: Le Cheval Ailé, 1946–48).

J. M. Borrás Llop, *Francia ante la guerra civil española: burguesía, interés nacional e interés de clase* (Madrid: Centro de Investigaciones Sociológicas, 1981).

C. Bowers, *My Mission to Spain: Watching the Rehearsal for World War Two* (London: Gollancz, 1954).

A. Boyle, *The Climate of Treason* (London: Hodder/Coronet, 1980).

P. Broué, 'La non-intervention de l'URSS en Espagne', *Cahiers Léon Trotsky* XXVIII (December 1986), pp. 39–45.

A. Brown and C. MacDonald, *On a Field of Red: the Communist International and the Coming of World War Two* (New York: G. Putnam's Sons, 1981).

R. Buell, 'US neutrality in the Spanish conflict', *Foreign Policy Reports* (Vol. XIII, 17: 15 November 1937).

C. Burdick, 'The American military attachés in the Spanish Civil War' (*Militärgeschichtliche Mitteilungen* (XLVI, 1989).

M. Burgos Madroñero, 'La colonia española en Portugal y la Guerra Civil' (Madrid: *Historia* 16, No 172, August 1990).

J. Cable, *The Royal Navy and the Siege of Bilbco* (Cambridge: Cambridge University Press).

R. Cantalupo, *Fu la Spagna* (Milan: Mondadori, 1948).

V. Cárcel, *Historia de la Iglesia en España*, Vol. 5 (Madrid: BAC, 1979).

D. Carlton, 'Eden, Blum and the origins of Non-Intervention', *Journal of Contemporary History* (VI), 3 (1971), pp. 40–55.

D. Carlton, *Anthony Eden: a Biography* (London: Allen and Unwin, 1986 paperback ed.).

E. H. Carr, *The Twilight of Comintern 1930–1935* (London: Macmillan, 1982).

E. H. Carr, *The Comintern and the Spanish Civil War* (London: Macmillan, 1984).

W. Carr, *Arms, Autarky and Aggression: a Study in German Foreign Policy 1933–1939* (London: E. Arnold, 1979).

A. Castells, *Las brigades internacionales en la guerra de España* (Barcelona: Ariel, 1974).

D. Cattell, *Communism and the Spanish Civil War* (Berkeley: University of California Press, 1955).

D. Cattell, *Soviet Diplomacy and the Spanish Civil War* (Berkeley: University of California Press, 1957).

G. Ceretti, *A l'ombre des deux T.: 40 ans avec Maurice Thorez et Palmiro Togliatti* (Paris: Julliard, 1973).

N. Chamberlain, *The Struggle for Peace* (London: Hutchinson, n.d.).

Chatfield, Lord, *The Navy and Defence: the Autobiography of Admiral of the Fleet Lord Chatfield*, Vol. II (London: Heinemann, 1942).

R. de la Cierva, *Historia Ilustrada de la guerra civil española* (Barcelona: Danae, 1970).

O. Conforti, *Guadalajara, la primera derrota del fascismo* (Barcelona: Oikos-Tau, 1977). Translation of *Guadalajara, la prima sconfitta del fascismo* (Milan: Mursia, 1967).

T. Conley, 'Broken Blockage: Notas sobre la guerra civil española en el cine de Hollywood (1937–1944), (Madrid: *Revista de Occidente*, No. 53, October 1985).

J. Cortada, *Spain in the Twentieth Century: Essays on Spanish Diplomacy 1898–1978* (Westport, Ct: Greenwood Press, 1979).

P. Cot, *The Triumph of Treason* (Chicago: Ziff-Davis Publishing Co., 1944).

J. Coverdale, *La intervención fascista en la guerra civil española* (Madrid: Alianza, 1979).

R. Dallek, *Franklin D. Roosevelt and American Foreign Policy 1932–1945* (New York: Oxford University Press, 1979).

H. Dalton, *The Fateful Years: Memoirs 1931–45* (London: Muller, 1957).

I. Delgado, *Portugal e a guerra civil de Espanha* (Lisbon: Publicacaos Europa–America, n.d.).

I. Deutscher, *Stalin, a Political Biography* (Oxford: Oxford University Press, 1967).

192   *Bibliography*

D. Dilks, *Retreat from Power: Studies in Britain's Foreign Policy of the Twentieth Century*, Vol. I, 1906–1939 (London: Macmillan, 1981).

A. Dixon, *Señor Monopolio: la asombrosa vida de Juan March* (Barcelona: Planeta, 1985).

J. Dreifort, *Yvon Delbos at the Quai D'Orsay: French Foreign Policy during the Popular Front 1936–38* (Lawrence: University Press of Kansas, 1973).

J. Duroselle, *La Décadence 1932–39* (Paris: Imprimerie Nationale, 1979).

A. Eden, *Facing the Dictators* (London: Cassell, 1962).

J. Edwards, *The British Government and the Spanish Civil War* (London: Macmillan, 1979).

P. G. Edwards, 'The Foreign Office and Fascism 1924–1929' (*Journal of Contemporary History*, No. 5, 1970).

M. Egido León, *La concepción de la política exterior española durante la Segunda República* (Madrid: UNED, 1987).

H. Errock, *The Attitude of the Labour Party to the Spanish Civil War* (MA: Keele, 1980).

G. Fee, *The Course of US Government Policy towards the Spanish Civil War* (B. Litt: Oxford, 1959).

K. Feiling, *The Life of Neville Chamberlain* (London: Macmillan, 1946).

R. de Felice, *Mussolini il Duce*, Vol. II, *Lo Stato totalitario 1936–1940* (Turin: Einaudi 1981).

A. Fernández Garcia, 'La Iglesia española y la guerra civil' (Salamanca: *Studia Historica*, III, No. 4, 1985).

L. Fischer, *Men and Politics* (London: Cape, 1941).

J. Flint, '"Must God go Fascist?" English Catholic Opinion and the Spanish Civil War' (*Church History* (LVI) 1987).

M. Foot, *Aneurin Bevan* (London: Granada, 1975).

H. Footitt, *Intellectuals of the French Right and the Spanish Civil War* (M. Phil: Reading, 1972).

Foreign Intervention in Spain (Ed. 'Hispanicus') Vol. 1 (London: United Editorial, n.d.).

M. Gallagher, 'Léon Blum and the Spanish Civil War', *Journal of Contemporary History* (VI), (1971), pp. 56–64.

A. Galland, *The First and the Last* (London: Methuen, 1955).

G. Gamelin, *Servir* (Paris: Plon, 1946).

F. Gannon, *The British Press and Germany 1936–1939* (Oxford: Clarendon Press, 1971).

J. M. Gárate, 'Las tropas de Africa en la Guerra Civil Española' (*Revista de Historia Militar* (LXX) 1991.

A. Garosci, *Vita di Carlo Rosselli* (Florence: Edizioni Unite, 1948).

R. Garriga, *Guadalajara y sus consecuencias* (Madrid: Gregorio del Toro, 1974).

F. Gordón-Ordás, *Mi politica fuera de España* (Mexico City: Talleres Gráficos Victoria, 1965).

D. Grandi, *Il mio paese* (Bologna: I Mulino, 1985).

P. Gretton, *El factor olvidado: la marina británica y la guerra civil española* (Madrid: San Martin, 1984).

D. Grisoni and D. Herzog, *Les brigades de la mer* (Paris: Grasset, 1979).

R. Guariglia, *Ricordi 1922–1946* (Naples: Edizioni Scientifichi Italiani, 1950).

A. Guttman, *The Wound in the Heart: American Neutrality and the Spanish Civil War* (New York: The Free Press of Glencoe, 1962).

R. Haigh *et al.*, *Soviet Foreign Policy, The League of Nations and Europe 1917–1939* (Aldershot: Gower, 1986).

C. Halstead, "'A somewhat Machiavellian face": Colonel Juan Beigbeder as High Commissioner in Spanish Morocco 1937–1939' (*The Historian* XXXVIII, 1, 1974).

G. Harper, *German Economic Policy in Spain during the Spanish Civil War* (The Hague: Mouton, 1967).

C. Harvey, 'Politics and Pyrites during the Spanish Civil War', *Economic History Review* (XXXI) 1978, pp. 89–104.

O. Harvey, *The Diplomatic Diaries of Oliver Harvey 1937–1940* (ed. John Harvey) (London: Collins, 1970).

J. Haslam, *The USSR and the Struggle for Collective Security in Europe 1933–39* (London: Macmillan, 1984).

J. Haslam, 'The Soviet Union, the Comintern and the demise of the Popular Front 1936–1939', in *The Popular Front in Europe*.

P. Heaton, *Welsh Blockade Runners in the Spanish Civil War* (Newport, Gwent: Starling Press, 1985).

N. Henderson, *Failure of a Mission* (London: Hodder and Stoughton, 1940).

G. Hermet, *Los católicos en la España franquista* (Madrid: Siglo XXI, 1986).

J. Hernández, *Yo fui un ministro de Stalin* (Madrid: Gregorio del Toro, 1974).

I. Hidalgo de Cisneros, *Cambio de rumbo*, Vol. II (Bucharest: no. publ., 1964).

R. Hidalgo Salazar, *La ayuda alemana a España 1936–1939* (Madrid: San Martín, 1975).

K. Hildebrand, *The Foreign Policy of the Third Reich* (London: Batsford, 1973).

G. Hills, *Gibraltar: Rock of Contention* (London: Robert Hale, 1974).

R. Hodgson, *Spain Resurgent* (London: Hutchinson, 1953).

G. Howson, *Aircraft of the Spanish Civil War 1936–1939* (London: Putnam, 1990).

C. Hull, *The Memoirs of Cordell Hull* (London: Hodder and Stoughton, 1948).

H. Ickes, *The Secret Diary of Harold L. Ickes*, Vol. II (London: Weidenfeld and Nicolson, 1955).

Italia y la guerra civil española: Simposio celebrado en la escuela española de Historia y Arqueología de Roma (Madrid: CSIC, 1986).

Italian Aggression in Spain: Documents captured from Italian troops in action at Guadalajara (Summary prepared by the Press Bureau of the Spanish delegation) (London: Union of Democratic Control, 1937).

J. Jackson, *The Popular Front in France: Defending Democracy 1934–1938* (Cambridge: Cambridge University Press, 1988).

D. Jerrold, *Georgian Adventure* (London: Collins, 1937).

T. Jones, *A Diary with Letters* (Oxford: Oxford University Press, 1954).

H. Kay, *Salazar and Modern Portugal* (London: Eyre and Spottiswoode, 1970).

G. Kennan, *Russia and the West under Lenin and Stalin* (London: Hutchinson, 1971).

P. Kennedy, *The Realities behind Democracy: Background and Influences on British External Policy 1865–1980* (London: Fontana, 1981).

P. Kent, 'The Vatican and the Spanish Civil War', *European History Quarterly*, XVI, 4 (1986), pp. 441–65.

W. Kleine-Ahlbrandt, *The Policy of Simmering: a Study of British Policy during the Spanish Civil War* (Geneva: Institut Universitaire des Hautes Etudes Internationales, 1961).

A. Koestler, *Spanish Testament* (London: Gollancz, 1937).

A. Koestler, *The Invisible Writing* (London: Hamish Hamilton, 1954).

W. Krivitsky, *I was Stalin's Agent* (London: Hamish Hamilton, 1939).

N. Kuznetsov, *Na Dalyokom Meridiane* (Moscow: Nauta, 1966).

J. Lacouture, *Léon Blum*, (Paris: Seuil, 1977).

D. Lammers, 'Fascism, Communism and the Foreign Office 1937–1939, *Journal of Contemporary History*, VI (1971), pp. 66–86.

D. Lancien, *British Left-Wing Attitudes to the Spanish Civil War* (B. Litt: Oxford, 1965).

F. Lannon, 'The Church's Crusade against the Republic', in *Revolution and War in Spain* (ed. Preston) (London: Methuen, 1984).

F. Lannon, *Privilege, Persecution and Prophecy: the Church in Spain 1895–1975* (Oxford: Clarendon Press, 1987).

G. Lefranc, *Histoire du Front Populaire 1934–1938* (Paris: Payot, 1965).

Léon Blum, Chef de Gouvernement 1936–1937 (Paris: Colin, 1967).

D. Little, 'Claude Bowers and his Mission to Spain: the Diplomacy of a Jeffersonian Democrat', in K. P. Jones, *US Diplomats in Europe 1919–1946* (Santa Barbara: ABC–Clio, 1976).

D. Little, *Malevolent Neutrality: the US, Great Britain and the Origins of the Spanish Civil War* (Ithaca: Cornell University Press, 1985).

D. Little, 'Red Scare 1936: Anti-Bolshevism and the Origins of British Non-Intervention in the Spanish Civil War', *Journal of Contemporary History*, XXIII, (1988), pp. 291–311.

A. de Lizarra, *Los vascos y la República española. Contribución a la historia de la Guerra Civil* (Buenos Aires: Vasca Ekin, 1944).

C. Lowe and F. Marzari, *Italian Foreign Policy 1870–1940* (London: Routledge and Kegan Paul, 1975).

D. MacKinnon, 'The Spanish Civil War 1936–1939: Catholicism's minority voice' (*New Blackfriars*, November 1986).

I. Maisky, *Spanish Notebooks* (London: Hutchinson, 1966).

A. Manent and J. Raventós, *L'Església clandestina a Catalunya durant la guerra civil (1936–1939). Els intents de restabler el culte pùblic* (Montserrat: Publicacions de l'Abadia, 1984).

M. Manning, *The Blueshirts* (Dublin: Gill and Macmillan, 1987 edn).

J. Margenat, 'Manuel de Irujo: la política religiosa de los gobiernos de la República en la Guerra Civil', *Cuadernos de Historia Moderna y Contemporánea* (IV) (Madrid: Facultad de Historia, 1983).

A. Marquina, *La diplomacia vaticana y la España de Franco 1936–1945* (Madrid: CSIC, 1983).

J. Martínez Parrilla, *Las fuerzas armadas francesas y la guerra civil española (1936–1939)* (Madrid: Ediciones Ejército, 1987).

F. McCullagh, *In Franco's Spain*, (London: Burns, Oates and Washbourne, 1987).

M. Mazzetti, 'I contatti del governo italiano con i cospiratori militari spagnoli prima del luglio 1936' (*Storia Contemporanea*, November–December 1979).

F. de Meer, 'Una carta de José Antonia de Aguirre al Cardenal Gomá (9 de marzo de 1937): nota documental, *Boletín de la Real Academia de la Historia*, (CLXXXIV), iii, pp. 521–9.

F. de Meer, *El Partido Nacionalista Vasco ante la Guerra de España* (1936–1937) (Pamplona: Eunsa, 1992).

M. Merkes, *Die Deutsche Politik gegenüber dem Spanischen Bürgerkrieg* (Bonn: Ludwig Röhrscheid, 1961).

M. Meshcheryatov, 'The Soviet Union and the Antifascist struggle of the Spanish People', *Istoriya SSSR* (January–February, 1988).

K. Middlemass, *Diplomacy of Illusion, The British Government and Germany 1937–1939* (London: Weidenfeld and Nicolson, 1972).

J. Moch, *Rencontres avec Léon Blum* (Paris: Plon, 1970).

J. Moch, *Le Front Populaire... grande espérance* (Paris: Perrin, 1971).

I. Montanelli and M. Cervi, *Storia d'Italia*, Vol. XLII, *La Guerra di Spagna e il patto di Monaco* (Milan; Rizzoli, 1984).

A. Montero, *Historia de la persecución religiosa en España 1936–1939* (Madrid: Biblioteca de Autores Cristianos, 1961).

C. de la Mora, *In Place of Splendour: the Autobiography of a Spanish Woman* (New York: Harcourt, Brace and Co., 1939).

E. Moradiellos, *Neutralidad benévola: El Gobierno británico y la insurrección militar española de 1936* (Oviedo: Pentalfa, 1990).

F. Moravec, *Master of Spies* (London: The Bodley Head, 1975).

C. Mowat, *Britain between the Wars* (London: Methuen, 1968).

E. O'Duffy, *Crusade in Spain* (London: Robert Hale, 1938).

F. Olaya, *El oro de Negrín* (Móstoles: Ediciones Madre Tierra, 1990).

C. Oliveira, *Salazar e a Guerra Civil de Espanha* (Lisbon: O Jornal, 1987).

V. Palacio Atard, *Cinco Historias de la República y de la Guerra* (Madrid: Editora Nacional, 1973).

L. Paselli, 'Sul numero e la nazionalità dei volontari antifascisti stranieri nella guerra di Spagna (1936–1939)' (*Archivio Trimestrale* VIII, no. 1, May 1982).

Paths to War: New Essays on the Origins of the Second World War (ed. Boyce and Robertson) (London: Macmillan, 1989).

D. Pike, *Les Français et la guerre d'Espagne* (Paris: PUF, 1975).

The Popular Front in Europe (ed. H. Graham and P. Preston) (London: Macmillan, 1987).

T. Powell, *Mexico and the Spanish Civil War* (Albuquerque: University of New Mexico Press, 1980).

L. Pratt, *East of Malta, West of Suez: Britain's Mediterranean crisis 1936–39* (Cambridge: Cambridge University Press, 1975).

I. Preito, 'Cómo y por qué salí del ministerio de Defensa Nacional' in *Convulsiones de España* (Mexico City: Oasis 1967–9)

R. Proctor, *Hitler's Luftwaffe in the Spanish Civil War* (Westport, Ct: Greenwood Press, 1983).

D. Puzzo, *Spain and the Great Powers 1936–1941* (New York: Columbia University Press, 1962).

R. Quartararo, *Roma tra Londra e Berlino: la politica estera fascista dal 1930 al 1940* (Roma: Bonacci, 1980).

R. Quatrefages, 'La politique française de non-intervention et le soutien matériel à la République pendant la guerre civile' in *Les Armées françaises et espagnoles: modernisation et réforme entre les deux guerres mondiales* (Madrid: Casa de Velázquez, 1989).

H. Raguer, *La espada y la cruz: la Iglesia 1936–1939* (Barcelona: Bruguera, 1977).

R. Rémond, *Les catholiques, le communisme et les crises 1929–1939* (Paris: Colin, 1960).

A. Rhodes, *The Vatican in the Age of the Dictators 1922–45* (London: Hodder and Stoughton, 1973).

M. Rodríguez Aisa, *El Cardenal Gomá y la Guerra de España: aspectos de la gestión pública del Primado 1936–1939* (Madrid: CSIC, 1981).

L. Romero, *El final de la Guerra* (Barcelona; Ariel, 1976).

Russian Foreign Policy: Essays in Historical Perspective (ed. I. Lederer) (New Haven: Yale University Press, 1962).

P. Sainz Rodríguez, *Testimonia y recuerdos* (Barcelona: Planeta, 1978).

J. Salas Larrazábal, *La intervención extranjera en la guerra de España* (Madrid: Editora Nacional, 1974).

J. Sánchez, *The Spanish Civil War as a Religious Tragedy* (Notre Dame: Notre Dame University Press, 1987)

E. Sanz, 'Hollywood y la guerra civil de España', *Revista de Occidente*, no. 53 (1985), pp. 33–46.

I. Saz, *Mussolini contra la Segunda República* (Valencia: Edicions Alfons el Magnánim, 1986).

F. Schwartz, *La Internacionalización de la Guerra civil Española* (Barcelona: Ariel, 1971).

C. Serrano, 'Las estrategias internacionales en torno a Marruecos y la guerra civil española'. *Perspectiva Contemporánea*, I.i. (1988) (Madrid: Facultad de Geogafía e Historia), pp. 33–49.

C. Serrano, *L'enjeu espagnol: PCF et la Guerre d'Espagne* (Paris: Messidor, 1987).

W. Shirer, *Berlin Diary: the Journal of a Foreign Correspondent 1934–41* (London: Hamish Hamilton, 1941).

W. Shirer, *The Rise and Fall of the Third Reich* (London: Secker and Warburg, 1959).

W. Shirer, *The Collapse of the Third Republic* (New York: Simon and Shuster, 1969).

D. Smyth, 'Reflex action: Germany and the onset of the Spanish Civil War' in *Revolution and War in Spain* 1936–39 (ed. Preston) (London: Methuen, 1984).

D. Smyth, *Diplomacy and Strategy of Survival: British Policy and Franco's Spain 1940–1941* (Cambridge: Cambridge University Press, 1986).

H. Southworth, *Guernica! Guernica! A Study of Journalism, Diplomacy, Propaganda and History* (Berkeley; University of California Press, 1977).

Soviet Shipping in the Spanish Civil War (New York: Research Program on the USSR, 1954).

The Spanish Civil War: American Hemisphere Perspectives (ed. Falcoff and Pike) (Lincoln: University of Nebraska Press, 1982).

P. Spriano, *Storia del partito comunista italiano*, Vol. 3, *I fronti popolari, Stalin, la guerra* (Turin: Einaudi, 1970).

P. Spriano, *Togliatti, segretario dell' Internazionale* (Milan: Mondadori, 1988).

G. Steer, *The Tree of Gernika: a Field Study of Modern War* (London: Hodder and Stoughton, 1938).

G. Stone, 'Britain, Non-Intervention and the Spanish Civil War', *European Studies Review*, X, (1979), pp. 129–49.

S. Tanner, *German Naval Intervention in the Spanish Civil War as Reflected in the German Records* (Ph.D. The American University, Washington DC, 1976).

F. de Tarr, *The French Radical Party from Herriot to Mendès-France* (Oxford: Oxford University Press, 1961).

F. Jay Taylor, *The US and the Spanish Civil War* (New York: Bookman Associates, 1956).

H. Thomas, *The Spanish Civil War* (Harmondsworth: Penguin Books, rev. edn, 1977).

H. de la Torre, *La relación peninsular en la antecámara de la guerra civil de España (1931–1936)* (Mérida: UNED, n.d.).

R. Traina, *American Diplomacy and the Spanish Civil War* (Bloomington: Indiana University Press, 1968).

A. Ulam, *Expansion and Co-existence: Soviet Foreign Policy 1917–1973* (New York: Holt, Rinehart and Winston, 2nd edn, 1974).

J. D. Valaik, 'Catholics, Neutrality and the Spanish Embargo 1937–39'. *The Journal of American History* (June 1967), pp. 73–85.

P. Van der Esch, *Prelude to War: The International Repercussions of the Spanish Civil War* (The Hague: Mouton, 1951).

R. Veatch, 'The League of Nations and the Spanish Civil War 1936–1939, *European History Quarterly*, XX (1990), pp. 181–207.

J. Vidarte, *Todos fuimos culpables* (Mexico City: Fondo de Cultura Económica, 1973).

A. Viñas, *La Alemania Nazi y el 18 de Julio* (Madrid: Alianza, 2nd edn, 1977).

A. Viñas, *El oro de Moscú* (Barcelona: Grijalbo, 1979)

A. Viñas et al. *Política Comercial Exterior en España 1931–1975* (Madrid: Banco Exterior de Espana, 1979).

A. Viñas, 'Guernica, ¿Quién lo hizo?', *Historia General de la Guerra Civil en Euzcadi*, Vol. III (San Sebastián: L. Haramburu, 1979), pp. 165–220.

A. Viñas, 'Los condicionantes internacionales'. *La guerra civil 50 años después* (ed. Tuñón de Lara et al.) (Barcelona: Labor, 1985).

A. Viñas, 'Blum traicionó a la República', *Historia 16*, XXIV, (1978), pp. 41–54.

F. P. Walters, *A History of the League of Nations* (Oxford: Oxford University Press, 1960 edn).

G. Ward Price, *I Know These Dictators* (London: Harrap, 1938).

G. Warner, 'France and Non-Intervention in Spain, July–August 1936, *International Affairs* (XXXVIII), 1962, pp. 203–20.

K. Watkins, *Britain Divided* (London: Nelson, 1963).

W. E. Watters, *An International Affair: Non-Intervention in the Spanish Civil War* (New York: Exposition Press, 1971).

G. Weinberg, *The Foreign Policy of Hitler's Germany: Diplomatic Revolution in Europe 1933–36* (Chicago: University of Chicago Press, 1970).

E. Von Weizsaecker, *Memoirs* (London: Gollancz, 1951).

A. Werth, *The Twilight of France 1933–40* (London: Hamish Hamilton, 1942).

R. Wesson, *Soviet Foreign Policy in Perspective* (Homewood, Ill.: The Dorsey Press, 1969).

R. Whealey, *Hitler and Spain: the Nazi Role in the Spanish Civil War 1936–39* (Louisville: The University Press of Kentucky).

Index